The Science of Salvation

Forty-nine Instant Sermons

"Especially for lay-pastors"

Add your own personality and your life experiences, and stir hearts with the aid of the Holy Spirit.

Compiled by
Jacque Lafleur*

*(nom de plume)

TEACH Services, Inc.
www.TEACHServices.com

World rights reserved. This book or any portion thereof may not be copied or reproduced in any form or manner whatever, except as provided by law, without the written permission of the publisher, except by a reviewer who may quote brief passages in a review.

This book was written to provide truthful information in regard to the subject matter covered. The author assumes full responsibility for the accuracy of all facts and quotations as cited in this book. The opinions expressed in this book are the author's personal views and interpretation of the Bible, Spirit of Prophecy, and/or contemporary authors and do not necessarily reflect those of TEACH Services, Inc.

This book is sold with the understanding that the publisher is not engaged in giving spiritual, legal, medical, or other professional advice. If authoritative advice is needed, the reader should seek the counsel of a competent professional.

Copyright © 2009 Jack Blume and TEACH Services, Inc.
ISBN-13: 978-1-57258-586-7
Library of Congress Control Number: 2009928244

Published by
TEACH Services, Inc.
www.TEACHServices.com

FOREWORD

"*Reinforce the message with literature.*—The days in which we live are times that call for constant vigilance, times in which God's people should be awake to do a great work in presenting the light on the Sabbath question . . . This last warning to the inhabitants of the earth is to make men see the importance God attaches to His holy law. So plainly is the truth to be presented that no transgressor, hearing it, shall fail to discern the importance of obedience to the Sabbath commandment . . .

There is work for all to do in order that the simple truths of the Word of God may be made known. *The words of scripture should be printed and published just as they read.* It would be well if the nineteenth and greater portion of the twentieth chapters of Exodus, with verses twelve to eighteen of the thirty-first chapter, were printed just as they stand. Crowd these truths into small books and pamphlets, and let the word of God speak to the people. When a discourse concerning the law is preached that is right to the point, *if you have any means of doing so, get it into a printed leaflet.* Then when those who plead for Sunday laws meet you, place these leaflets in their hands. Tell them that you have no discussion over the Sunday question, for you have a plain 'thus saith the Lord' for the keeping of the seventh day."—Review and Herald, March 26, 1908.

Dear Reader:
 The quotation from Evangelism p. 232 by Mrs. Ellen G. White was brought to my attention by another church member. It seemed an excellent idea, so

I prepared a paper with texts on the Sabbath to carry in my Bible should the opportunity arise to share it with someone else.

I then started preparing pages on additional topics. There is very little narration. This book consists primarily of Bible texts strung together in such a fashion as to present studies on 49 different Bible topics.

I hope that this book will help church members reach out to other people. This book of texts is listed by topic and sub-headings, and can be useful in several of the following ways:

1. They can be used as "instant sermons" or as "Bible studies" when needed at a moment's notice. Keep these in your automobile or briefcase as you travel, so that you will have them with you at all times. We are told in 1 Peter 3:15, ". . . be ready always to give an answer to every man that asketh you a reason of the hope that is in you with meekness and fear," and in 2 Timothy 4:2, 3, Paul writes, "Preach the word; be "instant" in season, out of season; reprove, rebuke, exhort with all longsuffering and doctrine. For the time will come when they will not endure sound doctrine"

2. The book can be used to mark your Bible, so that you can more easily give a study to others on these topics directly from your Bible.

3. The pages can be copied to pass on to others.

4. The book can be read for inspiration, or as the basis for family or private worship.

5. I hope that many good uses can be found for this book, and that each reader will be blessed as I was blessed in bringing the texts together.

My prayer is that the same Holy Spirit who inspired the Bible writers of old will also inspire the minds and hearts of people who read these truths taken directly from the Bible.

Sincerely,

Jacque Lafleur*

*A pseudonym

TABLE OF CONTENTS

CHAPTER 1

(pages 1–7)

GOD—ATTRIBUTES OF THE GOD HEAD

    Omnipresence, Omniscience, Omnipotence
    Eternal, Immutable, Righteousness
    God the Ruler of the Universe
    God of Mercy, a Covenant God, a Redeemer God,
    A God of Refuge
    A God of Forgiveness, A God of Goodness,
    A God of Faithfulness
    A God of Salvation and Vengeance

CHAPTER 2

(pages 8–16)

AS CHRISTIANS WE BELIEVE IN ONE GOD (ONE GOD-HEAD)

    All Three Persons of the God-Head Active at Creation
    Additional Evidences of Plurality in Old Testament
    God the Father Spoke from Heaven Three Times While

Christ was a Man on Earth:
First: At Christ's Baptism.
Second: On the Mount of Transfiguration.
Third: During Jesus' Prayer Shortly Before His Crucifixion.
Holy Spirit Becomes Very Active in the Spread of the Gospel.
Evidence From N.T. of a Triune God.

CHAPTER 3

(pages 17–20)

GOD ABOVE TIME

God Exists Totally Apart from the Universe and Yet Can Be Everywhere within it.
Christ Spoke the Words That Brought Everything into Existence.
Christ's Existence Precedes Time, He is Not Created.
God Created the Universe from What Cannot be Detected With Our Senses.
Christ Has Extra dimensionality Since His Resurrection and Can Pass Through Walls.
God is Very Near, Yet We Cannot See Him, Because of Extra dimensionality.
Christ Now Reigns with God the Father.

CHAPTER 4

(pages 21–24)

A FATHER GOD

God the Father in the New Testament
The Father of All Creation
Jesus Reveals the Father.
A God Who Gives
A God Who Loves

CHAPTER 5

(pages 25–40)

GOD THE SON (CHRIST IS TRULY GOD)

1. His Divine Attributes
2. His Divine Power and Prerogatives
3. His Divine Names
4. His Divinity Acknowledged
5. His Personal Testimony
6. His Equality With God Assumed
7. He is Worshiped as God

(JESUS CHRIST IS TRULY MAN)

1. His Human Birth
2. His Human Development
3. He Was Called a "Man"
4. His Human Characteristics
5. His Identity with Human Nature
6. The Sinlessness of Jesus Christ's Human Nature
7. The Necessity of Christ's Taking Human Nature

(THE NECESSITY OF A UNION BETWEEN TWO

NATURES)
1. To Reconcile Humanity with God
2. To Veil Divinity with Humanity
3. To Live Victoriously
(THE OFFICES OF JESUS CHRIST ARE :)
A. Christ the Prophet.
B. Christ the Priest.
   1. Christ's Earthly Priesthood
   2. Christ's Heavenly Priesthood
C. Christ the King.

CHAPTER 6

(pages 41–49)

THE GREAT I AM

Y H W H = LORD = Jehovah = I AM
The Great I AM of the O.T. Is the Same Person as Jesus Christ of N.T.
Christ Reveals Himself to the Prophet John in the Book of Revelation as the Same Great I AM.
God Sees Future as We See Present.
Christ Spoke the World into Existence.
The Names Used for God Were Significant.

CHAPTER 7

(pages 50–57)

JEHOVAH

Jehovah Created the Earth.
Jehovah Seeks Adam and Eve After They Sinned.

Jehovah Provides for Their Needs.
Jehovah Calls Noah into the Ark of Safety.
Jehovah Promises Abraham a Son.
Jehovah Destroys Sodom.
Jehovah Wrestles with Jacob.
Jehovah Appears to Moses in Burning Bush.
Jehovah Sent Ten Plagues over Egypt.
Jehovah Parted the Red Sea.
Jehovah Leads by a Pillar of Cloud and of Fire.
Jehovah Gives Law on Mount Sinai.
Jehovah Meets with Joshua.
The "Angel of the Lord" is a Deity Who Later Becomes Christ.
The Rock Which Gave Water was Christ.
Christ in the N.T. is Revealed as Being Jehovah of the O.T.

CHAPTER 8

(pages 58–64)

CHRIST THE LORD OF GLORY

Christ had Godly Glory Before Creation.
In the Old Testament, Jehovah (Christ) Had Glory That No One Could Look Upon.
Moses Saw a Little of Christ's Glory.
Christ's Glory Filled Solomon's Temple.
Afterwards, Christ Gave Up His Heavenly Glory and Became a New Born Baby.

Certain Disciples Expected Christ to Set up an Earthly Kingdom.
Christ glorified on the Mount of Transfiguration.

> We Will See Christ in His Heavenly Glory at His Second Coming.
> We can Reflect the Glory of Christ by Accepting Him in Our Lives.
> Christ is Now Next to the Father With Godly Glory.
> At the Resurrection We Will See Christ in All His Glory and Live.
> Mankind Will Regain Their Spiritual Natures as Before Sin.
> Christ Will Live With Mankind Throughout Eternity.

CHAPTER 9

(pages 65–67)

JESUS GIVES US LIVING WATER

> We Must Believe in Christ to Receive the Living Water.
> To Those Who Forsake the LORD
> Living Water Will Not Fail Those Who Are Faithful.
> Living Water Given Israel in the Wilderness.

CHAPTER 10

(pages 68–70)

CHRIST IS THE LIGHT OF THE WORLD

> Christ is Our Light in the New Jerusalem.
> Christ the Light in Old Testament Times
> Word = Christ = Light = Commandments

CHAPTER 11

(pages 71–82)

THE ROCK OF AGES

    Upon This rock—Matthew 16:18. (See: 1, 2, 3, 4, and 5.)
    John and Peter Witness to the High Priest.
    1. Upon This Rock I Will Build My Church.
    In the O. T. Rock or Stone used for God
    GOD = LORD = Rock = Christ
    Christ is the Rock That Supplies Us Living Water.
    Christ is Our Foundation Stone.
    Christ a Stumbling Stone and a Rock of Offense To Those Who Refuse to Believe.
    Peter Named Head of the Church?

    2. The Gates of Hell Shall Not Prevail
    Satan Cannot Hold Those (In The Grave) Forever Who Believe in Christ.
    Christ Entered Satan's Stronghold and Bound Him.
    Peter is Martyred as Foretold by Christ.

    3. Give unto Thee the Keys (Knowledge).
    The "Word of God" is the "Key" to the New Birth Experience.
    "All" His Disciples Are to Pass on the Words of Functions Over the Early Church in Jerusalem.
    Paul Corrected Peter for a Wrong Course of Action.

    4. Kingdom of Heaven, Kingdom of Grace.
    We Cannot Enter Kingdom of Glory Until We First Enter His Kingdom of Grace.

    5. To Bind on Earth, to Loose on Earth.

CHAPTER 12

(pages 83–89)

THE HOLY SPIRIT AND HIS WORK
    The Holy Spirit Takes the Place of Jesus.
    The Holy Spirit the Comforter
    The Spirit of Truth
    The Spirit Beareth Witness.
    The Spirit Gives Gifts.
    The Holy Spirit Invites the Sinner.
    A Limit to the Holy Spirit's Strivings.
    Spirit Does Not Give Up on Man Easily.
    Holy Spirit Exhibits Personal Attributes.
    He Appoints People for Service.
    Holy Spirit in the Old Testament.
    Personality of Holy Spirit in O.T.
    The Holy Spirit Clearly Referred to as God.
    All the Lost Have Sinned Against the Holy Spirit.

CHAPTER 13

(pages 90–103)

ANGELS
    Not Self-Existent or Self-Sustaining
    Existed Before Our Earth or Humanity
    Angles Are Subject to God's Authority.
    Angels Are a Higher Order Than Humans.
    Angel's Nature Differ From Humans.
    Angels are Powerful, Quick, and Mighty
    Angels Obey God's Commandments.
    Angels Have Freedom of Choice.

We Each Have a Guardian Angel.
Travel Faster Than Speed of Light.
The Saved More Like Angels at 2nd Coming.
Angels Sometimes Appear as Humans.
There Are Different Orders of Angels.
There Are Also Evil Angels.
Angels Home is in Heaven.
Angels Have Access to God at All Times.
Angels Come and Go as God Commands.
Angels Are Innumerable.
Angels Are Interested in Our Salvation.
Angels Are God's Messengers.
They Know Our Name, Address, and Occupation.
Angels Instruct God's People.
They Help God's People Preach the Gospel.
God Uses Angels as Ministers of Justice.
They Guide, Direct, Protect, and Provide.
Angels Intervene in World Affairs, Hold Back Destructive Forces, Restrain Tyrants, and Punish Evil.
Angels Witness God's Judgment.
Angels Refuse Worship but Worship God.
They Will Accompany Christ at His Return.
Angels Are Our Companions in Heaven.

CHAPTER 14

(pages 104–112)

CREATION

The Worth of the Physical Universe
The Sacredness of Life
Has God Finished His Creation?
Christ and His Creative Word Today.

Christ Re-created While on Earth.

CHAPTER 15

(pages 113–119)

THE WORD OF GOD

Divine Revelation, General and Special
Authorship and the Inspiration of the Scriptures
Writers Sometimes Perplexed over Message.
Methods and Content of Revelation
The Claims of the Scriptures
Jesus and the Holy Spirit and the Authority of Scripture
The Scope of Spiritual Authority

CHAPTER 16

(pages 120–132)

THE NATURE OF MAN

God Created Woman From Man.
Man Became Subject to Death.
Man Crested After a Divine Type.
Man to Rule Other Creatures.
The Unity of the Human Race
The Breath of Life
Man, a Living Soul
The Soul, an Indivisible Unity
Nephesh Translated as Person or Self.
Nephesh Translated Life 100 Times.

Nephesh Refers to Desires, Appetite, Passions or Seat of Affections.
Nephesh (soul) Dies, is a Corpse.
The Greek Word "Psuche" in the N. T. is Used Similarly as Nephesh in O. T. for Both Animals as Well as Humans.
Sometimes Used to Mean "People", Refers to the Emotions, Mind or Heart.
Psuche is Subject to Death.
Ruach Used 377 Times in the O. T. Usually Translated Spirit, Wind, or Breath.
Rauch (Breath) Leaves Body at Death.
In N. T. the Greek Pneuma is Used and is Yielded to the Lord at Death.
Unity of Body, Soul and Spirit.
Man Created in the Image of God.
When Man Fell, God Didn't Cause Sin.
The Author of Sin
The Origin of Sin in the Human Race
Impact of Sin, Immediate Consequences
The Definition of Sin
Sin Causes Guilt.
The Control Center of Sin
The Universal Sinfulness of Man.
Is Sin Inherited or Acquired?
The Eradication of Sinful Behavior
The Bible View of Evolution
The Original Plan for Man
The Covenant Given at the Fall
The Covenant Established Before Creation
The Covenant Renewal Through Abraham
The New Covenant

CHAPTER 17

(pages 133–139)

THE GREAT CONTROVERSY

(A BATTLE BETWEEN CHRIST AND SATAN)
    Angels a Higher Order Than Humans.
    The Origin of the Controversy
    Earth, The Theater of the Universe
    The Cosmic Issue—God's Government and Law.
    Showdown at Calvary
    The Most Crucial Question
    The Center of Biblical Doctrines
    Evil Did Not Originate with God.
    Upon Christ's Return to Heaven He Provided for Us By:
        The Holy Spirit, by Teachers and Angles.

CHAPTER 18

(pages 140–152)

THE LIFE, DEATH, AND RESURRECTION OF CHRIST
    Only Christ Lived the Perfect Life.
    God's Saving Grace
    The Divine Initiative
    A Blend of Grace and Justice
    A God of Forgiveness
    God's Wrath is Against Sin Not People.
    The Human Response
    Christ's Ministry of Reconciliation
    Christ's Death a Necessity

What Does the Atoning Sacrifice Accomplish?
Christ the Vicarious Sin-Bearer
What is the Role of the Blood?
Christ the Ransom
What Did the Ransom Accomplish?
Christ the Representative of Humanity
His Perfect Life Our Salvation
The Inspiration of Christ's Life
Christ's Resurrection and Salvation
Reconciliation Throughout the Universe
The Vindication of God's Law
Justification
Salvation Through Right Connection
The Motivation For Mission

CHAPTER 19

(pages 153–159)

REPENTANCE/CONFESSION AND FORGIVENESS

There Can Be No Repentance Without Reformation. Repentance Is a Change of Mind, Reformation is a Change of Life.

CHAPTER 20

(pages 160–166)

JUSTIFICATION AND SANCTIFICATION

Sanctification is the Work of the Holy Spirit upon the Character of Those Who are Justified, In Order That We May Be Glorified.

CHAPTER 21

(pages 167–173)

GRACE

    Grace Is a Gift
    Salvation by Grace Alone
    God Was a God of Grace Also in the O. T.
    Grace = Mercy Also in the New Testament
    Grace and Obedience
    The Limits of Grace

CHAPTER 22

(pages 174–177)

FAITH

CHAPTER 23

(pages 178–181)

HOPE

CHAPTER 24

(pages 182–200)

THE CHURCH

    Church Built Upon Christ the Rock

The Church Existed Before N. T. Times.
Christ Called His People a Church While He Was on Earth as a Man.
The Mission of the Church
The Church as a Body
The Church as a Temple
The Church as a Bride
The Church as "Jerusalem Above:
The Church as a Family
The Church an Army, Militant and Triumphant
The Visible Church
The Invisible Church
The Organization of the Church
Membership Qualifications
Equality and Service
Priesthood of all Believers
Allegiance to God and State
Worship and Exhortation
Christian Fellowship
Instruction in the Scriptures
Worldwide Proclamation of the Gospel
The Government of the Church
Christ is Head of Church
Christ the Source of all its Authority
The Scriptures Carry Christ's Authority
The New Testament Officers of the Church
Qualifications of an Elder
The Deacons and Deaconesses
Dealing with Private Offences
Dealing with Division Persons
Restoration of Offenders

CHAPTER 25

(pages 201–211)

UNITY IN THE BODY OF CHRIST AND SPIRITUAL GIFTS AND MINISTRIES

Unity of the Spirit
Unity in Diversity
Unity of Faith
Strength in Unity
Unity Transcends Human Differences
Unity Through Different Gifts
Avoid Attitudes of Divisiveness
Spiritual Gifts and Ministries
The Gifts of the Holy Spirit
Harmony within the Church
The Indispensable Dimension
Living in God's Glory
The Growth of the Church
A common Ministry
The Failure to Use Spiritual Gifts
Spiritual Preparation and Guidance

CHAPTER 26

(pages 212–215)

BAPTISM

Part of Our Christian Confession
Jesus baptized in Jordan by Immersion.
The Apostles Baptized by Immersion.
No Record in Bible of Infant Baptism.

Table of Contents   xxiii

We are to be Buried (Covered over) With Christ in Baptism.
Before Baptism a Person Must be Taught to Observe All Things for a Christian to Follow.
When a Person Receives the Full Christian Message it is Well to be re-Baptized.
After Baptism we Rise to Walk in Newness of Life.
Through Baptism we "Put on Christ".
After Baptism we are to Walk as Jesus Walked.

CHAPTER 27

(pages 216–222)

BORN AGAIN CHRISTIANS

God has a Spiritual Nature.
God Created the Man and woman with a Spiritual Nature.
When Man Sinned the Spiritual Nature Died That Very Day.
All That was Left was a Body of Flesh.
When Born Again We are Given Back Our Spiritual Nature through Christ and the Holy Spirit.
We Can Get Back Our Spiritual Nature by Believing on Jesus Christ.
Belief is the Exercise of Faith.
If You have Jesus You have Everything.
A New Born Babe Must be Nourished and Instructed, to Grow up in Christ.
The Old Man of Sin Must be Starved Out.
The Spiritual Nature of a Born Again Christian Does Not Sin but it is the Fleshly Nature That Wars Against the Spiritual Nature That Sins.

New Infant Christians Need the Simple Milk of the Word and Not Heavy Food.

It is the Word of God That Gives Us Nourishment and Instruction.

To Stay Healthy a Person Must Have Nourishment (Bible Reading), Air to Breath (Prayer) and Exercise (Witnessing).

Focusing on Christ Makes Us Like Him.

The Flesh Nature Wars Against the New Born Spiritual Nature.

CHAPTER 28

(pages 223–230)

THE GIFT OF TONGUES

Christ Commissions the Preaching of the Gospel.

The Lord Will Protect Those Who Follow the Gospel Commission.

First They Must Wait for Holy Spirit.

The Holy Spirit Will Give Power to Witness.

These Gifts were the Former Rain Spoken of by the Prophet Joel.

Peter's First Mission Trip to Gentiles.

Gift of Prophecy More Important than Gift of Tongues.

Edify = Enlighten, Elevate, Uplift

There are Many Gifts of the spirit Some Have One, Others Have Another.

The More Excellent Way is Love.

How Long Will the Gifts be Needed?

When Will the Gifts of the Holy Spirit No Longer be Needed?

The Fruit of the Spirit is Different Than the Gift of the Spirit.

CHAPTER 29

(pages 231–237)

THE GIFT OF PROPHECY
>The Prophetic Gift in Old Testament Times.
>The Prophetic Gift in the New Testament Church.
>Prophets Assisted in the Founding of the Church.
>Prophets Edified and United the Church.
>Prophets Warned of Future Difficulties.
>Continuation of Spiritual Gifts
>Prophetic Gift Prior to the Second Advent.
>The Prophetic Gift in the Remnant Church.
>Help in the Final Crisis
>Testing the Prophetic Gift
>Is Christ's Incarnation Recognized?
>Does the Prophet Bear Good or Bad Fruit?

CHAPTER 30

(pages 238–244)

THE LORD'S SUPPER
>Seeking Ascendancy
>The Supper
>The Ordinance of Foot Washing
>A Memorial of Christ's Condescension
>A Fellowship of Forgiveness
>A Fellowship with Christ and Believers
>The Celebration of the Lord's Supper
>Commemoration of Deliverance of Sin
>The Bread and the Fruit of the Vine

Anticipation of the Second Advent
Qualification for Participation

CHAPTER 31

(pages 245–254)

CHRISTIAN BEHAVIOR

Behavior and Salvation
The Blessing of Physical Work
The Blessing of Rest
The Effect of Viewing Movies, T.V., Etc.
We Must be Careful of Our Music and Reading.
Careful of Our Activities
Careful About Our Food
What About Alcoholic Beverages?
Drunkenness
How Should a Christian Dress?
Gaudy Cosmetics Associated with Paganism and Apostasy.
Principles of Christian Standards
Living with the Mind of Christ.
Living to Praise and Glorify God.
Living to be an Example and to Minister.

CHAPTER 32

(pages 255–261)

MARRIAGE AND THE FAMILY

Male and Female in the Image of God
Marriage and Biblical Love

The Family
The Father and Mother
Children Committed to the Lord
The Extended Family

CHAPTER 33

(pages 262–265)

WHAT THE BIBLE SAYS ABOUT SINFUL SEXUAL BEHAVIOR

Adultery and Fornication
Homosexuality and Lesbianism
Bestiality

CHAPTER 34

(pages 266–269)

THE REMNANT CHURCH

A Remnant is a Small Portion Left from a Larger Whole.
Noah and Family were the First Remnant.
Paul Compares His Own Day With the Remnant of Elijah's Time.
Only a Remnant was Left in Judea During the Babylonian Captivity.
A Remnant Returned from Babylon to Judea.
Paul Predicted a Falling away from the Church After His Time.
The True Church (A Remnant) was in Hiding During the Dark Ages.
How is the Remnant Church Identified?

What is the Testimony of Jesus Christ?
The Remnant Church Keeps the Commandments of God and has the Spirit of Prophecy.

CHAPTER 35

(pages 270–276)

HELL FIRE, WHEN? WHERE? HOW?
Everlasting Fire and Unquenchable Fire

CHAPTER 36

(pages 277–284)

WHERE ARE THE DEAD?
Dust + Breath of Life = Living Soul
Where Does the Spirit go at Death?
The Dead Know Not What the Living are doing.
Will the Dead Live Again?
There Will by a Resurrection
Only God has Inherent Immortality.
God Gives Immortality to the Righteous at the Second Coming of Christ.
God Considers Death a Sleep.
Who are the Dead Brought up by Mediums?
What Does God Think of Spirit Mediums?
Does Man Continue to Live after Death?

CHAPTER 37

(pages 285–291)

THE SECOND COMING OF CHRIST—MATTHEW 24

Christ Returns to Heaven.
Christ Wants Us with Him.
We have a Future Home in Heaven.
Christ Will Not Come in Secret.
The Righteous Living Will be Caught up with the Righteous Dead.

CHAPTER 38

(pages 292–299)

THE NEARNESS OF THE RETURN OF JESUS

Signs Tell Us His Coming is Near.
People Lose Interest in Church Going.
False Christs and False Prophets.
The Rich Will Pile up Great Fortunes.
There Will be Many Poor on the Earth.
Knowledge and Travel Will be Increased.
Fearful Calamities on the Increase.
A Craze for Pleasure, A Decline in True Religion.
Crime and Wickedness on the Increase.
Missionaries Spread Gospel World Wide.
Nations Will Talk Peace.
Nations Will Prepare for War.
When These Things are Happening Christ's Coming is Near.

CHAPTER 39

(pages 300–308)

THE TIME OF THE END AND THE MILLENNIUM

When is the End of Prophetic Time?
How Do We Know That Prophetic Time Begins With the Year 457 B.C.?
In the Days of the Time of the End the Books of Daniel and Revelation Would Begin to be Understood by God's People.
Christ Came Right on Time at His First Advent.
Jesus' Crucifixion Happened on the Very Hour for Which it was Prophesied.
Most of the World Will Not Expect His Second Coming.
Following is a Description of Society on Earth Just Before Christ Returns.
Events During the Millennium
A Description of the Earth During the Millennium.

CHAPTER 40

(pages 309–315)

THE MILLENNIUM

Two Resurrections Separated by 1000 Years.
Righteous Dead Raised in the First Resurrection.
The Righteous Will Judge the Wicked Dead.
The Wicked Dead Will Remain Dead Another 1000 Years.
Satan Will be Left on the Earth with No One to Tempt for 1000 Years.
There is No Second Chance for the Wicked.

The New Jerusalem Descends After 1000 Years.
Resurrected Wicked Agree, God is Just.
Satan and Resurrected Wicked, Will Attempt to Capture the New Jerusalem.
A New Earth is Created after the Fire.

CHAPTER 41

(pages 316–322)

THE LAW OF GOD
The Ten Commandments in Full
The Perpetuity of the Law
Meaning of "to Fulfill the Law"

CHAPTER 42

(pages 323–330)

THE SABBATH
Sabbath Importance Re-Confirmed
God Gives Ten Commandments
Sabbath a Sign Between God and Man
What Prophets Said about the Sabbath
Sabbath to be observed in the New Earth
Christians Today are Israelites.
Christ Observed the Sabbath.
Christ is Lord of the Sabbath.
Christ is Lord of the Commandments.
The Commandments are Not Changeable.
Christ Rested on the Sabbath in the Tomb.
The Apostle Paul Observed the Sabbath.
The Sabbath Kept in the New Jerusalem.

CHAPTER 43

(pages 331–338)

THE CHANGE OF THE SABBATH AND THE FIRST DAY OF THE WEEK
A Day in Prophecy = A Calendar Year.
Sabbath Truth Made Known at End Time.
Past Sunday Keeping Not Condemned.
Eight N. T. Tests that Mention the First Day.

CHAPTER 44

(pages 339–344)

THE TRUTH ABOUT THE SABBATH
The Bible = Absolute Truth
There are Three Special Words in the Bible: Hallowed 23 Times, Sanctified 40 Times, Blessed 307 Times.
The Only Place Where All Tree Words are Found is Where God Speaks of the Sabbath.
Ancient Israel Also had Trouble Hallowing the Sabbath.
Christ is the Lord of the Sabbath.
Christ is the word Who Created Worlds.
Christ Demonstrated to Us What God the Father is Like.
God Promised a Great Blessing on those Who Honor His Sabbath.
How Do We Know for Sure Which Day is the Seventh Day?

CHAPTER 45

(pages 345–354)

THE EVERLASTING COVENANT

Christ Wishes to Have a Covenant in the Hearts and Minds of His People.
Covenant = Agreement = Will = Testament
The Rainbow is an Everlasting Covenant.
God has Another Everlasting Covenant
Mankind's Part Toward the Covenant is to Obey His Commandments.
A Covenant for All People Not Just Israel.
John in vision sees the original Ark of the testament in heaven.
Christ Made a New Covenant at the Last Supper Then Ratified it With His Death.
Gentile Christians are Abraham's Seed by Adoption Through Christ.
Why Do We Need a New Covenant?
The Old Covenant was Obedience by Works.
Christ is Testator of the New Covenant.
Christ Lived a Perfect Life for Us.
Through the Blood of the Everlasting Covenant
Christians Continued to Keep the Sabbath After Christ Died.
The Sabbath Will be Kept in the New Earth.

CHAPTER 46

(pages 355–361)

BIBLE PLAN TO SUPPORT GOD'S WORK

Everything in the World Belongs to God.
We Each Belong to God.
The Ministers of the Gospel are to be Supported by the Tithes.
Christ Endorsed Tithing.
We are to Give Offerings in Addition to the Tithe as We are Able.
When the Lord Speaks to Our Hearts We Should Give Willingly.
Generous Giving Would Provide Enough Funds to Spread the Gospel.
Many Men Rob God.
God Blesses Tithe Givers and He Will Provide for Our Needs.
If We Do Our Part God Will Keep His Promise.
Hard for a Rich Man to Enter Heaven.
Our Giving is Means Tested.

CHAPTER 47

(pages 362–368)

FOOD GIVEN TO MAN BY GOD

Animals and Sea Life Allowed as Food.
Fowls Not Allowed as Food.
Peter's Dream of Sheet Full of Creatures.
Romans 14, 1 Tim. 4, and Mark 7 Examined.
Modern Medicine Agrees with Leviticus.

CHAPTER 48

(pages 369–386)

CHRIST'S MINISTRY IN THE HEAVENLY SANCTURY

    The Earthly Sanctuary Replica
    The Heavenly Sanctuary
    The Substitutionary Sacrifice
    God's Judgment On Sin
    The Ministry (Work) of Earthly Priests
    LORD = Jehovah = Christ = Veil
    The Result of Being Forgiven and Forgiving
    Ministry in the Earthly Most Holy Place.
    Azazel, The Scapegoat, its Function.
    The Three Phases of the Judgment
    The Cleansing of the Heavenly Sanctuary.
    The Vindication of God's People.
    Judgment and Salvation
    Both Genuine and False Believers in the Church

CHAPTER 49

(pages 387–393)

HEAVEN

    There is a First Heaven, a Second Heaven and a Third Heaven.
    Jesus Prepares a Place for His People.
    The New Jerusalem Size
    A City of Perfect Health
    We Will have Glorious Spiritual Bodies.

We Will Recognize One Another in Heaven.
After the Millennium God Will Make a New 1st Heaven with a New Atmosphere.
New Jerusalem Will Become Earth's Capital.
A Description of the New Earth.

CHAPTER 1
GOD
ATTRIBUTES OF THE GOD HEAD

OMNIPRESENCE—Everywhere present

7. Whither shall I go from thy spirit? Or whither shall I flee from thy presence?
8. If I ascend up unto heaven, Thou art there; if I make my bed in hell, behold, Thou art there.
9. If I take the wings of the morning, and dwell in the uttermost parts of the sea;
10. Even there shall Thy hand lead me and Thy right hand shall hold me.
11. If I say, Surely the darkness shall cover me; even the night shall be light about me.
12. Yea, the darkness hideth not from thee; but the night shineth as the day; the darkness and the light are both alike to thee.
—Psalms 139:7-12

OMNISCIENCE—knows all things

1. O LORD, Thou hast searched me, and known me.
2. Thou knowest my downsitting and mine uprising, Thou understandest my thought afar off.
3. Thou compassest my path and my lying down, and art acquainted with all my ways.

4. For there is not a word in my tongue, but lo, O LORD, Thou knowest it altogether.
—Psalm 139:1-4

OMNIPOTENCE—All Powerful

26. But Jesus beheld them, and said unto them, With men this is impossible; but with God all things are possible.
—Matthew 19:26

ETERNAL—God has always been there

2. Before the mountains were brought forth, or ever Thou hadst formed the earth and the world, even from everlasting to everlasting, Thou art God.
—Psalm 90:2

IMMUTABLE—God never changes

6. For I AM the LORD, I change not;
—Malachi 3:6

GOODNESS—God is good.

9. The LORD is good to all: and His tender mercies are over all His works.
—Psalm 145:9

RIGHTEOUSNESS—God is righteous and Holy.

7. The law of the LORD is perfect, converting the soul: the testimony of the LORD is sure, making wise the simple.
8. The statutes of the LORD are right, rejoicing the heart: The commandment of the LORD is pure, enlightening the eyes.
9. The fear of the LORD is clean, enduring for ever: the judgment of the LORD are true and righteous altogether.
—Psalms 19:7-9

GOD THE RULER OF THE UNIVERSE

9. I beheld till the thrones were cast down (put in place), and the ANCIENT OF DAYS did sit whose garments was white as snow, and hair of His head like pure wool: His throne was like the fiery flame, and His [margin = its] wheels as burning fire.
10. A fiery stream issued and came forth from before Him: thousands thousand ministered unto Him, and ten thousand times ten thousand [100 million] stood before Him: the judgment was set, and the books were opened.
—Daniel 7:9, 10

A GOD OF MERCY

20. And He said, Thou canst not see my face: for there shall no man see me, and live.
21. And the LORD said, Behold, there is a place by me, and thou shalt stand upon a rock:
22. And it shall come to pass, while My glory passeth by, that I will put thee in a clift [cleft] of the rock, and will cover thee with My hand while I pass by:
23. And I will take away mine hand, and thou shalt see My back parts: but My face shall not be seen.
—Exodus 33:20-23
6. And the LORD passed by before him, and proclaimed, the LORD, the LORD God, merciful and gracious, long-suffering, and abundant in goodness and truth.
7. Keeping mercy for thousands, forgiving iniquity and transgression and sin, and that will by no means clear the guilty: visiting the iniquity of the fathers upon the children, and upon the children's children, unto the third and to the fourth generation.
—Exodus 34:6, 7
26. For if we sin willfully after that we have received the knowledge of the truth, there remaineth no more sacrifice for sin.

27. But a certain fearful looking for of judgment and fiery indignation, which shall devour the adversaries.
—Hebrews 10:26, 27
8. And let them make Me a Sanctuary that I may dwell among them.
—Exodus 25:8

A COVENANT GOD

9. ... I establish My Covenant with you, and with your seed after you;
11. ... neither shall all flesh be cut off any more by the waters of a flood; ...
12. And God said, This is the token of the covenant which I make between me and you and every creature that is with you, for perpetual generations:
13. I do set My bow in the cloud, and it shall be for a token of a covenant between Me and the earth.
—Genesis 9:9, 11, 12, 13
(Read Also: Genesis 9:1-17)
2. And I will make thee [Abram] a great nation, and I will bless thee, and make thy name great; and thou shalt be a blessing:
—Genesis 12:2
(Also Read: Genesis 12:1-3, 7; 13:14-17;15:1, 5, 6; 17:18; 22:15-18)
22. While the earth remaineth, seedtime and harvest, and cold and heat, and summer and winter, and day and night shall not cease.
—Genesis 8:22
8. And I will give unto thee, and to thy seed after thee, the land wherein thou art a stranger, all the land of Canaan, for an everlasting possession; and I will be their God.
—Genesis 17:8
(Also Read: Genesis 15:5-7, 18)

A REDEEMER GOD

3. When I consider thy heavens, the work of thy fingers, the moon and the stars, which Thou hast ordained;
4. What is man, that Thou art mindful of him? And the son of man, that Thou visitest him:
—Psalms 8:3, 4
1. I will love thee, O LORD, my strength.
2. The LORD is my rock, and my fortress, and my deliverer; my God, my strength, in whom I will trust; my buckler [hand-shield], and the horn of my salvation, and my high tower.
—Psalms 18:1, 2
24. For He hath not despised nor abhorred the affliction of the afflicted; neither hath He hid His face from him; but when he cried unto Him, He heard.
—Psalm 22:24

A GOD OF REFUGE

5. For in the time of trouble He shall hide me in His pavilion: in the secret of His tabernacle shall He hide me; He shall set me up upon a rock.
—Psalm 27:5
1. God is our refuge and strength, a very present help in trouble.
—Psalms 46:1
2. As the mountains are round about Jerusalem, so the LORD is round about His people from henceforth even for ever.
—Psalm 125:2
1. Blessed is he that considereth the poor: the LORD will deliver him in time of trouble.
2. The LORD will preserve him, and keep him alive; and he shall he blessed upon the earth: and thou wilt not deliver him unto the will of his enemies.
—Psalms 41:1, 2

22. Cast thy burden upon the LORD, and He shall sustain thee: He shall never suffer the righteous to be moved.
—Psalm 55:22
8. Trust in Him at all times; ye people, pour out your heart before Him: God is a refuge for us.
—Psalm 62:8
15. But thou, O Lord, art a God full of compassion, and gracious, long suffering, and plenteous in mercy and truth.
—Psalm 86:15

A GOD OF FORGIVENESS

1. Have mercy upon me, O God, according to thy loving kindness; according unto the multitudes of thy tender mercies blot out my transgressions.
11. Cast me not away from thy presence; and take not thy Holy Spirit from me.
—Psalms 51:1, 11
11. For as the heaven is high above the earth, so great is His mercy toward them that fear Him.
12. As far as the east is from the west, so far hath He removed our transgressions from us.
13. Like as a father pitieth his children, so the LORD pitieth them that fear Him.
14. For He knoweth our frame; He remembereth that we are dust.
—Psalms 103:11-14

A GOD OF GOODNESS

7. Which executeth judgment for the oppressed: which giveth food to the hungry. The LORD looseth the prisoners:
8. The LORD openeth the eyes of the blind: the LORD raiseth them that are bowed down: the LORD loveth the righteous:
9. The LORD preserveth the strangers; He relieveth the fatherless and widow: but the way of the wicked He turneth upside down.
—Psalms 146:7-9

A GOD OF FAITHFULNESS

9. Thou whom I have taken from the ends of the earth, and called thee from the chief men thereof, and said unto thee, Thou art My servant; I have chosen thee, and not cast thee away.
10. Fear thou not; for I AM with thee: be not dismayed; for I AM God: I will strengthen thee; yea, I will help thee; yea, I will uphold thee with the right hand of My righteousness.
—Isaiah 41:9, 10
12. Go and proclaim these words toward the north, and say, Return, thou backsliding Israel, saith the LORD: and I will not cause mine anger to fall upon you: for I AM merciful, saith the LORD, and I will not keep anger forever.
—Jeremiah 3:12
21. Remember there, O Jacob and Israel; for thou art my servant; I have formed thee, thou art My servant: O Israel, thou shalt not be forgotten of me.
22. I have blotted out, as a thick cloud, thy transgressions, and, as a cloud, thy sins: return unto Me; for I have redeemed thee.
—Isaiah 44:21, 22
22. Look unto Me, and be ye saved all the ends of the earth: for I AM God, and there is none else.
—Isaiah 45:22
(Read Also: Leviticus 26 and Deuteronomy 28)

A GOD OF SALVATION AND VENGEANCE

4. Say to them that are of a fearful heart, Be strong, fear not: behold, your God will come with a recompense; He will come and save you.
—Isaiah 35:4

CHAPTER 2
ONE GOD

AS CHRISTIANS WE BELIEVE IN ONE GOD (ONE GOD-HEAD) OR (THE TRIUNE GOD)

4. Hear, O Israel: The LORD our God is one LORD:
   —Deuteronomy 6:4
20. O LORD, there is none like thee, neither is there any God beside thee . . .
    —1 Chronicles 17:20
10. Have we not all one father? Hath not one God Created us?
    —Malachi 2:10
    (Note: These scriptures from the Old Testament makes it difficult for the Jews to accept Jesus as the Messiah in His day and in our day.)
17. And He said unto him? Why callest thou me good? There is none good but one, that is, God: . . .
    —Matthew 19:17
29. And Jesus answered him, The first of all the commandments is, Hear, O Israel; The Lord our God is one LORD:
    —Mark 12:29
41. . . . we have one Father, even God.
    —John 8:41
19. Thou believest that there is one God; thou doest well: the devils also believe, and tremble.

—James 2:19

BUT AS CHRISTIANS WE ALSO BELIEVE THAT THE GOD-HEAD IS MADE UP OF THREE PERSONS. A TRIUNE GOD. WE BELIEVE IN THE TRINITY. HOW CAN ONE GOD BE MORE THAN ONE PERSON?

6. But to us there is but one God, the Father, of whom are all things, and we in Him: and one Lord Jesus Christ, by whom are all things, and we by Him.
—1 Corinthians 8:6

WE BELIEVE THAT ALL THREE PERSONS OF THE GOD HEAD WERE ACTIVE AT THE CREATION.

26. And God [Elohim] said, Let US make man in OUR image, after OUR likeness: . . .
—Genesis 1:26 (Elohim is plural)

THE LORD IS ONE (One—English = Echod—Hebrew)

CONCERNING CREATION:

5. And the evening and the morning were the first day [one [echod] day].
—Genesis 1:5 (Two parts make one whole.)

CONCERNING MARRIAGE

24. Therefore shall a man leave his father and his mother, and shall cleave unto his wife: and they shall be one [echod] flesh.
—Genesis 2:24

PLURALITY IN THE GODHEAD

1. In the beginning God [Elohim] created the heavens and the earth.
—Genesis 1:1 (Elohim is the plural form of Eloah or YHWH.)
2. And the earth was without form, and void; and darkness

was upon the face of the deep. And the SPIRIT of God moved upon the face of the waters.
—Genesis 1:2

ADDITIONAL EVIDENCES OF PLURALITY IN THE OLD TESTAMENT

22. And the LORD God said, Behold, the man is become as one of US, to know good and evil: ...
—Genesis 3:22

7. Go to, let US go down, and there confound their language, ...
—Genesis 11:7

20. And the LORD said [to Abraham], Because the cry of Sodom and Gomorrah is great, and because their sin is very grievous: ...

22. And the men (angels) turned their faces from thence, and went toward Sodom: but Abraham stood yet before the LORD.
—Genesis 18:20, 22

13. For we [angels speaking] will destroy this place, because the cry of them is waxen great before the face of the LORD; and the LORD hath sent us to destroy it.
—Genesis 19:13

24. Then the LORD [who visited Abraham] rained upon Sodom and upon Gomorrah brimstone and fire from the LORD [Jehovah] out of heaven:
—Genesis 19:24
(For complete story read: Genesis 18:16-19:29)

ANOTHER EXAMPLE IN DEUTERONOMY

17. For the LORD your God is God of gods, and LORD of lords, a great God, a mighty, and a terrible, which regardeth not persons, nor taketh reward:
—Deuteronomy 10:17 (Here the true God speaks of Himself as being the Gods [plural] of Israel.)

THE MESSIAH IN PSALM 45

3. Gird thy sword upon thy thigh, O most mighty, with thy glory and thy majesty.
4. And in thy majesty ride prosperously because of truth and meekness and righteousness; and thy right hand shall teach thee terrible things.
5. Thine arrows are sharp in the heart of the king's enemies; whereby the people fall under thee.
6. The throne, O God [Elohim], is for ever and ever: the sceptre of thy kingdom is a right scepter
7. Thou lovest righteousness, and hatest wickedness: therefore God [Elohim] thy God, hath anointed thee with the oil of gladness above thy fellows.
—Psalms 45:3-7

(The Messiah is twice addressed as Elohim, which is plural in form but in this context has a singular connotation.)

SOLOMON IN ECCLESIASTES DECLARES;

1. Remember now your Creator [Hebrew word for Creator here is plural.] in the days of your youth.
—Ecclesiastes 12:1

THE GREAT MESSIANIC PROPHET ISAIAH DECLARED:

6. For unto us a child is born, unto us a Son is given, and the government shall be upon His shoulders: His name shall be Wonderful, Counsellor, the Mighty God, the Everlasting Father, the Prince of Peace.
7. Of the increase of his government and peace there will be no end, upon the throne of David and over His kingdom, to order it and establish it with judgment and justice from that time forward even forever. The zeal of the Lord of Hosts will perform this.
—Isaiah 9:6, 7

14. . . . Behold a virgin shall conceive, and bear a Son, and shall call His name Immanuel.
   —Isaiah 7:14
8. Also I heard the voice of the LORD, saying, Whom shall I send, and who will go for US? Then said I, Here am I; send me:
   —Isaiah 6:8

GOD THE FATHER SPOKE FROM HEAVEN THREE TIMES WHILE CHRIST WAS A MAN ON EARTH. FIRST AT CHRIST'S BAPTISM

11. And there came a voice from heaven, saying, Thou art my beloved Son, in whom I am well pleased.
12. And immediately the Spirit driveth Him into the wilderness.
    —Mark 1:11,12
22. And the Holy Ghost descended in a bodily shape like a dove upon Him, and a voice from heaven, which said, Thou art my beloved Son; in thee I am well pleased.
    —Luke 3:22

SECOND, ON THE MOUNT OF TRANSFIGURATION

5. While he yet spake, behold, a bright cloud overshadowed them: and behold a voice out of the cloud, which said, Thou art my beloved Son, in whom I am well pleased; hear ye Him.
   —Matthew 17:5
7. And there was a cloud that overshadowed them: and a voice came out of the cloud, saying, This is my beloved Son: hear Him.
   —Mark 9:7

THIRD, DURING JESUS' PRAYER SHORTLY BEFORE HIS CRUCIFIXION.

28. Father, glorify thy name. Then came there a voice from heaven, saying, I have both glorified it, and will glorify it again.
—John 12:28

SHORTLY AFTER CHRIST RETURNED TO HIS FATHER THE HOLY SPIRT BECAME VERY ACTIVE IN THE SPREAD OF THE GOSPEL.

26. But the comforter, which is the Holy Ghost [Holy Sprit], whom the Father will send in my name, He shall teach you all things, . . .
—John 14:26

2. And suddenly there came a sound from heaven as of a rushing mighty wind, and it filled all the house where they were sitting.
3. And there appeared unto them cloven tongues like as of fire, and it sat upon each of them.
4. And they were all filled with the Holy Ghost, . . .
—Acts 2:2-4

MORE EVIDENCES OF TRIUNE GOD FROM NEW TESTAMENT.

19. Go ye therefore, and teach all nations, baptizing them in the name of the Father, and of the Son, and of the Holy Ghost:
—Matthew 28:19

14. The grace of the Lord Jesus Christ, and the love of God, and the communion of the Holy Ghost, be with you all. Amen.
—2 Corinthians 13:14
(Read Also: Ephesians 3:14-21)

17. For the kingdom of God is not meat and drink; but righteousness, and peace, and joy in the Holy Ghost.
18. For he that in these things serveth Christ is acceptable to God, and approved of men.
—Romans 14:17, 18
(Read Also: Ephesians 2:11-22)

16. That I [Paul] should be the minister of Jesus Christ to the Gentiles, ministering the gospel of God, that the offering up of the Gentiles might be acceptable, being sanctified by the Holy Ghost.
—Romans 15:16
3. For we are the circumcision, which worship God in the Spirit, and rejoice in Christ Jesus, and have no confidence in the flesh.
—Philippians 3:3
14. If ye be reproached for the name of Christ, happy are ye; for the Spirit of glory and of God resteth upon you: on their part he is evil spoken of, but on your part he is glorified.
—1 Peter 4:14
2. Elect according to the foreknowledge of God the Father, through Sanctification of the Spirit, unto obedience and sprinkling of the blood of Jesus Christ: Grace unto you, and peace, be multiplied.
—1 Peter 1:2
20. But ye, beloved, building up yourselves on your most holy faith, praying in the Holy Ghost,
21. Keeping yourselves in the love of God, looking for the mercy of our Lord Jesus Christ unto eternal life.
—Jude 20, 21
3. Wherefore I give you to understand, that no man speaking by the Spirit of God calleth Jesus accursed: and that no man can say that Jesus is the Lord, but by the Holy Ghost.
—1 Corinthians 12:3
4. There is one body, and one Spirit, even as ye are called in one hope of your calling.
5. One Lord, one faith, one baptism,
6. One God and Father of all, who is above all, and through all, and in you all.
—Ephesians 4:4-6
(Read Also: 1 Corinthians 12:4-6)
13. But we are bound to give thanks always to God for you,

brethren beloved of the LORD, because God hath from the beginning chosen you to salvation through sanctification of the Spirit and belief of the truth:
14. Whereunto He called you by our gospel, to the obtaining of the glory of our Lord Jesus Christ.
—2 Thessalonians 2:13, 14
6. And because ye are sons, God hath sent forth the Spirit of His Son into your hearts, crying, Abba, Father.
7. Wherefore thou art no more a servant, but a son; and if a son, then an heir of God through Christ.
—Galatians 4:6, 7
21. Now He which stablisheth us with you in Christ, and hath anointed us, in God;
22. Who hath also sealed us, and given the earnest of the Spirit in our hearts.
—2 Corinthians 1:21, 22
(Read Also: Hebrews 6:4-6)
3. Forasmuch as ye are manifestly declared to be the epistle of Christ ministered by us, written not with ink, but with the Spirit of the living God; not in tables of stone, but in fleshly tables of the heart.
—2 Corinthians 3:3
14. That the blessing of Abraham might come on the Gentiles through Jesus Christ; that we might receive the promise of the Spirit through faith.
—Galatians 3:14
16. That I should be the minister of Jesus Christ to the Gentiles, ministering the gospel of God, that the offering up of the Gentiles might be acceptable, being sanctified by the Holy Ghost.
17. I have therefore whereof I may glory through Jesus Christ in those things which pertain to God.
18. For I will not dare to speak of any those things which Christ hath not wrought by me, to make the Gentiles obedient, by word and deed,
—Romans 15:16-18
4. But after that the kindness and love of God our Saviour toward man appeared,

5. Not by works of righteousness which we have done, but according to His mercy He saved us, by the washing of regeneration, and renewing of the Holy Ghost;
6. Which He shed on us abundantly through Jesus Christ our Saviour;
—Titus 3:4-6

CHRIST OUR ADVOCATE

1. My little children, these things write I unto you, that ye sin not. And if any man sin, we have an advocate with the Father, Jesus Christ the righteous:
—1 John 2:1

[after Christ returned to heaven we have Him working on behalf of repentant sinners before God the Father. God the Father the first person, God the Son the Second person and God the Holy Spirit the Third person of the God-Head; Have worked together at creation, when Jesus was on earth and after Jesus returned to Heaven. It is reasonable to believe that they also worked together during Old Testament Times.]

Y H W H = JEHOVAH = GOD = LORD so there was in the Old Testament times:

(1.) JEHOVAH the FATHER, (2.) JEHOVAH who later became JESUS CHRIST, and (3.) JEHOVAH the HOLY SPIRIT. *[Jehovah the Father seems to work primarily from Heaven. Jehovah the Son and Jehovah the Holy Spirit are the members of the God-Head who have worked on earth directly with mankind.]*

29. The secret things belong unto the LORD our God: but those things which are revealed belong unto us and to our children for ever, that we may do all the words of this law.
—Deuteronomy 29:29
(Read Also: Psalms 131:1)

CHAPTER 3
GOD ABOVE TIME

GOD ABOVE TIME

[Numerous scriptural references underscore a God without beginning or ending: God exists totally apart from the universe and yet can be everywhere within it.]

1. In the beginning God created the heaven and the earth.
   —Genesis 1:1

GOD IS MADE UP OF THREE PERSONS. AT CREATION ALL THREE WERE PRESENT.

26. And God said, Let US make man in *OUR* image, . . .
    [More than one person]
    —Genesis 1:26

THE HOLY SPIRIT WAS PRESENT

2. . . . And the Spirit of God moved upon the face of the waters.
   —Genesis 1:2

CHRIST SPOKE THE WORDS THAT BROUGHT EVERYTHING INTO EXISTENCE.

1. In the beginning was the Word, and the Word was with God, and the Word was God.
2. The same was in the beginning with God.

3. All things were made by Him; and without Him was not any thing made that was made.
4. In Him was life; and the life was the light of men.
5. And the light shineth in darkness; and the darkness comprehended it not.
—John 1:1-5
16. For by Him [Christ] were all things created, that are in heaven, and that are in earth, visible and invisible, whether they be thrones, or dominions, or principalities, or power: all things were created by Him, and for Him:
17. And He is before all things, and by Him all things consist (Greek: Hold together).
—Colossians 1:16, 17
1. God . . . .
2. Hath in these last days spoken unto us by His Son, by whom He hath appointed heir of all things, by whom *also He made the worlds;*
—Hebrews 1:1, 2

CHRIST'S EXISTENCE PRECEDES TIME.

CHRIST HAS NO BEGINNING AND WAS NOT CREATED.

2. But thou, Bethlehem Ephratah; though thou be little among the thousands of Judah, yet out of thee shall He come forth unto me that is to be ruler in Israel; whose goings forth have been from of old, from everlasting.
—Micah 5:2
9. Who hath saved us, and called us with an holy calling, not according to our works, but according to His own purpose and grace, which was given us in Christ Jesus before the world began.
—2 Timothy 1:9
2. In hope of eternal life, which God, that cannot lie, promised before the world began.
—Titus 1:2

GOD CREATED THE UNIVERSE FROM WHAT CANNOT BE DETECTED WITH THE FIVE SENSES.

3. Through faith we understand that the worlds were framed by the word of God, so that things which are seen were not made of things which do appear.
—Hebrews 11:3

CHRIST HAS EXTRADIMENSIONALITY SINCE HIS RESURRECTION AND CAN PASS THROUGH WALLS.

36. And as they thus spoke, Jesus Himself stood in the midst of them, and saith unto them, Peace be unto you.
37. But they were terrified and affrighted, and supposed that they has seen a spirit.
38. And He said unto them, Why are ye troubled? And why do thoughts arise in your hearts?
39. Behold My hands and My feet, that is I Myself: handle Me, and see; for a spirit hath not flesh and bones, as ye see Me have.
40. And when He had thus spoken, He showed them His hands and His feet.
41. And while they yet believed not for joy, and wonder, He said unto them, Have ye here any meat [food].
42. and they gave Him a piece of a broiled fish, and of an honeycomb.
43. And he took it, and did eat before them.
—Luke 24:36-43
26. And after eight days again His disciples were within, and Thomas with them: then came Jesus, the doors being shut, and stood in the midst, and said, Peace be unto you.
27. Then saith He to Thomas, Reach hither thy finger, and behold My hands; and reach hither thy hand, and thrust it into My side: and be not faithless, but believing.
28. And Thomas answered and said unto Him, My Lord and my God.
—John 20:26-28

GOD IS VERY NEAR, YET WE CANNOT SEE HIM.

20. And He said, Thou canst not see My face: for there shall no man see Me, and live.
—Exodus 33:20
11. For this commandment which I command thee this day it is not hidden from thee, neither is it far off.
12. It is not in heaven, that thou shouldest say, Who shall go up for us to heaven, and bring it unto us, that we may hear it, and do it?
13. Neither is it beyond the sea, that thou shouldest say, Who shall go over the sea for us, and bring it unto us, that we may hear it, and do it?
14. But the word is very nigh unto thee, in thy mouth, and in thy heart, that thou mayest do it.
—Deuteronomy 30:11-14
46. Not that any man hath seen the Father, save he which is of God he hath seen the Father.
—John 6:46

CHIRST NOW REIGNS WITH GOD THE FATHER.

3. Who being the brightness of His glory, and the express image of His person, and upholding all things by the word of His power, when He had by Himself purged our sins, *sat down on the right hand of the Majesty on high;*
—Hebrews 1:3

CHAPTER 4
A FATHER GOD

A FATHER GOD

6. Do ye thus requite the LORD, O foolish people and unwise? is not He thy father that hath bought thee? hath He not made thee, and established thee?
—Deuteronomy 32:6

8. But now, O LORD, thou art Our father; we are the clay, and thou our potter; and we all are the work of thy hand.
—Isaiah 64:8

16. ... Thou, O LORD art our father, our redeemer; thy name is from everlasting.
—Isaiah 63:16

6. A son honoureth his father, and a servant his master: if then I be a father, where is mine honour? And if I be a master, where is my fear? Saith the LORD of hosts ...
—Malachi 1:6

10. Have we not all one father? hath not one God created us? Why do we deal treacherously every man against his brother, by profaning the covenant of our father:
—Malachi 2:10

GOD THE FATHER IN THE NEW TESTAMENT

14. For if ye forgive men their trespasses, your heavenly Father will also forgive you:

15. But if ye forgive not men their trespasses, neither will your Father forgive your trespasses.
—Matthew 6:14, 15.
17. Jesus saith unto her [Mary], Touch me not; for I am not yet ascended to My Father: but go to My brethren, and say unto them, I ascend unto My Father, and your Father: and to My God, and your God.
—John 20:17

THE FATHER OF ALL CREATION

6. But to us there is but one God, the Father, of whom are all things, and we in Him; and one Lord Jesus Christ, by whom are all things, and we by Him.
—1 Corinthians 8:6
9. Furthermore we have had fathers of our flesh which corrected us, and we gave them reverence: shall we not much rather be in subjection unto the Father of spirits, and live?
—Hebrews 12:9
(Read Also: Galatians 4:6)
14. For this cause I bow my knees unto the Father of our Lord Jesus Christ,
15. Of whom the whole family in heaven and earth is named,
—Ephesians 3:14, 15
15. For ye have not received the spirit of bondage again to fear; but ye have received the Spirit of adoption, whereby we cry Abba, Father.
—Romans 8:15

JESUS REVEALS THE FATHER

18. No man hath seen God at any time; the only begotten Son, which is in the bosom of the Father, He hath declared Him.
—John 1:18
(Read Also: John 1:1, 14)
38. For I came down from heaven, not to do mine own will, but the will of Him that sent me.
—John 6:38

9. Jesus saith unto him, Have I been so long time with you, and yet hast thou not known Me, Philip? He that hath seen Me hath seen the Father; and how sayest thou then, Show us Father?
—John 14:9
1. God, . . .
2. Hath in these last days spoken unto us by His Son, whom He hath appointed heir of all things, by whom also He made the worlds;
3. Who being the brightness of His glory, and the express image of His person, and upholding all things by the word of His power, when He had by Himself purged our sins sat down on the right hand of the Majesty on high;
—Hebrews 1:1-3

A GOD WHO GIVES AND WHO LOVES

16. For God so loved the world, that He gave His only begotten Son, that whosoever believeth in Him should not perish, but have everlasting life:
—John 3:16
8. But God commendeth His love toward us, in that, while we were yet sinners, Christ died for us. Romans 5:8
7. Casting all your care upon Him; for He careth for you.
—1 Peter 5:7
7. Beloved, let us love one another: for love is of God; and every one that loveth is born of God; and knoweth God.
—1 John 4:7
16. And we have known and believed the love that God hath to us. God is love; and he that dwelleth in love dwelleth in God, and God in him.
—1 John 4:16
44. But I say unto you, Love your enemies, bless them that curse you, do good to them that hate you, and pray for them which despitefully use you, and persecute you;
45. That ye may be the children of your Father which is in heaven: for He maketh His sun to rise on the evil and on

the good, and sendeth rain on the just and on the unjust.
—Matthew 5:44, 45
35. But love ye your enemies, and do good, and lend, hoping for nothing again; and your reward shall be great, and ye shall be the children of the Hightest: for He is kind unto the unthankful and to the evil.
36. Be ye therefore merciful, as your Father also is merciful.
—Luke 6:35, 36
4. Or despisest thou the riches of His goodness and forbearance and longsuffering; not knowing that the goodness of God leadeth thee to repentance?
—Romans 2:4
27. For the Son of man shall come in the glory of His Father with His angels; and then He shall reward every man according to his works.
—Matthew 16:27
64. Jesus saith, unto him, Thou hast said: nevertheless I say unto you, hereafter shall ye see the Son of man sitting on the right hand of [Father's] power, and coming in the clouds of heaven.
—Matthew 26:64

CHAPTER 5
GOD THE SON
(JESUS CHRIST IS TRULY GOD)
HIS DIVINE ATTRIBUTES

(1.) HIS DIVINE ATTRIBUTES

18. And Jesus came and spake unto them, saying, All power is given unto me in heaven and in earth.
—Matthew 28:18
2. As Thou hast given Him power over all flesh, that He should give eternal life to as many as Thou hast given Him.
—John 17:2
3. In Whom are hid all the treasures of wisdom and knowledge.
—Colossians 2:3
8. Jesus Christ the same yesterday, and to day, and for ever.
—Hebrews 13:8
26. For as the Father hath life in Himself; so hath He given to the Son to have life in Himself;
27. And hath given Him authority to execute judgment also, because He is the Son of man.
—John 5:26, 27
(Read Also: Matthew 18:20; 28:20)
25. Jesus said unto her, I am the resurrection, and the life: he that believeth in Me, though he were dead, yet shall he live.
—John 11:25
(Read Also: John 1:4)

35. And the angel answered and said unto her, The Holy Ghost [Holy Spirit] shall come upon thee: and the power of the Highest shall overshadow thee: therefore also that Holy Thing which shall be born of thee shall be called the Son of God.
—Luke 1:35

24. [Unclean spirit speaking] Saying, Let us alone; what have we to do with thee, Thou Jesus of Nazareth? Art Thou come to destroy us? I know Thee who Thou art, the Holy One of God.
—Mark 1:24

6. For unto us a child is born, unto us a son is given: and the government shall be upon His shoulder: and His name shall be called Wonderful, Counselor, The mighty God, The everlasting Father, The Prince of Peace.
—Isaiah 9:6

(2.) HIS DIVINE POWER AND PREROGATIVES

2. The same was in the beginning with God.
3. All things were made by Him; and without Him was not anything made that was made.
—John 1:2, 3

16. For by Him were all things created, that are in heaven, and that are in earth, visible and invisible, whether they be thrones, or dominions, or principalities, or powers: all things were created by Him, and for Him:

17. And He is before all things, and by Him all things consist [hold together].
—Colossians 1:16, 17

3. Who being the brightness of His glory, and the express image of His person, and upholding all thing by the word of His power, when He had by Himself purged our sins, sat down on the right hand of the Majesty on high;
—Hebrews 1:3

28. Marvel not at this: for the hour is coming, in the which all that are in the graves shall hear His voice.

29. And shall come forth; they that have done good, unto the resurrection of life; and they that have done evil, unto the resurrection of damnation.
—John 5:28, 29

6. But that ye may know that the Son of man hath power on earth to forgive sins, (then saith He to the sick of the palsy,) Arise, take up thy bed, and go unto thine house.
—Matthew 9:6
(Read Also: Mark 2:5)

(3.) HIS DIVINE NAMES

23. ... they shall call His name Emmanuel, which being interpreted is, God with us.
—Matthew 1:23

29. ... Jesus, thou Son of God ...
—Matthew 8:29

7. ... Jesus, thou Son of the most high God ...
—Mark 5:7
(Read Also: Mark 1:1)

3. ... Prepare ye the way of the LORD [Jehovah or Yahweh], make straight in the desert a highway for our God;
—Isaiah 40:3

3. For this is He [John the Baptist speaking] that was spoken of by the prophet Esaias [Isaiah], saying, The voice of one crying in the wilderness, Prepare ye the way of the LORD [CHRIST], make His paths straight.
—Matthew 3:3

1. In the year that king Uzziah died I saw also the Lord sitting upon a throne, high and lifted up, and His train filled the temple.

3. And one cried unto another, and said, Holy, holy, holy, is the LORD [Jehovah] of hosts: the whole earth is full of His glory.
—Isaiah 6:1, 3

41. These things said Esaias [Isaiah], when he saw His [Jesus'] glory, and spake of Him.
—John 12:41

(4.) HIS DIVINTY ACKNOWLEGED

1. In the beginning was the Word, and the Word was with God, and the Word was God,
14. And the Word was made flesh, and dwelt among us, (and we beheld His glory, the glory as of the only begotten of the Father,) full of grace and truth.
—John 1:1, 14
28. And Thomas answered and said unto Him my Lord and my God.
—John 20:28
5. . . . Christ came, who is over all, the eternally blessed God.
—Romans 9:5, NKJV
8. But to the Son He says: "Your Throne, O God, is forever and ever; a scepter of righteousness is the scepter of Your kingdom.
9. You have loved righteousness and hated lawlessness; Therefore God, Your God, has anointed You With the oil of gladness more that Your companions"
10. And: "You, LORD [Jehovah], in the beginning laid the foundation of the earth, and the heavens are the work of Your hands;
—Hebrews 1:8-10, NKJV
(Quoted from: Psalms 45:6, 7; Isaiah 61:1, 3; Psalms 102:25-27)

(5.) HIS PERSONAL TESTIMONY

58. Jesus said unto them, Verily, verily, I say unto you, Before Abraham was, I AM.
—John 8:58
17. Jesus said to her, "Do not cling to Me, for I have not yet ascended to My Father; but go to My brethren and say to them, 'I am ascending to My Father and your Father, and to My God and to your God.' "
—John 20:17, NKJV
30. I and My Father are one.
—John 10:30

(6.) HIS EQUALITY WITH GOD ASSUMED

19. Go ye therefore, and teach all nations, baptizing them in the name of the Father, and the Son, and of the Holy Ghost:
—Matthew 28:19

9. Jesus saith unto him, Have I been so long time with you, and yet hast thou not known Me, Philip? he that hath seen Me hath seen the Father; and how sayest thou then, Show us the Father.
—John 14:9
(Read Also: 2 Corinthians 13:14; 1 Corinthians 12:4-6; Hebrews 1:3; John chapters 14-16, Jesus' parting counsel.)

14. The grace of the Lord Jesus Christ, and the love of God, and the communion of the Holy Ghost, be with you all. Amen.
—2 Corinthians 13:14

3. Who being the brightness of His glory, and the express image of His [the Father's] person, and upholding all things by the word of His power, when He [Christ' had by Himself purged our sins, sat down on the right hand of the Majesty [God the Father] on high;
—Hebrews 1:3

(7.) HE IS WORSHIPED AS GOD

6. . . . when He (God) bringeth in the first begotten into the world, He saith, and let all the angels of God worship Him.
—Hebrews 1:6

17. And when they saw Him [Jesus], they worshipped Him: . . .
—Matthew 28:17

10. That at the name of Jesus every knee should bow, of things in heaven, and things in earth, and things under the earth;

11. And that every tongue should confess that Jesus Christ is Lord, to the glory of God the Father.
—Philippians 2:10, 11

(Read Also: Luke 14:33; 2 Timothy 4:18; Hebrews 13:21; 2 Peter 3:18)

(8.) HIS DIVINE NATURE A NECESSITY

18. No man hath seen God at any time; the only begotten Son, which is in the bosom of the Father, He hath declared Him.
—John 1:18
19. And the whole multitude sought to touch Him: for there went virtue (power) out of Him, and healed them all.
—Luke 6:19
14. And the Word was made flesh, and dwelt among us, (and we beheld His glory, the glory as of the only begotten of the Father,) full of grace and truth.
—John 1:14
11. This beginning of miracles did Jesus in Cana of Galilee, and manifested forth His glory; and His disciples believed on Him.
—John 2:11
(Read Also: John 17:6; 14:9; 5:30; 5:1-15, 36; 11:41-45; 14:11; 8:3-11)

JESUS CHRIST IS TRULY MAN

2. Hereby know ye the Spirit of God: Every spirit that confesseth that Jesus Christ is come in the flesh is of God:
3. And every spirit that confesseth not that Jesus Christ is come in the flesh is not of God: . . .
—1 John 4:2, 3

(1.) HIS HUMAN BIRTH

4. But when the fullness of time was come, God sent forth His Son, made of a woman, made under the law, . . .
—Galatians 4:4
3. Concerning His Son Jesus Christ our Lord, which was made of the seed of David according to the flesh;

—Romans 1:3
15. And I will put enmity between thee [satan] and the woman, and between thy seed and her seed [Christ]; it shall bruise thy head [lethal], and thou shalt bruise His heel [non-lethal].
—Genesis 3:15
3. Is not this the carpenter, the son of Mary, the brother of James, and Joses, and of Juda, and Simon? And are not His sisters here with us? And they were offended at Him.
—Mark 6:3
(Read Also: John 1:14; Romans 9:5; Matthew 1:20-23; Luke 1:31-37)
7. But made Himself of no reputation, and took upon Him the form of a servant, and was made in the likeness of men:
8. And being found in fashion as a man, He humbled Himself, and became obedient unto death, even the death of the cross.
—Philippians 2:7, 8
16. And without controversy great is the mystery of godliness: God was manifest in the flesh, justified in the Spirit, seen of angels, preached unto the Gentiles, believed on in the world, received up into glory.
—1 Timothy 3:16

(2.) HIS HUMAN DEVELOPMENT

52. And Jesus increased in wisdom and stature, and in favour with God and man.
—Luke 2:52
40. And the child grew, and waxed strong in spirit, filled with wisdom: and the grace of God was upon Him.
—Luke 2:40
51. And He went down with them, and came to Nazareth, and was subject unto them: but His mother kept all these sayings in her heart.
—Luke 2:51

18. For in that He Himself hath suffered being tempted, He is able to succour them that are tempted.
—Hebrews 2:18
(Read Also: Luke 2:46-49; Hebrews 5:8, 9; 2:10)

(3.) HE WAS CALLED A "MAN"

30. (John the Baptist speaking) This is He of whom I said, after me cometh a man which is preferred before me: for He was before me.
—John 1:30
21. For since by man came death, by man came also the resurrection of the dead.
—1 Corinthians 15:21
5. For there is one God, and one mediator between God and men, the man Christ Jesus;
—1 Timothy 2:5
(Read Also: Acts 2:22; Romans 5:15; John 8:40)
20. And Jesus saith unto him, The foxes have holes, and the birds of the air have nests; but the Son of man hath not where to lay His head.
—Matthew 8:20
2. Ye know that after two days is the feast of the Passover, and the Son of man is betrayed to by crucified.
—Matthew 26:2
[Christ called himself Son of Man 77 times.]

(4.) HIS HUMAN CHARACTERISTICS

9. But we see Jesus, who was made a little lower than the angels for the suffering of death, crowned with glory and honour; that He by the grace of God should taste death for every man.
—Hebrews 2:9
(Read Also: Psalms 8:5)
14. Forasmuch then as the children are partakers of flesh and blood, He also Himself likewise took part of the same;

that through death He might destroy him that had the power of death, that is, the devil;
—Hebrews 2:14

Jesus suffered hunger, thirst, weariness, and anxiety.
(See: Matthew 4:2; John 19:28; John 4:6; Matthew 26:21; 8:24)

Christ felt compassion, righteous anger, and grief.
(See: Matthew 9:36; Mark 3:5)

He felt troubled, sorrow and wept.
(See: Matthew 26:38; Luke 19:41; 22:44; John 12:27; 11:33, 35; Hebrews 5:7)

He was completely dependent on God.
(See: Matthew 26:39-44; Mark 1:35; Mark 6:46; Luke 5:16; 6:12)

(5.) HIS IDENTITY WITH HUMAN NATURE

38. For I came down from heaven, not to do mine own will, but the will of Him that sent me.
    —John 6:38

45. . . . the first man Adam was made a living soul; the last Adam was made a quickening spirit.
    —1 Corinthians 15:45

2. Who can have compassion of the ignorant, and on them that are out of the way; for that He Himself also is compassed with infirmity.
   —Hebrews 5:2

17. That it might be fulfilled which was spoken by Esaias the prophet, saying, Himself took our infirmities, and bore our sicknesses.
    —Matthew 8:17
    (Read Also: Isaiah 53:4; Hebrews 5:7, 8; Hebrews 4:15; 1 Corinthians 10:13)

18. For in that He Himself hath suffered being tempted, He is able to succour them that are tempted.
    —Hebrews 2:18

(6.) THE SINLESSNESS OF JESUS' HUMAN NATURE

21. For He hath made Him (Christ) to be sin for us, who knew no sin; that we might be made the righteousness of God in Him.
—2 Corinthians 5:21
22. Who did no sin, neither was guile found in His mouth;
—1 Peter 2:22
(Read Also: 1 Peter 1:19; Hebrews 9:24; 1 John 3:5-7; 14:30)

(7.) THE NECESSITY OF CHRIST'S TAKING HUMAN NATURE

14. Seeing then that we have a great high priest, that is passed into the heavens, Jesus the Son of God, let us hold fast our profession.
15. For we have not an high priest which cannot be touched with the feelings of our infirmities; but was in all points tempted like as we are, yet without sin.
16. Let us therefore come boldly unto the throne of grace, that we may obtain mercy, and find grace to help in time of need.
—Hebrews 4:14-16
(Read Also: Hebrews 5:2; 2:17; Zechariah 6:13)
7. But made Himself of no reputation, and took upon Him the form of a servant, and was made in the likeness of men:
—Philippians 2:7.
(Read Also: Romans 6:23; 1 Corinthians 15:3; Hebrews 2:9; John 16:33)
15. For I have given you an example, that ye should do as I have done to you.
—John 13:15
(Read Also: 1 Peter 2:21; Hebrews 12:2, 3; 2 Corinthians 3:18)

CHRIST A UNION OF TWO NATURES

6. [Christ] thought it not robbery to be equal with God:
7. But made Himself of no reputation, and took upon Him the form of a servant, and was made in the likeness of men:
—Philippians 2:6, 7
14. And the Word was made flesh, and dwelt among us, (and we beheld His glory, the glory as of the only begotten of the Father,) full of grace and truth.
—John 1:14
3. For what the law could not do, in that it was weak through the flesh, God sending His own Son in the likeness of sinful flesh, and for sin, condemned sin in the flesh:
—Romans 8:3
(Read Also:1 Timothy 3:16; 1 John 4:2)

THE BLENDING OF THE TWO NATURES

5. Wherefore when He cometh into the world, He saith, Sacrifice and offering Thou wouldest not, but a body hast Thou prepared Me:
—Hebrews 10:5
9. For in Him dwelleth all the fullness of the Godhead bodily.
—Colossians 2:9

NECESSITY OF UNION BETWEEN THE TWO NATURES

(1.) TO RECONCILE HUMANITY WITH GOD

4. Whereby are given unto us exceeding great and precious promises: that by these ye might be partakers of the divine nature, having escaped the corruption that is in the world through lust.
—2 Peter 1:4

(2.) TO VEIL DIVINITY WITH HUMANITY

6. Who, being in the form of God, thought it not robbery to be equal with God:
7. But made Himself of no reputation, and took upon Him the form of a servant, and was made in the likeness of men:
8. And being found in fashion as a man, He humbles Himself, and became obedient unto death, even the death of the cross.
—Philippians 2:6-8

(3.) TO LIVE VICTORIOUSLY

19. Then answered Jesus . . . The Son can do nothing of Himself, but what He seeth the Father do: for what things soever He doeth, these also doeth the Son likewise.
—John 5:19
30. I can of mine own self do nothing: as I hear, I judge: and my judgment is just; because I seek not mine own will, but the will of the Father which hath sent Me.
—John 5:30
(Read Also: John 8:28; Ephesians 3:19)
3. According as His divine power hath given unto us all things that pertain unto life and godliness, through the knowledge of Him that hath called us to glory and virtue:
—2 Peter 1:3
(Read Also: Verse 4)
21. To him that overcometh will I grant to sit with Me in My throne, even as I also overcame, and Am set down with My Father in His throne.
—Revelation 3:21

THE OFFICES OF JESUS CHRIST

CHRIST THE PROPHET

14. Then those men, when they had seen the miracle that Jesus did, said, This is of a truth that prophet that should come into the world.
—John 6:14

40. Many of the people therefore, when they heard this saying, said, Of a truth this is the Prophet.
—John 7:40
22. For Moses truly said unto the fathers, A prophet shall the Lord your God raise up unto you of your brethren, like unto Me; Him shall ye hear in all things whatsoever He shall say unto you.
23. And it shall come to pass, that every soul, which will not hear that prophet, shall be destroyed from among the people.
—Acts 3:22, 23
(Read Also: Deuteronomy 18:18; Luke 13:33.)
(Jesus sees future: Matthew 24:1-51; Luke 19:41-44.)

CHRIST THE PRIEST

6. As He saith also in another place, Thou are a priest for ever after the order of Melchisedec.
—Hebrews 5:6
(Read Also: Psalms 110:4)

(1.) CHRIST'S EARTHLY PRIESTHOOD

10. Called of God as high priest after the order of Melchisedec.
—Hebrews 5:10

(2.) CHRIST'S HEAVENLY PRIESTHOOD

17. Wherefore in all things it behooved Him to be made like unto His brethren, that He might be a merciful and faithful high priest in things pertaining to God, to make reconciliation for the sin of the people.
18. For in that He Himself hath suffered being tempted, He is able to succour them that are tempted.
—Hebrews 2:17, 18
15. For we have not an high priest which cannot be touched

with the feelings of our infirmities; but was in all points tempted like as we are, yet without sin.
—Hebrews 4:15

(Read Also: Hebrews 5:2; Zechariah 6:13)

1. ... We have such a high priest, who is set on the right hand of the throne of the Majesty in the heavens;
2. A minister of the sanctuary, and of the true tabernacle, which the Lord pitched, and not man.
—Hebrews 8:1, 2

25. Wherefore He is able also to save them to the uttermost that come unto God by Him, seeing He ever liveth to make intercession for them.
—Hebrews 7:25

1. My little children these things write I unto you, that ye sin not. And if any man sin, we have an advocate with the Father, Jesus Christ the righteous:
—1 John 2:1

(Read Also: Zechariah 3rd Chapt.)

34. ... (Christ who is even at the right hand of God, who also maketh intercession for us.
—Romans 8:34

(Read Also: John 16:23)

CHRIST THE KING

19. The LORD hath prepared His throne in the heavens; and His kingdom ruleth over all.
—Psalms 103:19

8. But unto the Son He saith, Thy throne, O God, is for ever and ever: a sceptre of righteousness is the sceptre of thy kingdom.
—Hebrews 1:8

(Prophesied in Psalms 45:6)

9. Thou hast loved righteousness, and hated iniquity; therefore God, even thy God, hath anointed thee with the oil of gladness above thy fellows.

—Hebrews 1:9

5. For unto which of the angels said He at any time, Thou art My Son, this day have I begotten thee? And again, I will be to Him a Father, and He shall be to Me a Son?
—Hebrews 1:5
(Prophesied: Psalms 2:6, 7)

33. And He shall reign over the house of Jacob for ever; and of His kingdom there shall be no end.
—Luke 1:33
(Read Also: Jeremiah 23:5, 6)

31. When the Son of man shall come in His glory, and all the holy angels with Him, *then shall* He sit upon the throne of His glory:
—Matthew 25:31

(1.) THE KINGDOM OF GRACE

20. And when He was demanded of the Pharisees, when the kingdom of God should come, He answered them and said, The kingdom of God cometh not with observation:
21. Neither shall they say, Lo here! Or lo there! For, behold, the kingdom of God is within you.
—Luke 17:20, 21

37. Pilate therefore said unto Him, Art thou a king then? Jesus answered, Thou sayest that I Am a king. To this end was I born, and for this cause came I into the world, that I should bear witness unto the truth. Every one that is of the truth heareth My voice.
—John 18:37

17. For the Kingdom of God is not meat and drink; but righteousness, and peace, and joy in the Holy Ghost.
—Romans 14:17

9. . . . behold, thy King cometh unto thee: He is just, and

having salvation; lowly, and riding upon an ass, and upon a colt the foal of an ass.
—Zechariah 9:9 (Fulfilled in Matthew 21:7-10)
(Read Also: Luke 23:3; John 18:33-37; 19:2,3; 19:14, 15; Psalms 2:7, 8; Hebrews 1:3-5; Philippians 2:9-11; Ephesians 1:20-23.)

(2.) THE KINGDOM OF GLORY

2. And [Christ] was transfigured before them; and His face did shine as the sun, and His raiment was white as the light.
—Matthew 17:2

27. For as the lightning cometh out of the east, and shineth even unto the west; so shall also the coming of the Son of man be.

30. And then shall appear the sign of the Son of man in heavens: and then shall all the tribes of the earth mourn, and they shall see the Son of man coming in the clouds of heaven with power and great glory.
—Matthew 24:27, 30
(Read Also: Matthew 25:31, 32.)

9. I beheld till the thrones were cast down, and the Ancient of days did sit, whose garment was white as snow, and the hair of His head like the pure wool: His throne was like the fiery flame, and His [Its] wheels as burning fire.

10. A fiery stream issued and came forth from before Him: thousands thousands ministered unto Him, and ten thousand times ten thousand stood before Him:

14. And there was given Him dominion, and glory, and a kingdom, that all people, nations, and languages, should serve Him: His dominion is an everlasting dominion, which shall not pass away, and His kingdom that which shall not be destroyed.
—Daniel 7:9, 10, 14
(Read Also: Daniel 7:27; Revelation 20; 21)

CHAPTER 6
THE GREAT I AM

THE GREAT I AM

The covenant name of God in the Old Testament, represented by the Hebrew consonants Y H W H, is translated "LORD" or "GOD" in the King James Bible and many others. Y H W H is pronounced Je-ho-vah by English speaking people.

1. After these things the word of the LORD came unto Abram in a vision, saying, Fear not, Abram; *I AM* thy shield, and thy exceeding great reward.
—Genesis 15:1

NOTICE THAT Y H W H (LORD) SAID *I AM*.

7. And He God said unto Him, *I AM* the LORD that brought thee out of Ur of the Chaldees . . .
—Genesis 15:7

1. . . . The LORD appeared to Abram, and said unto him, *I AM* the Almighty God . . .
—Genesis 17:1

24. And the LORD appeared unto him (Isaac) the same night and said, *I AM* the God of Abraham thy father:
—Genesis 26:24

13. And, behold, the LORD stood above it, and said, *I AM* the LORD God of Abraham thy father, and the God of Isaac: the land whereon thou (Jacob) liest, to thee will I give it, and to thy seed;
—Genesis 28:13

15. And, behold, *I AM* with thee, and will keep thee in all places whither thou goest . . .
—Genesis 28:15
11. And God said unto him, *I AM* God almighty: . . .
13. *I AM* the God of Bethel, where thou [Jacob] anointedst the pillar . . .
—Genesis 31:11, 13
3. And He said, *I AM* God, the God of thy father: fear not to go down into Egypt;
—Genesis 46:3
6. Moreover He said, *I AM* the God of thy father, the God of Abraham, the God of Isaac, and the God of Jacob. And Moses hid His face; for He was afraid to look upon God,
—Exodus 3:6
13. And Moses said unto God, Behold, when I come unto the children of Israel, and shall say unto them, The God of your fathers hath sent me unto you: and they shall say to me, What is His name? What shall I say unto them?
14. And God said unto Moses, *I AM that I AM*: And He said, Thus shalt thou say unto the children of Israel, *I AM* hath sent me unto you.
15. And God said moreover unto Moses, Thus shalt thou say unto the children of Israel. The LORD God of your fathers, the God of Abraham, the God of Isaac, and the God of Jacob, hath sent me unto you: this is my name *for ever* and this is my memorial unto all generations.
—Exodus 3:13-15

I AM that I AM God explained to Moses the name by which He had made Himself known to Abraham at the making of the covenant.
In Hebrew as in English, this name (*I AM*) is a form of the verb "to be", and implies that its possessor is the eternal, self-existing one.]—Seventh-day Adventist Bible Commentary, Volume 1, pg. 511, Review and Herald Publishing Association, Washington, D.C.

2. And God spake unto Moses, and said unto him, *I AM* the LORD:
3. And I appeared unto Abraham, unto Isaac, and unto Jacob, by the name of God almighty, but my name JEHOVAH (Y H W H) was I not known to them.
—Exodus 6:2, 3
6. Wherefore say unto the children of Israel, *I AM* the LORD, and I will bring you out from under the burdens of the Egyptians . . .
8. And I will bring you in unto the land concerning the which I did swear to give it to Abraham, to Isaac, and to Jacob; and I will give it you for an heritage: *I AM* the LORD.
—Exodus 6:6, 8
29. That the LORD spake unto Moses, saying *I AM* the LORD: speak thou unto Pharaoh King of Egypt all that I say unto thee.
—Exodus 6:29

THE PROPHETS SPOKE OF HIM AS BEING ETERNAL, IMMORTAL.

22. The LORD possessed me in the beginning of His way, before His works of old.
23. I was set up from everlasting, from the beginning, or ever [before] the earth was.
—Proverbs 8:22, 23
2. But thou, Bethlehem Ephratah, though thou be little among the thousands of Judah, yet out of thee shall He come forth unto me that is to be ruler in Israel; whose goings forth have been from of old, from everlasting.
—Micah 5:2

THE GREAT I AM OF THE O. T. IS THE SAME PERSON AS JESUS CHRIST OF THE N. T.

39. Search the scriptures; for in them ye think ye have eternal life: and they are they which testify of me:
—John 5:39

ALL THROUGH THE N. T. JESUS CALLS HIMSELF THE *I AM*.

56. Your father Abraham rejoiced to see My day: and he saw it, and was glad.
57. Then said the Jews unto Him, Thou art not yet fifty years old, and hast thou seen Abraham?
58. Jesus said unto them, Verily, verily, I say unto you, Before Abraham was *I AM*.
59. Then took they up stones to cast at Him: but Jesus hid himself . . .
    —John 8:56-59
15. He saith unto them, But whom say ye that *I AM*?
16. And Simon Peter answered and said, Thou art the Christ, the Son of the living God.
    —Matthew 16:15, 16
5. . . . *I AM* the light of the world.
7. . . . *I AM* the door of the sheep.
9. *I AM* the door: by me if any man enter in, he shall be saved . . .
10. . . . *I AM* come that they might have life, and that they might have it more abundantly.
11. *I AM* the good shepherd: the good shepherd giveth His life for the sheep.
    —John 9:5; 10:7, 9, 10, 11
35. And Jesus said unto them, *I AM* the bread of life: . . .
    —John 6:35
51. *I AM* the living bread which came down from heaven:
    —John 6:51
12. Then spake Jesus again unto them, saying, *I AM* the light of the world:
24. . . . for if ye believe not that *I AM He*, ye shall die in your sins.
    —John 8:12, 24
28. Then said Jesus, unto them, When ye have lifted up the Son of man, then shall ye know that *I AM He*, and that I

do nothing of myself; but as my Father hath taught me, I speak these things.
—John 8:28

14. *I AM* the good shepherd, and know my sheep . . .
—John 10:14

25. Jesus said unto her, *I AM* the resurrection, and the life: he that believeth in me, though he were dead, yet shall he live:
—John 11:25

46. *I AM* come a light into the world, that whosoever believeth on me should not abide in darkness.
—John 12:46

6. Jesus saith unto him, *I AM* the way, the truth, and the life: no man cometh unto the Father, but by me.
—John 14:6

20. At that day ye shall know that *I AM* in my Father, and ye in me, and I in you.
—John 14:20

1. *I AM* the true vine, and my Father is the husbandman.
—John 15:1

5. *I AM* the vine, ye are the branches: He that abideth in me, and I in him, the same bringeth forth much fruit: for without me ye can do nothing.
—John 15:5

CHRIST SAID THE FOLLOWING ABOUT HIMSELF

26. For as the Father hath life in Himself; so hath He given to the Son to have life in Himself;
—John 5:26

17. Therefore doth My Father love Me, because I lay down My life, that I might take it again.
—John 10:17

5. And now, O Father, glorify thou Me with Thine Own Self with the glory which I had with Thee before the world was.
—John 17:5

HOW JESUS IDENTIFIED HIMSELF TO THOSE ARRESTING HIM

6. As soon then as He had said unto them, *I AM He*, they went backward, and fell to the ground.

8. Jesus answered, I have told you that *I AM He*: if therefore ye seek Me, let these go their way.
—John 18:6, 8

61. ... Again the high priest asked Him, and said unto Him, Art thou the Christ, the Son of the Blessed?

62. And Jesus said, *I AM*: and ye shall see the Son of man sitting on the right hand of power, and coming in the clouds of heaven.

63. Then the high priest rent his clothes, and said, What need we any further witnesses?
—Mark 14:61-63

37. Pilate therefore said unto Him, Art thou a King then: Jesus answered, Thou sayest that *I AM* a King.
—John 18:37

WHAT THE APOSTLE PAUL HAD TO SAY ABOUT CHRIST

6. But to us there is but one God, the Father, of whom all things, and we in Him; and one Lord Jesus Christ, by whom are all things, and we by Him.
—1 Corinthians 8:6

15. Who is the image of the invisible God, the firstborn of every creature:

16. For by Him were all things created that are in heaven, and that are in earth, visible and invisible, whether they by thrones, or dominions, or principalities, or powers: all things were created by Him, and for Him:

17. And He is before all things, and by Him all things consist [hold together].
—Colossians 1:15-17

9. And to make all men see what is the fellowship of the

mystery, which from the beginning of the world hath been hid in God, who created all things by Jesus Christ:
—Ephesians 3:9
6. Who, being in the form of God, thought it not robbery to be equal with God:
7. made Himself of no reputation, and took upon Him the form of a servant, and was made in the likeness of men:
8. And being found in fashion as a man, He humbled Himself, and became obedient unto death, even the death of the cross.
—Philippians 2:6-8

CHIRST REVEALS HIMSELF TO THE PROPHET JOHN IN THE BOOK OF REVELATION AS THE SAME *GREAT I AM*.

8. *I AM* Alpha and Omega, the beginning and the ending, saith the LORD, which is, and which was, and which is to come, the Almighty.
—Revelation 1:8
17. And when I [John] saw Him, I fell at His feet as dead. And He laid His right hand upon me, saying unto me, Fear not; *I AM* the first and the last:
—Revelations 1:17
18. *I AM He* that liveth, and was dead; and behold, *I AM* alive for evermore, Amen; and have the keys of hell and of death.
—Revelation 1:18
6. And He said unto me, It is done. *I AM* Alpha and Omega, the beginning and the end. I will give unto Him that is athirst of the fountain of the water of life freely.
—Revelation 21:6
13. *I AM* Alpha and Omega the beginning and the end, the first and the last.
16. . . . *I AM* the root and the offspring of David, and the bright and morning star.
—Revelation 22:13, 16

19. And if any man shall take away from the words of the book of this prophecy, God shall take away his part out of the book of life, and out of the holy city, and from the things which are written in this book.
—Revelation 22:19

GOD SEES FUTURE AS WE SEE PRESENT

I AM means an eternal presence; the past, present, and future are alike to God. He sees the most remote events of past history, and the far distant future with as clear a vision as we do those things that are transpiring daily.
—Ellen G. White, Manuscript 5a, 1895.

CHIRST SPOKE THE WORLD INTO EXISTENCE

1. In the beginning was the Word [Christ], and the Word [Christ] was with God, and the Word [Christ] was God.
2. The same was in the beginning with God.
3. All things were made by Him [Christ]; and without Him [Christ] was not any thing made that was made.
14. And the Word was made flesh, and dwelt mong us, (and we beheld His glory as of the only begotten of the Father,) full of grace and truth.
—John 1:1-3, 14
16. For by Him [Christ] were all things created, that are in heaven, and that are in earth, visible and invisible, whether they be thrones, or dominions, or Principalities, or power: all things were created by Him, and for Him:
—Colossians 1:16
1. God, who at sundry times and in divers manners spake in time past unto the fathers by the prophets,
2. Hath in these last days spoken unto us by His Son, whom He hath appointed heir of all things, by whom also *He made the worlds*;
8. But unto the Son He saith, Thy throne, O God, is for ever and ever: a sceptre of righteousness is the sceptre of Thy kingdom.
—Hebrews 1:1, 2, 8

THE NAME USED FOR GOD WERE SIGNIFICANT

Elohim was the generic term for Deity. Jehweh (YAHWEH) the personal name of the God of Israel. The word "generic" means having a wide or general application. Elohim also used to speak of non Hebrew gods or idols. YAHWEH means "self-existent one."

HIS NEW TESTAMENT NAME:

21. Thou shalt call His name Jesus (YESHUA).
    —Matthew 1:21

"Yeshua" means "God's Salvation." Yeshua is the Hebrew for Jesus. 'Lesous (pronounced YESOUS) the Greek name. Jesus is the Latin name brought over into English. All three of these names appeared on the cross above the head of our crucified LORD.

19. And Pilate wrote a title, and put it on the cross. And the writing was, JESUS OF NAZARETH THE KING OF THE JEWS.
    —John 19:19

Y H W H, Yahweh, or Jahweh, Jehovah of the Old Testament is the same person as Yeshua [Hebrew], Yesous, 'Lesous [Greek] or Jesus [Latin] of the New Testament.

CHAPTER 7
JEHOVAH

JEHOVAH (If A = B and A = C then C = B)

The name JEHOVAH is only found four times in the King James Bible.

> 2. And God spake unto Moses, and said unto him, I AM the LORD:
> 3. And I appeared unto Abraham, unto Isaac, and unto Jacob, by the name of God almighty, but by my name JEHOVAH was I not known to them.
> —Exodus 6:2, 3

> 18. That men may know that thou, whose name alone is JEHOVAH, art the most high over all the earth.
> —Psalms 83:18

> 2. Behold, God is my salvation; I will trust, and not be afraid: for the LORD JEHOVAH is my strength and my song; He also is become my salvation.
> —Isaiah 12:2

> 4. Trust ye in the LORD for ever: for in the LORD JEHOVAH is everlasting strength:
> —Isaiah 26:4

These texts show that Y H W H = JEHOVAH = I AM = LORD. Y H W H is translated "LORD" or GOD" using capital letters as shown in the KJV and many others.

When you find "LORD" or "GOD" in capital letters you may substitute the name JEHOVAH.

Y H W H is found in every book of Old Testament except the books of Esther, Ecclesiastes and the Song of Solomon—about 6,823 times.

JEHOVAH CREATED THE EARTH

4. These are the generations of the heavens and of the earth when they were created, in the day that the LORD God [JEHOVAH] made the earth and the heavens,
7. And the LORD God [JEHOVAH] formed man of the dust of the ground, and breathed into his nostrils the breath of life: and man became a living soul.
—Genesis 2:4, 7

JEHOVAH SEEKS ADAM AND EVE AFTER THEY SINNED

8. And they heard the voice of the LORD God [JEHOVAH] walking in the garden in the cool of the day: and Adam and his wife hid themselves from the presence of the LORD God amongst the trees of the garden.
9. And the LORD God [JEHOVAH] called unto Adam, and said unto him, Where art thou?
—Genesis 3:8, 9

JEHOVAH PROVIDES FOR THEIR NEEDS

21. Unto Adam also and to his wife did the LORD God [JEHOVAH] make coats of skins, and clothed them.
—Genesis 3:21

JEHOVAH CALLS NOAH INTO THE ARK OF SAFETY

1. And the LORD [JEHOVAH] said unto Noah, Come thou and all thy house into the ark . . .
—Genesis 7:1

JEHOVAH PROMISES ABRAHAM A SON

13. And the LORD [JEHOVAH] said unto Abraham, Wherefore did Sarah laugh, saying, Shall I of a surety bear a child, which am old?
14. Is any thing too hard for the LORD? At the time appointed I will return unto thee, according to the time of life, and Sarah shall have a son.
—Genesis 18:13, 14

JEHOVAH DESTROYS SODOM

13. For we will destroy this place, because the cry of them is waxen great before the face of the LORD [JEHOVAH] and the LORD hath sent us to destroy it.
—Genesis 19:13
24. Then the LORD [JEHOVAH] rained upon Sodom and upon Gomorrah brimstone and fire from the LORD [JEHOVAH] out of heaven.
—Genesis 19:24

JACOB WRESTLES WITH GOD

24. And Jacob was left alone; and there wrestled a man with him until the breaking of the day.
26. And He said, Let Me go, for the day breaketh. And he said, I will not let Thee go, except Thou bless me.
29. And Jacob asked Him, and said, Tell me, I pray Thee, Thy name. And He said, Wherefore is it that thou dost ask after My name? And He blessed him there.
30. And Jacob called the name of the place Peniel: for I have seen God face to face, and my life is preserved.
—Genesis 32:24, 26, 29, 30

JEHOVAH APPEARS TO MOSES IN BURNING BUSH

2. And the angel of the LORD appeared unto him in a flame of fires out of the midst of a bush: and he looked, and, behold, the bush burned with fire, and the bush was not consumed.

4. And when the LORD [JEHOVAH] saw that he turned aside to see, God called unto him out of the midst of the bush and said, Moses, and he said, Here am I.
—Exodus 3:2, 4

JEHOVAH SENT TEN PLAGUES OVER EGYPT

21. And the LORD said to Moses, Stretch out thine hand toward heaven, that there may be darkness over the land of Egypt, even darkness which may be felt.
—Exodus 10:21

JEHOVAH PARTED THE RED SEA

21. . . . Sing ye to the LORD [JEHOVAH], For He hath triumphed gloriously; the horse and his [Egyptian] rider hath He thrown into the sea.
—Exodus 15:21

JEHOVAH LEADS BY A PILLAR OF CLOUD & FIRE

21. And the LORD [JEHOVAH] went before them by day in a pillar of a cloud, to lead them the way; and by night in a pillar of fire, to give them light; to go by day and night:
—Exodus 13:21

JEHOVAH GIVES LAW ON MOUNT SINAI

16. Wherefore the children of Israel shall keep the Sabbath, to observe the Sabbath throughout their generations, for a perpetual covenant.
17. It is a sign between me and the children of Israel for ever: for in six days the LORD made heaven and earth, and on the seventh day He rested, and was refreshed.
18. And He gave unto Moses, when He had made an end of communing with him upon mount Sinai, two tables of testimony [law], tables of stone, written with the finger of God.
—Exodus 31:16-18

Note: The same LORD [JEHOVAH] who created the Seventh day Sabbath of creation week gave the tables of stone containing the fourth [or Sabbath] commandments on Mount Sinai.
(Read Also: Genesis 2:2, 3)

JEHOVAH ON MERCY SEAT OF THE ARK

89. And when Moses was gone into the tabernacle of the congregation to speak with Him, then he heard the voice of one speaking unto him from off the mercy seat that was upon the ark of testimony, from between the two cherubims: and He spake unto him.
   —Numbers 7:89
1. And the LORD [JEHOVAH] spake unto Moses, . . .
   —Numbers 8:1
   (Read Also: Leviticus 16:13)

JEHOVAH MEETS WITH JOSHUA

13. And it came to pass, when Joshua was by Jericho, that he lifted up his eyes and looked, and, behold, there stood a man over against him with His sword drawn in His hand: and Joshua went unto Him, and said unto Him, Art thou for us, or for our adversaries?
14. And He said, Nay: but as captain of the host of the LORD [JEHOVAH] *Am I* now come. And Joshua fell on his face to the earth, and did worship, and said unto Him, What saith my Lord unto His servant?
15. And the captain of the LORD's [JEHOVAH's] host said unto Joshua, Loose thy shoe form off thy foot; for the place whereon thou standest is holy. And Joshua did so.
    —Joshua 5:13-15
    The Angel of the LORD [JEHOVAH] confronts Balaam.
    (See: Numbers 22:21-35)
    The Angel of the LORD comes to Manoah's wife, Samson's mother.
    (Read Also: Judges 13:2-25)

The Angel of the LORD appears to Gideon.
(Read Also: Judges 6:11-22)
Joshua the High Priest stands before the Angel of the LORD.
(Read Also: Zechariah 3:1-10)
The Angel of the LORD appears to Moses out of the burning bush. (Read Also: Exodus 3:2-4)
[The "Angel of the LORD" is Deity and accepts worship. This is the Second Member of the God-Head and He later becomes Christ.]

1. And an Angel of the LORD [JEHOVAH] . . . said, I made you to go up out of Egypt, and have brought you unto the land which I sware unto your fathers; and I said, I will never break My covenant with you . . .
   —Judges 2:1
   (Read Also: Judges 2:2-4)

THE ROCK WHICH GAVE THEM WATER WAS CHRIST

4. And did all drink the same spiritual drink: for they drank of that spiritual ROCK that followed them: and that ROCK was Christ.
   —1 Corinthians 10:4
   (Read Also: Exodus 17:6; Numbers 20:6-11; Nehemiah 9:15)

CHIRST IN THE NEW TESTAMENT IS REVEALED AS BEING JEHOVAH OF THE OLD TESTAMENT

1. In the beginning was the Word [Christ], and the Word [Christ] was with God, and the Word [Christ] was God.
2. The same was in the beginning with God.
3. All things were made by *Him [Christ]*; and without *Him [Christ]* was not any thing made that was made.
4. In *Him [Christ]* was life; and the life was the light of men.
   —John 1:1-4

3. .... Prepare ye the way of the LORD [JEHOVAH or YAHWEH], make straight in the desert a highway for our God;
—Isaiah 40:3

3. For this is He [John the Baptist speaking] that was spoken of by the prophet Esaias [Isaiah], saying The voice of one crying in the wilderness, Prepare ye the way of the LORD [CHRIST], make His paths straight.
—Matthew 3:3

1. In the year that King Uzziah died I saw also the Lord sitting upon a throne, high and lifted up, and His train filled the temple.

3. And one cried unto another, and said, Holy, holy, holy, is the LORD [Jehovah] of hosts: the whole earth is full of His glory.
—Isaiah 6:1, 3

41. These things said Esaias [Isaiah], when he saw His [Jesus'] glory, and spake of Him.
—John 12:41

37. ... Moses, ... said unto the children of Israel, a prophet shall the Lord your God raised up unto you of your brethren, like unto me; Him [Christ] shall ye hear.

38. This is He [Christ], that was in the church in the wilderness with the Angel which spake to him [Moses] in the mount Sina, and with our fathers: who received the lively [living] oracles [Ten Commandments] to give unto us.
—Acts 7:37, 38

1. GOD, who at sundry times and in divers manners spake in times past unto the fathers by the prophets,

2. Hath in these last days spoken unto us by His Son, whom He hath appointed heir of all things, by whom also He [Christ] made the worlds;
—Hebrews 1:1, 2

8. But to the Son He says: "Your Throne, O God, is forever & ever; a scepter of righteousness is the scepter of Your Kingdom.

9. You have loved righteousness and hated lawlessness;

Therefore God, Your God, has anointed You With the oil of gladness more than Your companions"
10. And "You, LORD (JEHOVAH), in the beginning hast laid the foundation of the earth, and the heavens are the works of Your [Christ's] hands:
—Hebrews 1:8-10, NKJV
(Quoted from: Psalms 45:6, 7; Isaiah 61:1, 3; Psalms 102:25-27)

Conclusion: Since Christ is the one who spoke the words that brought all the world(s) into existence it is consistent to believe He is the [Jehovah] active with mankind throughout the Old Testament.

CHAPTER 8

CHRIST THE LORD OF GLORY

CHRIST HAD GODLY GLORY BEFORE CREATION

CHRIST HAD GODLY GLORY BEFORE CREATION

5. And now, O Father, glorify thou Me [Christ] with Thine own self with the *glory* which I had with Thee *before the world was.*

22. And the *glory* which thou gavest me I have given them; that they may be one, even as We are one:

24. Father, I will that they also, whom thou hast given Me, be with Me where I am; that they may behold My *glory*, which thou hast given Me: for Thou lovedst Me *before the foundation of the world.*
—John 17:5, 22, 24

IN THE OLD TESTAMENT JEHOVAH [CHRIST] HAD GLORY THAT NO ONE COULD LOOK UPON

10. . . . they looked toward the wilderness, and, behold, the *glory* of the LORD appeared in the cloud.
—Exodus 16:10

16. And the *glory* of the LORD abode upon mount Sinai, and the cloud covered it six days: and the seventh day He [Christ] called unto Moses out of the midst of the cloud.

17. And the sight of the *glory* of the LORD was like devour-

ing fire on the top of the mount in the eyes of the children of Israel.
—Exodus 24:16, 17

MOSES SAW A LITTLE OF CHRIST'S GLORY

18. And He (Moses) said, I beseech thee, show me Thy *glory*.
22. And it shall come to pass, while My *glory* passeth by, that I will put thee in a clift [cleft] of the rock, and will cover thee with My hand while I pass by:
—Exodus 33:18, 22
34. Then a cloud covered the tent of the congregation, and the *glory* of the LORD filled the tabernacle.
35. And Moses was not able to enter into the tent of the congregation, because the cloud abode thereon, and the *glory* of the LORD filled the tabernacle.
—Exodus 40:34, 35

CHRIST'S GLORY FILLED SOLOMON'S TEMPLE

11. So that the priests could not stand to minister because of the cloud: for the glory of the LORD had filled the house of the LORD.
—1 Kings 8:11

AFTERWARDS, CHRIST GAVE UP HIS HEAVENLY GLORY AND BECAME A NEW BORN BABY

9. And, lo, the angel of the Lord came upon them, and the *glory* of the Lord shone round about them: and they were sore afraid.
14. *Glory* to God in the highest, and on earth peace, good will toward men.
—Luke 2:9, 14

CERTAIN DISCIPLES EXPECTED CHRIST TO SET UP AN EARTHLY KINGDOM

37. They said unto Him, Grant unto us that we may sit, one on thy right hand, and the other on thy left hand, in Thy *glory*.
—Mark 10:37

CHRIST WAS GLORIFIED BRIEFLY ON THE MOUNT OF TRANSFIGURATION PARTLY TO HELP HIS DISCIPLES TO UNDERSTAND THAT HIS KINGDOM WAS NOT OF THIS WORLD.

26. For whosoever shall be ashamed of Me and of My words, of him shall the Son of man be ashamed, when He shall come in his Own *glory*, and in His Father's and of the holy angels.
31. Who appeared in *glory*, and spake of his decease [death] which he should accomplish at Jerusalem.
32. But Peter and they that were with him were heavy with sleep: and when they were awake, they saw his *glory*, and the two men (Moses & Elias) that stood with him.
—Luke 9:26, 31, 32
14. And the Word was made flesh, and dwelt among us, (and we beheld His *glory*, the *glory* as of the only begotten of the Father,) full of grace and truth.
—John 1:14

WE WILL SEE CHRIST IN HIS HEAVENLY GLORY AT HIS SECOND COMING

30. And then shall appear the sign of the Son of man in heaven: and then shall all the tribes of the earth mourn, and they shall see the Son of man coming in the clouds of heaven with power and great *glory*.
—Matthew 24:30

31. When the Son of man shall come in His *glory*, and all the holy angels with him, then shall He sit upon the throne of His *glory*:
    —Matthew 25:31
38. Whosoever therefore shall be ashamed of Me and of My words in this adulterous and sinful generation; of him also shall the Son of man be ashamed, when He cometh in the *glory* of His Father with the holy angels.
    —Mark 8:38
27. And then shall they see the Son of man coming in a cloud with power and great *glory*.
    —Luke 21:27
26. Ought not Christ to have suffered these things, and to enter into His *glory*?
    —Luke 24:26

WE CAN REFLECT THE GLORY OF CHRIST BY ACCEPTING HIM IN OUR LIVES

18. But we all, with open face beholding as in a glass [mirror] the *glory* of the Lord, are changed into the same image from *glory* to *glory*, even as by the Spirit of the Lord.
    —2 Corinthians 3:18
27. For the Son of man shall come in the *glory* of His Father with His angels; and then He shall reward every man according to His works.
    —Matthew 16:27
28. And Jesus said unto them, Verily I say unto you, That ye which have followed Me, in the regeneration when the Son of man shall sit in the throne of His *glory*, ye also shall sit upon twelve thrones, judging the twelve tribes of Israel.
    —Matthew 19:28

CHRIST IS NOW NEXT TO THE FATHER WITH GODLY GLORY

55. But he [Stephen], being full of the Holy Ghost, looked up stedfastly into heaven, and saw the *glory* of God, and Jesus standing on the right hand of God,
—Acts 7:55

AT THE RESURRECTION WE WILL SEE CHRIST IN ALL HIS GLORY AND LIVE

18. For I reckon that the sufferings of this present time are not worthy to be compared with the *glory* which shall be revealed in us.
—Romans 8:18

43. It [our bodies] is sown in dishonour: it is raised in *glory*: it is sown in weakness; it is raised in power:
—1 Corinthians 15:43

17. For our light affliction, which is but for a moment, worketh for us a far more exceeding and eternal weight of *glory*;
—2 Corinthians 4:17

19. But my God shall supply all your need according to His riches in *glory* by Christ Jesus.
—Philippians 4:19

4. When Christ, who is our life, shall appear, then shall ye also appear with him in *glory*.
—Colossians 3:4

12. That ye would walk worthy of God, who hath called you unto His kingdom and *glory*.
—1 Thessalonians 2:12

9. Who shall be punished with everlasting destruction from the presence of the Lord, and from the *glory* of His power;
—2 Thessalonians 1:9

14. Whereunto He called you by our gospel, to the obtaining of the *glory* of our Lord Jesus Christ.
—2 Thessalonians 2:14

16. And without controversy great is the mystery of godliness: God was manifest in the flesh, justified in the Spirit, seen of angels, preached unto the Gentiles, believed on in the world, received up into *glory*.
—1 Timothy 3:16
3. Who being the brightness of His *glory*, and the express image of His person, and upholding all things by the word of His power, when He had by Himself purged our sins, sat down on the right hand of the Majesty on high;
—Hebrews 1:3

MANKIND WILL REGAIN THEIR SPIRITUAL NATURES AS BEFORE SIN

6. But one in a certain place testified, saying, What is man, that Thou art mindful of him? Or the son of man, that thou visitest him?
7. Thou madest him a little lower than the angels; thou crownedst him with *glory* and honour, and didst set him over the works of Thy hands:
9. But we see Jesus, who was made a little lower than the angels for the suffering of death, crowned with *glory* and honour; that He by the grace of God should *taste death for every man.*
10. For it became him, for whom are all things, and by whom are all things, in bringing many sons unto *glory*, to make the captain of their salvation perfect through sufferings.
—Hebrews 2:6, 7, 9, 10
7. That the trial of your faith, being much more precious than of gold that perisheth, though it be tried with fire, might be found unto praise and honour and *glory* at the appearing of Jesus Christ:
11. Searching what, or what manner of time the Spirit of Christ which was in them did signify, when it testified beforehand the sufferings of Christ, and the *glory* that should follow.

21. Who by Him do believe in God, that raised Him up from the dead, and gave Him *glory*; that your faith and hope might be in God.
   —1 Peter 1:7,11, 21

CHRIST WILL LIVE WITH MANKIND THROUGH OUT ETERNITY

3. And I heard a great voice out of heaven saying, Behold, the tabernacle of God [Christ Himself] is with men, and He will dwell with them, and they shall be His people, and God himself shall be with them, and be their God.
4. And God shall wipe away all tears from their eyes; and there shall be no more death, neither sorrow nor crying, neither shall there be any more pain: for the former things are passed away.
26. And they shall bring the *glory* and honour of the nations into it [The New Jerusalem].
   —Revelations 21:3, 4, 26

CHAPTER 9
JESUS GIVES US LIVING WATER

WE MUST BELIEVE IN CHRIST TO RECIEVE THE LIVING WATER

38. He that *believeth* on me, as the scripture hath said, out of his belly shall flow rivers of *living water*.
—John 7:38

1. Ho, every one that thirsteth, come ye to the *waters*, and he that hath no money; come ye, *Buy*, and eat; yea, come, buy wine and milk *without money* and without price.
—Isaiah 55:1

17. And the Spirit and the bride say, Come. And let him that heareth say, Come. And let him take the *water of life* freely.
—Revelation 22:17

10. Jesus answered and said unto her, If thou knewest the gift of God, and who it is that saith to thee, Give me to drink; thou wouldest have asked of him, and he would have given thee *living water*.
—John 4:10

13. Jesus answered and said unto her, Whosoever drinketh of this [well] *water* shall thirst again:

14. But whosoever drinketh of the *water* that I shall give him shall never thirst; but the *water* that I shall give him shall be in him a well of *water* springing up into *everlasting life*.
—John 4:13, 14

TO THOSE WHO FORSAKE THE LORD

13. For My people have committed two evils; they have forsaken Me the *fountain of living waters*, and hewed them out cisterns, broken cisterns, that can hold no *water*.
—Jeremiah 2:13

12. These are spots in your *feasts of charity*, when they feast with you, feeding themselves without fear: *clouds* they are *without water*, carried about of winds; trees whose fruit withereth, without fruit, twice dead, plucked up by the roots;
—Jude 12

30. For ye shall be as an oak whose leaf fadeth, and as a garden that hath no *water*.
—Isaiah 1:30

LIVING WATER WILL NOT FAIL THOSE WHO ARE FAITHFUL

11. And the LORD shall guide thee continually, and satisfy thy soul in drought, and make fat thy bones: and thou shalt be like a *watered garden*, and like a *spring of water*, whose *waters* fail not.
—Isaiah 58:11

6. And he said unto me, It is done. I Am Alpha and Omega, the beginning and the end. I will give unto him that is athirst of the *fountain of the water of life* freely.
—Revelation 21:6

LIVING WATER GIVEN ISRAEL IN THE WILDERNESS

7. And the LORD spake unto Moses, saying,
8. Take the rod, and gather thou the assembly together, thou, and thy brother, and speak ye unto the rock before their eyes; and *it shall give forth His water*, and thou shalt bring forth to them *water out of the rock*: so thou shalt give the congregation and their beasts drink.
11. And Moses lifted up his hand, and with his rod he smote

the rock twice: and the *water came out abundantly*, and the congregation drank, and their beasts also.
—Numbers 20:7, 8, 11

15. Who led thee through that great and terrible wilderness, wherein were fiery serpents, and scorpions, and drought, where there was no *water*; who brought thee forth *water* out of the rock of flint;
—Deuteronomy 8:15

15. And gavest them bread from heaven for their hunger, and *broughtest forth water* for them out of the rock for their thirst, and promisedst them that they should go in to possess the land which thou hadst sworn to give them.
—Nehemiah 9:15

8. Which turned the rock into a *standing water*, the flint into a *fountain of waters*.
—Psalms 114:8

1. And he showed me a pure river of *water of life*, clear as crystal, proceeding out of the throne of God and of the Lamb [Christ].
—Revelation 22:1

5. Who is he that overcometh the world, but he that believeth that Jesus is the Son of God?

6. *This is He that came by water and blood, even Jesus Christ; not by water only but by water and blood.*
And it is the Spirit that beareth witness, because the Spirit is truth.
—1 John 5:5, 6

34. But one of the [Roman] soldiers with a spear pierced His [Christ's] side, and forthwith came there out b*lood and water.*
—John 19:34

7. For there are three that bear record in heaven, *the Father, the Word [Christ], and the Holy Ghost: and These Three are One.*

8. And there are three that bear witness in earth, *the Spirit, and the Water, and the Blood: and These Three agree in One.*
—1 John 5:7, 8

CHAPTER 10
THE LIGHT OF THE WORLD

CHRIST IS THE LIGHT OF THE WORLD

30. For mine eyes have seen Thy salvation,
31. Which Thou hast prepared before the face of all people;
32. A *light* to *lighten* the Gentiles, and the glory of Thy people Israel.
    —Luke 2:30-32

4. In Him was life; and the life was the *light* of men.
5. And the *light* shineth in darkness; and the darkness comprehended [grasped] it not.
6. There was a man sent from God, whose name was John.
7. The same came for a witness, to bear witness of the *light*, that all men through him might believe,
8. He was not that *light*, but was sent to bear witness of that *light*.
9. That was the true *light*, which *lighteth* every man that cometh into the world.
    —John 1:4-9

19. And this is the Condemnation, that *light* is come into the world, and men loved darkness rather than *light*, because their deeds were evil.
20. For every one that doeth evil hateth the *light*, neither cometh to the *light*, lest his deeds should be reproved.
21. But he that doeth truth cometh to the *light*, that his deeds may be made manifest, that they are wrought in God.
    —John 3:19-21

12. Then spake Jesus again unto them, saying, I AM the *light* of the world: he that followeth Me shall not walk in darkness, but shall have the *light* of life.
—John 8:12
5. As long as I AM in the world, I AM the *light* of the world.
—John 9:5
35. Then Jesus said unto them, Yet a little while is the *light* with you. Walk while ye have the *light*, lest darkness come upon you: for he that walketh in darkness knoweth not whither he goeth.
36. While ye have *light*, believe in the *light*, that ye may be the children of *light* . . .
—John 12:35, 36
46. I AM come a *light* into the world, that whosoever believeth on Me should not abide in darkness.
—John 12:46
16. Who only hath immortality, dwelling in the *light* which no man can approach unto; whom no man hath seen, nor can see: to whom be honour and power everlasting. Amen.
—1 Timothy 6:16

CHRIST IS OUR LIGHT IN NEW JERUSALEM

23. And the city had no need of the sun, neither of the moon, to shine in it: for the glory of God did *lighten* it, and the *lamb [Christ]* is the *light* thereof.
—Revelation 21:23
5. And there shall be no night there; and they need no candle [lamp], neither light of the sun; for the Lord God giveth them *light*; and they shall reign for ever and ever.
—Revelation 22:5

CHRIST THE LIGHT IN OLD TESTAMENT TIMES

21. And the LORD [CHRIST] went before them by day in a pillar of a cloud, to lead them the way; and by night in a pillar of fire, to give them *light*; to go by day and night:
—Exodus 13:21

20. And it came between the camp of the Egyptians and the camp of Israel; and it was a cloud and darkness to them, but It [*Christ*] gave *light* by night to these: so that the one came not near the other all the night.
   —Exodus 14:20

1. The LORD [CHRIST] is my *light* and my salvation; whom shall I fear? the LORD is the strength of my life; of whom shall I be afraid?
   —Psalms 27:1

15. Blessed is the people that know the joyful sound: they shall walk, O LORD, in the *light* of thy countenance.
    —Psalms 89:15

WORD = CHRIST = LIGHT = COMMANDMENTS

105. Thy WORD is a *lamp* unto my feet, and a LIGHT unto my path.
     —Psalms 119:105

20. To the law and to the testimony: if they speak not according to this word, it is because there is no *light* in them.
    —Isaiah 8:20

2. The people that walked in darkness have seen a great *light*: they that dwell in the land of the shadow of death, upon them hath the *light* shined.
   —Isaiah 9:2

17. And the *light* of Israel *[Christ]* shall be for a fire, and His Holy One for a flame:
    —Isaiah 10:17

8. Rejoice not against me, O mine enemy: when I fall, I shall arise; when I sit in darkness, the LORD shall be a *light* unto me.

9. I will bear the indignation of the LORD, because I have sinned against him, until he plead my cause, and execute judgment for me: he will bring me forth to the *light*, and I shall behold his righteousness.
   —Micah 7:8, 9

29. For thou art my *lamp*, O LORD: and the LORD will *lighten* my darkness.
    —2 Samuel 22:29

CHAPTER 11
THE ROCK OF AGES

UPON THIS ROCK—Matthew 16:18

[Some have interpreted this as meaning that Peter is the *rock* but what does the Bible say.]

13. When Jesus came into the coast of Caesarea Philippi, He asked His disciples, saying, Whom do men say that I the Son of man Am?
14. And they said, some say that Thou art John the Baptist: some Elias; and others, Jeremias, or one of the prophets.
15. He [Christ] saith unto them, But whom say ye that I Am?
16. And Simon Peter answered and said, Thou art the Christ, the Son of the living God.
17. And Jesus answered and said unto him, Blessed art thou, Simon Barjona [son of Jona]: for flesh and blood hath not revealed it unto thee, but My Father which is in heaven. [Let us divide up verses 18 and 19 into several parts and study each part.]
18. And I say also unto thee, That thou art Peter, and [Part # 1. *Upon this rock* I will build My church]; and [Part # 2. The gates of hell shall not prevail against it].
19. And I will give unto thee [Part # 3, the keys (understanding)] of [Part # 4. the kingdom of heaven]: and [Part # 5. whatsoever thou shalt bind on earth shall be bound in heaven: and whatsoever thou shalt loose on earth shall be loosed in heaven.]
—Matthew 16:13-19

(Read Also: John 1:42)
[explanation to follow]
[Peter and John were eyewitnesses to this conversation. What do they say.]

16. For we have not followed cunningly devised fables, when we made known unto you the power and coming of our Lord Jesus Christ, but were eyewitnesses of His majesty.
—2 Peter 1:16

1. That which was from the beginning, which we have heard which we have seen with our eyes, which we have looked upon, and our hands have handled of the Word of life;
2. For the life was manifested, and we have seen it, and bear witness, and show unto you that eternal life, which was with the Father, and was manifested unto us;
3. That which we have seen and heard declare we unto you, that ye also may have fellowship with us: and truly our fellowship is with the Father, and with His Son Jesus Christ.
—1 John 1:1-3

JOHN AND PETER WITNESS TO HIGH PRIEST

6. And Annas the high priest, and Caiaphas, and *John*, and Alexander, and as many as were of the kindred of the high priest, were gathered together at Jerusalem.
7. And when they had set them (Peter and John) in the midst, they asked, By what power, or by what name, have ye done this?
8. Then Peter, filled with the Holy Ghost, said unto them. Ye rulers of the people, and elders of Israel,
9. If we this day be examined of the good deed done to the impotent [crippled] man, by what means he is made whole;
10. Be it known unto you all, and to all the people of Israel, that by the name of Jesus Christ of Nazareth, whom ye crucified, whom God raised from the dead, even by Him doth this man stand here before you whole.
11. This [Christ] is the *Stone* which was set at nought of you builders, which is become the head of the corner.

12. Neither is there salvation in any other: for there is none other name under heaven given among men, whereby we must be saved.
—Acts 4:6-12

PART # 1. UPON THIS ROCK I WILL BUILD MY CHURCH

4. To whom coming, as unto a living *Stone*, disallowed indeed of men, but chosen of God, and precious,
7. Unto you therefore which believe He is precious: but unto them which be disobedient, the *Stone* which the builders disallowed, the same is made the head of the corner,
8. And a *Stone* of stumbling and a *Rock* of offence, even to them which stumble at the word, being disobedient:
—1 Peter 2:4, 7, 8

JESUS USES THE SAME FIGURE OF SPEECH

42. Jesus saith unto them, Did ye never read in the scriptures, The *Stone* which the builders rejected the same is become the head of the corner: this is the Lord's doing and it is marvelous in our eyes?
—Matthew 21:42
(Read Also: Luke 20:17)

IN THE OLD TESTAMENT ROCK OR STONE USED FOR GOD MANY TIMES

4. He is the *Rock*, His work is perfect: for all His ways are judgment: a God of truth and without iniquity, just and right is He.
—Deuteronomy 32:4
(Read Also: Deuteronomy 32:15, 18, 37)
2. There is none holy as the LORD: for there is none beside thee: neither is there any *Rock* like our God.
—1 Samuel 2:2
2. . . . The LORD is my Rock, and my fortress, and my deliverer . . .
—Psalms 18:2

GOD = LORD = ROCK = CHRIST

31. For who is God save the LORD? Or who is a *Rock* save our God?
—Psalms 18:31
(Read Also: Psalms 18:46; 28:1; 31:1-3; 62:2-7; 71:3; 78:16; 89:26; 92:15; 94:22; 95:1; 105:41; 114:7, 8)

CHRIST IS THE ROCK THAT SUPPLIES US THE WATER OF LIFE

4. And did all drink the same spiritual drink: for they drank of that spiritual *Rock* that followed them: and that *Rock* was *Christ*.
—1 Corinthians 10:4

6. Behold, I will stand before thee there upon the *Rock* in Horeb; and thou shalt smite the *Rock*, and there shall come water out of it, that the people may drink.
—Exodus 17:6

15. ... who brought thee forth water out of the *Rock* of flint;
—Deuteronomy 8:15

7. And the LORD spake unto Moses, saying ...

8. ... speak ye unto the *Rock* before their eyes; and it shall give forth His water, and thou shalt bring forth to them water out of the rock: so thou shalt give the congregation and their beasts drink.
—Numbers 20:8
(Read Also Numbers 20:9-11)

41. He *[Christ]* opened the *Rock*, and the water gushed out; they ran in the dry places like a river.
—Psalms 105:41

7. ... the God of Jacob;

8. Which turned the *Rock* into a standing water, the flint into a fountain of water.
—Psalms 114:7, 8
(Read Also: Nehemiah 9:15)

CHRIST IS OUR FOUNDATION STONE

24. Therefore whosoever heareth these sayings of Mine, and doeth them, I will liken him unto a wise man, which built his house upon a *Rock (Petra = Christ)*:
25. And the rain descended, and the floods came, and the winds blew, and beat upon that house: and it fell not: for it was founded upon a *Rock (petra = Christ): (not petros = peter)*.
—Matthew 7:24, 25
(Read Also: Luke 6:48)

CHRIST THE CHIEF CORNER STONE

10. And have ye not read this scripture; The *Stone* which the builders rejected is become the head of the corner:
—Mark 12:10
17. And He [Christ] beheld them, and said, What is this then that is written, the *Stone* which the builders rejected the same is become the head of the corner?
18. Whosoever shall fall upon that *Stone* shall be broken; but on whomsoever it shall fall, it will grind him to powder.
—Luke 20:17, 18
11. This is the *Stone* which was set at nought of you builders, which is become the head of the corner.
12. Neither is there salvation in any other: for there is none other name under heaven given among men, whereby we must be saved.
—Acts 4:11, 12

CHRIST A STUMBLING STONE AND A ROCK OF OFFENSE TO THOSE WHO REFUSE TO BELIEVE

22. The *Stone* which the builders refused is become the *head Stone* of the corner.
—Psalms 118:22
14. And He [Christ] shall be for a sanctuary; but for a *Stone* of stumbling and for a *Rock* of offence to both the houses

of Israel, for a gin [trap] and for a snare to the inhabitants of Jerusalem.
—Isaiah 8:14
(Read Also: Isaiah 17:10; 48:21; 51:1)

16. Therefore thus saith the Lord GOD, Behold, I lay in Zion for a foundation a *Stone*, a tried *Stone*, a precious *corner Stone*, a sure foundation: he that believeth shall not make haste.
—Isaiah 28:16

33. . . . Behold, I lay in Sion a *Stumblingstone* and *Rock* of offence: and whosoever believeth on Him shall not be ashamed.
—Romans 9:33

19. Now therefore ye are no more strangers and foreigners, but fellowcitizens with the saints, and of the household of God;

20. And are built upon the foundations of the apostles and prophets, Jesus Christ Himself being the *Chief corner Stone*;

21. In whom all the building fitly framed together growth unto a holy temple in the Lord:

22. In whom ye also are builded together for a habitation of God through the Spirit.
—Ephesians 2:19-22

PETER NAMED HEAD OF THE CHURCH?

24. And there was also a strife among them, which of them should be accounted the greatest.
—Luke 22:24

1. At the same time came the disciples unto Jesus, saying, Who [among them] is [to be] the greatest in the [new] kingdom of heaven?
—Matthew 18:1

33. And He came to Capernaum: and being in the house He asked them, What was it that ye disputed among yourselves by the way?

34. But they held their peace: for by the way they had disputed among themselves, who should be the greatest.
35. And He sat down, and called the twelve, and saith unto them, If any man desire to be first, the same shall be last of all, and servant of all.
—Mark 9:33-35

[If Christ had made Peter first among the disciples, why were they still arguing who should be the greatest in the new kingdom they thought Christ was about to set up?]

[The name Peter comes from the Greek work "petros", a "stone" or small movable slab or small rock that can be thrown. The Greek word "petra" means a large mass of rock, a ledge, or shelf or rocky peak. A "petra" is a large, fixed immovable rock, whereas a "petros" is a small stone. Peter was called a small unstable stone. Christ could see in the future that Peter would deny his Lord three times.]

18. And I say unto thee, That thou art Peter [a "petros"—small unstable stone], and [—but] upon this Rock ["petra"—Christ] I will build My church; and the gates of hell [—grave] shall not prevail against It [—the Rock who is Christ].
—Matthew 16:18

PART # 2. THE GATES OF HELL SHALL NOT PREVAIL

[In ancient cities to capture the gates was to overcome the entire city. Christ overcame death, not Peter.]

24. Whom God hath raised up, having loosed the pains of death: because it was not possible that He [Christ] should be holden of it.
—Acts 2:24

[Just three verses down from, Matthew 16:18, Jesus begins to tell them He would die and be raised in three days.]

21. From that time forth began Jesus to show unto His disciples, how that He must go unto Jerusalem, and suffer many things of the elders and chief priests and scribes, and be killed, and be *raised again* the third day.
—Matthew 16:21
40. For as Jonas was three days and three nights in the whale's belly; so shall the Son of man be three days and three nights in the heart of the earth.
—Matthew 12:40
6. He is not here: for He is risen, as He said, Come, see the place where the Lord lay.
—Matthew 28:6
(Read Also: Matthew 28, Mark 16, Luke 24; John 20 and 21)

[But the gates of hell (the grave) did prevail against Peter]

BUT SATAN CANNOT HOLD THOSE (IN THE GRAVE) FOREVER WHO BELIEVE IN CHRIST

16. For God so loved the world, that He gave His only begotten Son, that whosoever believeth in Him should not perish, but have everlasting life.
—John 3:16
23. For the wages of sin is death; but the gift of God is eternal life through Jesus Christ our Lord.
—Romans 6:23

CHRIST ENTERED SATAN'S STRONGHOLD AND BOUND HIM

29. Or else how can one enter into a strong man's house, and spoil his goods, except he first bind the strong man? And then he will spoil his house.
—Matthew 12:29
26. The last enemy that shall be destroyed is death.
—1 Corinthians 15:26

14. And death and hell [grave] were cast into the lake of fire. This is the second death.
—Revelation 20:14

PETER IS MARTYRED AS FORETOLD BY CHRIST

18. Verily, verily, I say unto thee, When thou wast young, thou girdedst thyself, and walkedst whiter thou wouldest: but when thou shalt be old, thou shalt stretch forth thy hands, and another shall gird thee, and carry thee whither thou wouldest not.
19. This spake He, signifying by what death He should glorify God, And when He had spoken this, He saith unto Him, Follow Me.
—John 21:18, 19

PART # 3. GIVE UNTO THEE THE KEYS (KNOWLEDGE)

[Not a *key* to open a locked door.]

52. Woe unto you, lawyers! For ye have taken away the key of knowledge:
—Luke 11:52
3. And this is life eternal, that they might *know* thee the only true God, and Jesus Christ, whom thou hast sent.
—John 17:3
63. It is the spirit that quickeneth; the flesh profiteth nothing: the *words* that I speak unto you, they are spirit and they are life.
—John 6:63
68. Then Simon Peter answered Him, Lord, to whom shall we go? thou hast the *words* of eternal life.
—John 6:68
12. But as many as received Him [not just Peter] gave He power [the keys] to become the sons of God, even them that believeth on His name:
—John 1:12

THE "WORD OF GOD" IS THE "KEY" TO THE NEW BIRTH EXPERIENCE

23. Being born again, not of corruptible seed, but of incorruptible, by the *word* of God, which liveth and abideth for ever.
—1 Peter 1:23

"ALL" HIS DISCIPLES ARE TO PASS ON THE WORDS OF RECONCILIATION TO OTHERS

18. And all things are of God, who hath reconciled us to Himself by Jesus Christ, and that given to us the ministry of reconciliation.
19. To wit, that God was in Christ, reconciling the world unto Himself, not imputing their trespasses upon them; and hath committed unto us the word of reconciliation.
20. Now then we are ambassadors for Christ, as though God did beseech you by us: we pray you in Christ's stead, be ye reconciled to God.
21. For He hath made Him to be sin for us, who knew no sin; that we might be made the righteousness of God in Him.
—2 Corinthians 5:18-21

JAMES, NOT PETER, EXERCISED ADMINISTRATIVE FUNCTIONS OVER THE EARLY CHURCH IN JERUSALEM

13. . . . *James* answered, saying, Men and brethren, hearken unto me:
19. Wherefore my sentence is that we trouble not them, which from among the Gentiles are turned to God:
—Acts 15:13, 19
(Read Entire Account: Acts 15:1–35)
17. . . . And he [Peter] said, Go shew these things unto *James*, and to the brethren.
—Acts 12:17

18. And the day following Paul went in with us unto *James*; and all the elders were present.
—Acts 21:18
7. After that, He was seen of *James*; then all of the apostles.
—1 Corinthians 15:7

PAUL CORRECTED PETER FOR A WRONG COURSE OF ACTION

11. But when Peter was come to Antioch, I [Paul] withstood him to the face, because he was to be blamed.
12. For before that certain [men] came from *James*, he did eat with the Gentiles: but when they [these certain Jewish men] were come, he [Peter] withdrew and separated himself, fearing them which were of the circumcision [Jews].
—Galatians 2:11, 12
(Read Entire Account: Galatians 2:11-17)

PART # 4. KINGDOM OF HEAVEN, KINGDOM OF GRACE

17. From that time Jesus began to preach, and to say, Repent: for the *kingdom of heaven* is at hand.
—Matthew 4:17
2. . . . and taught them saying,
3. Blessed are the poor in spirit: for theirs is the *kingdom of heaven*.
—Matthew 5:2, 3

WE CANNOT ENTER KINGDOM OF GLORY UNTIL WE FIRST ENTER HIS KINGDOM OF GRACE

31. When the Son of man shall come in His *glory*, and all the holy angels with Him, then shall He sit upon the throne of His *glory*.
34. Then shall the King say unto them on His right hand, Come, ye blessed of My Father, inherit the *kingdom* prepared for you from the foundation of the world:
—Matthew 25:31, 34

PART # 5. TO BIND ON EARTH, TO LOOSE ON EARTH

19. ... and whatsoever thou shalt bind on earth shall be bound in heaven: and whatsoever thou shalt loose on earth shall be loosed in heaven.
—Matthew 16:19
(The meaning evidently is this, that the church on earth will require *only* what heaven requires and will prohibit only what heaven prohibits.)
24. Therefore Whosoever heareth these sayings of mine, and doeth them, I will liken him unto a wise man which built his house upon a Rock:
26. And every one that heareth these sayings of mine, and doeth them not, shall be likened unto a foolish man, which built his house upon the sand:
—Matthew 7:24, 26
(Read Also: Matthew 7:21-27)
7. Howbeit in vain do they worship me, teaching for doctrines the commandments of men, ...
8. For laying aside the commandment of God, ye hold the tradition of men, ...
9. ... Full well ye reject the commandment of God, that ye may keep your own tradition.
—Mark 7:7-9
(Read Also: Mark 7:6-13)

[They were to teach converts "to observe all things whatsoever" Christ commanded—no more no less.]
Pope Leo I, was the first Roman pontiff to claim (about 445 AD) that his authority came from Christ through Peter. He used Matthew 16:13-19 to prove his point. No Roman Bishop for four centuries, after Christ, had discovered this fact. Only when a fifth-century Roman bishop found it necessary to find a Biblical reason for papal authority did it happen.
—A History of Christianity, 1953, by Kenneth Scott Latourette, pg. 186

CHAPTER 12
THE HOLY SPIRIT AND HIS WORK

THE HOLY SPIRIT TAKES THE PLACE OF JESUS

16. I will pray the Father, and He shall give you another *Comforter*, that He may abide with you forever.
    —John 14:16
26. But the *Comforter*, even the *Holy Spirit*, whom the Father will send in My name, *He* shall teach you all things, and brings to your remembrance all that I said unto you.
    —John 14:26, RV
16. And I will pray the Father, and He shall give you another *Comforter*, that He may abide with you for ever;
17. Even the *Spirit of Truth*; whom the world cannot receive, because it seeth *Him* not, neither knoweth *Him*: but ye know *Him*; for *He* dwelleth with you, and shall be in you.
18. I [*Christ*] will not leave you *Comfortless*: I will come to you [via the *Holy Spirit*].
    —John 14:16-18
19. Go ye therefore, and teach all nations, baptizing them in the name of the Father, and of the Son, and of the *Holy Spirit*:
20. . . . Lo, I am with you always, even unto to the end of the world.
    —Matthew 28:19, 20
20. At that day ye shall know that I am in My Father, and ye in Me, and I in you.
    —John 14:20

(HOLY GHOST = HOLY SPIRIT)

20. Behold, I stand at the door, and knock: if any man hear My voice, and open the door, I will come in to him, and will sup with him, and he with Me.
—Revelation 3:20

7. Nevertheless I tell you the truth; It is expedient for you that I go away: for if I go not away, the *Comforter* will not come unto you; but if I depart, I will send *Him* unto you.
—John 16:7

8. And when *He* is come, *He* will reprove [convince] the world of sin, and of righteousness, and of judgment.
—John 16:8

26. But when the *Comforter* is come, whom I will send unto you from the Father, even the *Spirit of truth*, which proceedeth from the Father, *He* shall testify of Me.
—John 15:26

WHAT DID JESUS SAY THE SPIRIT WOULD DO?

13. Howbeit when HE, the *Spirit of Truth*, is come, *He* will *Guide* you into all truth: for *He* shall not speak of *Himself*; but whatsoever *He* shall hear, that shall *He* speak: and *He* will show you things to come.

14. *He* shall glorify Me: for *He* shall receive of Mine, and *He* will show you things to come.
—John 16:13, 14

1. Now the *Spirit speaketh expressly*, that in the latter times some shall depart from the faith, giving heed to seducing spirits, and doctrines of devils;
—1 Timothy 4:1

16. The *Spirit* itself *beareth witness* with our spirit, that we are the children of God:
—Romans 8:16

4. Now there are diversities of gifts, but the same *Spirit*.

8. For to one is given by the *Spirit* the word of wisdom; to another a word of *knowledge* by the same *Spirit*;

9. To another *faith* by the same *Spirit*; to another the gifts of *healing* by the same *Spirit*;
10. To another the working of *miracles*; to another prophecy; to another *discerning of Spirits*; to another *divers kinds of tongues*; to another *interpretation of tongues*:
11. But all these worketh that one and the selfsame *Spirit*, dividing to every man severally as he will.
—1 Corinthians 12:4, 8-11

THE HOLY SPIRIT INVITES THE SINNER.

17. And the Spirit and the bride say, Come. And let him that heareth say, Come. And let him that is athirst come, And whosoever will, let him take the water of life freely.
—Revelation 22:17
14. How much more shall the blood of Christ, who through the Eternal Spirit offered Himself without spot to God, purge your conscience from dead works to serve the living God?
—Hebrews 9:14
(Read Also: 1 Corinthians 2:7-16)
21. For the prophecy came not in old time by the will of man: but holy men of God spake as they were moved by the *Holy Ghost*.
—2 Peter 1:21
(Read Also: 1 Peter 1:11, 12)
13. . . . In whom also after that ye believed, ye were sealed with the *Holy Spirit of promise*.
—Ephesians 1:13

THERE IS A LIMIT TO HOLY SPIRIT STRIVINGS

30. Grieve not the *Holy Spirit* of God, whereby ye are sealed unto the day of redemption.
—Ephesians 4:30
3. And the Lord said My *Spirit* shall not always strive with man.
—Genesis 6:3

THE SPIRIT DOES NOT GIVE UP ON MAN EASILY.

11. [David prayed,] Cast me not away from Thy presence; and take not *Thy Holy Spirit* from me.
—Psalms 51:11
13. If ye then, being evil, know how to give good gifts unto your children: how much more shall your Heavenly Father give the *Holy Spirit* to them that ask Him.
—Luke 11:13
26. Likewise the *Spirit* also helpeth our infirmities: for we know not what we should pray for as we ought: but the *Spirit* itself maketh intercession for us with groanings which cannot be uttered.
27. And He that searcheth the hearts knoweth what is the mind of the *Spirit*, because He maketh intercession for the saints according to the will of God.
—Romans 8:26, 27

THE HOLY SPIRIT EXHIBITS PERSONAL ATTRIBUTES

12. . . . *shall teach* you in the same hour what ye ought to say.
—Luke 12:12
13. . . . which the *Holy Ghost* teacheth . . .
—1 Corinthians 2:13.
29. Then the *Spirit said* unto Philip, Go near . . .
—Acts 8:29
19. . . . the *Spirit said* unto him, Behold, three men seek thee.
20. Arise therefore, and get thee down, and go with them, doubting nothing: for I have sent them.
—Acts 10:19, 20
7. . . . the *Holy Ghost saith*, To day if ye will hear His voice, . . .
—Hebrews 3:7

HE APPOINTS PEOPLE FOR SERVICE

2. . . . the *Holy Ghost Said*, Separate me Barnabas and Saul for the work whereunto I have called them.

4. So they, being *Sent forth* by the *Holy Ghost*, departed . . .
—Acts 13:2, 4
28. Take heed . . . over the which the *Holy Ghost* hath *made you overseers*, to feed the church of God . . .
—Acts 20:28

HE FORBIDS

6. . . . were *forbidden* of the *Holy Ghost* to preach the word in Asia . . .
7. . . . they assayed to go into Bithynia, but the Spirit suffered them not.
—Acts 16:6, 7

HE WORKS MIRACLES

4. And they were *filled* with the *Holy Ghost*, and *began to speak* with other tongues, as the *Spirit gave them utterance*.
—Acts 2:4
39. . . . the *Spirit* of the Lord *caught away* Philip, that the eunuch saw him no more.
—Acts 8:39

THE HOLY SPIRIT IN THE OLD TESTAMENT

39. Search the scriptures; for in them ye think ye have eternal life: and they are they which testify of me.
—John 5:39
2. And the earth was without form, and void; and darkness was upon the face of the deep. And the *Spirit* of God moved upon the face of the waters.
—Genesis 1:2
4. The *Spirit* of God hath made me, and the breath of the Almighty hath given me life.
—Job 33:4
30. Thou sendest forth thy *Spirit*, they are created: and thou renewest the face of the earth.
—Psalms 104:30

PERSONALITY OF HOLY SPIRIT IN OLD TESTAMENT

2. The *Spirit* of the LORD spake by me, and His word was in my tongue.
—2 Samuel 23:2

24. But Zedekiah . . . went near, and smote Micaiah on the cheek, and said, Which way went the *Spirit* of the LORD from me to speak unto thee?
—1 Kings 22:24

10. But they rebelled and grieved His *Holy Spirit*; So He turned Himself against them as an enemy, And He fought against them.
—Isaiah 63:10, NKJV
(Read Also: Micah 2:7)

4. Whereby, when ye read, ye may understand my knowledge in the mystery of Christ
5. Which in other ages [Old Testament Times] was not made known unto the sons of men, as it is now revealed unto His holy apostles and prophets by the *Spirit*:
6. That the Gentiles should be fellow heirs, and of the same body, and partakers of His promise in Christ by the gospel:
—Ephesians 3:4-6

THE HOLY SPIRIT IS ALSO YAHWEH

2. The *Spirit* of the LORD [Yahweh] spake by me, and His word was in my tongue.
—2 Samuel 23:2

25. And when they agreed not among themselves, they departed, after that Paul had spoken one word, well spake the *Holy Ghost* by Esaias [Isaiah] the prophet unto our fathers.
26. Saying, Go unto this people, and say, Hearing ye shall hear, and shall not understanding; and seeing ye shall see, and not perceive:
27. For the heart of this people is waxed gross, and their ears are dull of hearing, and their eyes have they closed; lest

they should see with their eyes, and hear with their ears, and understand with their heart, and should be converted, and I should heal them.
28. Be it known therefore unto you, that the salvation of God is sent unto the Gentiles, and that they will hear it.
—Acts 28:25-28
(Quoting Isaiah 6:8-10)

HOLY SPIRIT CLEARLY REFERRED TO AS GOD

3. But Peter said, Ananias, why hath Satan filled thine heart to lie to the *Holy Ghost*, and to keep back part of the price of the land?
4. Whiles is remained, was it not thine own? And after it was sold, was it not in thine own power? why hast thou conceived this thing in thine heart? Thou hast not lied unto men, but unto God.
—Acts 5:3, 4
16. Know ye not that ye are the temple of God, and that the *Spirit* of God dwelleth in you?
17. If any man defile the temple of God, him shall God destroy; for the temple of God is holy, which temple ye are.
—1 Corinthians 3:16, 17
(Read Also: 1 Corinthians 6:19)
31. Wherefore I say unto you, all manner of sin and blasphemy shall be forgiven unto men: but the blasphemy against the *Holy Ghost* shall not be forgiven unto men.
—Matthew 12:31
29. Of how much sorer punishment, suppose ye, will he be thought worthy, who hath trodden under foot the Son of God, and hath counted the blood of the covenant, wherewith he was sanctified, and unholy thing, and hath done despite unto the *Spirit of Grace*?
—Hebrews 10:29
[*The lost will have sinned against the Holy Spirit by refusing to repent.*]
(Read Also: Revelation 22:17; Acts 28:27; Genesis 3:6; Ephesians 4:30)

CHAPTER 13
ANGELS

ANGELS WERE CREATED BY CHRIST

16. For by Him were all things created, that are in heaven, and that are in earth, visible and invisible, whether they be thrones, or dominions, or principalities, or power: *All things* were created by Him, and for Him:
—Colossians 1:16

ANGELS NOT SELF-EXISTENT OR SELF-SUSTAINING

2. [God] Hath in these last days spoken unto us by His Son, whom He hath appointed heir of all things, *BY WHOM ALSO HE MADE THE WORLDS*;
3. Who being the brightness of His glory, and the express image of His person, and upholding all things by the word of His power, when He had by Himself purged our sins, sat down on the right hand of the Majesty on high.
4. Being made so much better than the angels, as He hath by inheritance obtained a more excellent name than they.
—Hebrews 1:2-4

ANGELS EXISTED BEFORE OUR EARTH OR HUMANITY

4. Where wast thou when I laid the foundations of the earth? declare, if thou hast understanding.

7. When the morning stars sang together, and all the sons of God shouted for joy?
—Job 38:4, 7
24. So He drove out the man; and He placed at the east of the garden of Eden Cherubims, and a flaming sword which turned every ways . . .
—Genesis 3:24

SPIRIT ANGELS ARE SUBJECT TO GOD'S AUTHORITY

7. And of the angels He saith, Who maketh His angels spirits, and His ministers a flame of fire.
14. Are they not all ministering spirits, sent forth to minister for them who shall be heirs of salvation?
—Hebrews 1:7,14

ANGELS ARE A HIGHER ORDER THAN HUMANS

4. What is man, that thou art mindful of him? and the son of man, that thou visitest him?
5. For thou hast made him a little lower than the angels, and hast crowned him with glory and honour.
—Psalms 8:4, 5
7. Thou madest him a little lower than the angels; thou crownedst him with the glory and honour, and didst set him over the works of thy hands:
—Hebrews 2:7

ANGEL'S NATURE DIFFER FROM HUMANS

16. For verily He [Christ] took not on Him the nature of angles; but he took on Him the seed of Abraham.
—Hebrews 2:16

ANGELS ARE POWERFUL, QUICK AND MIGHTY

7. . . . when the Lord Jesus shall be revealed from heaven with His might angels,

8. In flaming fire taking vengeance on them that know not God, and that obey not the gospel of our Lord Jesus Christ . . .
—2 Thessalonians 1:7, 8

21. And a mighty angel took up a stone like a great millstone, and cast it into the sea saying, Thus with violence shall that great city Babylon be thrown down, and shall be found no more at all.
—Revelation 18:21

14. And the living creatures [angels] ran and returned as the appearance of a flash of lightning.
—Ezekiel 1:14

37. Then the angel of the LORD went froth, and smote in the camp of the Assyrians a hundred and fourscore and five thousand: and when they arose early in the morning, behold, they were all dead corpses.
—Isaiah 37:36

ANGELS OBEY GOD'S COMMANDMENTS

20. Bless the LORD, ye His angels, that excel in strength, that do His commandments, hearkening unto the voice of His word.
21. Bless ye the LORD, all ye His hosts; ye ministers of His, that do His pleasure.
—Psalms 103:20, 21

ANGELS HAVE FREEDOM OF CHOICE

6. And the angels which kept not their first estate, but left their own habitation, He hath reserved in everlasting chains under darkness unto the judgment of the great day.
—Jude 6

WE EACH HAVE A GUARDIAN ANGEL

10. Take heed that ye despise not one of these little ones; for I say unto you, That in heaven their angels do always behold the face of my Father which is in heaven.

—Matthew 18:10

15. And they said unto her, Thou art mad. But she constantly affirmed [insisted] that it was even so. Then said they, It is his angel.
—Acts 12:15
11. For He shall give His angels charge over thee, to keep thee in all thy ways.
12. They shall bear thee up in their hands, lest thou dash thy foot against a stone.
—Psalms 91:11, 12
22. My God hath sent His angel, and hath shut the lions' mouths, that they have not hurt me: for as much as before Him innocency was found in me; and also before thee, O King, have I done no hurt.
—Daniel 6:22

TRAVEL FASTER THAN THE SPEED LIGHT

21. Yea, whiles I was speaking in prayer, even the man Gabriel, whom I had seen in the vision at the beginning, being caused to fly swiftly, touched me about the time of the evening oblation.
22. And he informed me, and talked with me, and said, O Daniel, I am now come forth to give thee skill and understanding.
23. At the beginning of thy supplication the commandment came forth, and I am come to show thee; for thou art greatly beloved: therefore understand the matter, and consider the vision.
—Daniel 9:21-23
51. And He saith unto him, Verily, verily, I say unto you, Hereafter ye shall see heaven open, and the angels of God ascending and descending upon the Son of man.
—John 1:51

WE WILL BE MORE LIKE ANGELS AT SECOND COMING

34. And Jesus . . . said, The children of this world marry, and are given in marriage:
35. But they which shall be accounted worthy to obtain that world, and the resurrection from the dead, neither marry, nor are given in marriage:
36. Neither can they die any more: for they are equal unto the angels; and are the children of God, being the children of the resurrection.
—Luke 20:34-36
20. For our conversation [citizenship] is in heaven; from whence also we look for the Saviour, the Lord Jesus Christ:
21. Who shall change our vile [humble] body, that it may be fashioned like unto His glorious body, according to the working whereby He is able even to subdue all things unto himself.
—Philippians 3:20, 21

ANGELS SOMETIMES APPEAR AS HUMANS

1. . . . And he [Abraham] sat in the tent door in the heat of the day;
2. And he lift up his eyes and looked, and, lo, three men stood by him: and when he saw then, he ran to meet them [the angels] from the tent door, and bowed himself toward the ground.
—Genesis 18:1-2
(Read Also: Genesis 18:3-8 for full account.)
1. And there came two angels to Sodom: and Lot seeing them rose up to meet them; and the bowed himself with his face toward the ground;
10. But the men [angels] put forth their hand, and pulled Lot into the house to them, and shut the door.
—Genesis 19:10
(Read Also: Genesis 19:1-11)
4. And it came to pass, as they were much perplexed there

about, behold, two men stood by them in shining garments:
—Luke 24:4

12. ... Two angels in white sitting, the one at the head, and the other at the feet, where the body of Jesus had lain.
—John 20:12

5. And entering into the sepulcher, they saw a young man [angel] sitting on the right side, clothed in a long white garment; and they were affrighted.
—Mark 16:5

5. And the angel answered and said unto the women, Fear not ye: for I know that ye seek Jesus, which was crucified.
—Matthew 28:5

2. Be not forgetful to entertain strangers: for thereby some have entertained angels unawares.
—Hebrews 13:2

10. And while they looked stedfastly toward heaven as He went up, behold, two men stood by them in white apparel;
—Acts 1:10
(Read Also: Acts 1:9-11)

THERE ARE DIFFERENT ORDERS OF ANGELS

2. Above it [God's throne] stood the seraphims: each one had six wings; with twain he covered his face, and with twain he covered his feet, and with twain he did fly.
—Isaiah 6:2

10. As for the likeness of their faces, they four had the face of a man, and the face of a lion, on the right side: and they four had the face of an ox on the left side; they four also had the face of an eagle.
—Ezekiel 1:10

20. And the cherubims shall stretch forth their wings on high, covering the mercy seat with their wings, & their faces look one to another; toward the mercy seat shall the faces on the cherubims be.
—Exodus 25:20

24. , ... He [GOD] placed at the east of the garden of Eden cherubims ... to keep the way of the tree of life.
—Genesis 3:24

THERE ARE ALSO EVIL ANGELS

9. And the great dragon was cast out, that old serpent, called the Devil, and Satan, which deceiveth the whole world: he was cast out into the earth, and his angels were cast out with him.
—Revelation 12:9

HOW MANY ANGELS ARE THERE?

11. And I beheld, and I heard the voice of many angels round about the throne and the beasts and the elders: and the number of them was ten thousand times ten thousand, and thousands of thousands:
—Revelation 5:11

ANGELS' HOME IS IN HEAVEN

1. Give ear, O Shepherd of Israel [Christ], thou that leadest Joseph like a flock; thou that dwellest between the cherubims, shine forth.
—Psalms 80:1
1. The LORD reigneth; let the people tremble: He sitteth between the cherubims; let the earth be moved.
—Psalms 99:1
1. ... I saw also the LORD sitting upon a throne, high and lifted up, and His train filled the temple.
2. Above it stood the seraphims ...
—Isaiah 6:1-2
(Read Also: Isaiah 6:3, 4)

ANGELS HAVE ACCESS TO GOD AT ALL TIMES

19. And the angel answering said unto him, I am Gabriel, that stand in the presence of God; and am sent to speak unto thee, ...
—Luke 1:19
10. Take heed that ye despise not one of these little ones; for I say unto you, That in heaven their angels do always behold the face of My Father which is in heaven.
—Matthew 18:10

ANGELS COME AND GO AS GOD COMMANDS

17. The chariots of God are twenty thousand, even thousands of angels: the Lord is among them, as in Sinai ...
—Psalms 68:17
51. And He saith unto him [Nathanael], Verily, verily, I say unto you, Hereafter ye shall see heaven open, and the angels of God ascending and descending upon the Son of man.
—John 1:51

ANGELS ARE INNUMERABLE

10. A fiery stream issued and came forth from before Him: thousands thousands ministered unto Him and ten thousand times ten thousand stood before Him ...
—Daniel 7:10
22. But ye are come unto mount Sion, and unto the city of the living God, the heavenly Jerusalem, and to an innumerable company of angels.
—Hebrews 12:22

ANGELS, VERY INTERESTED IN OUR SALVATION

10. Likewise, I say unto you, there is joy in the presence of the angels of God over one sinner that repenteth.
—Luke 15:10

ANGELS ARE GOD'S MESSENGERS

20. Bless the LORD, ye His angels, that excel in strength, that do His commandments, hearkening unto the voice of His word.
21. Bless ye the LORD, all ye His hosts; ye ministers of His, that do His pleasure.
—Psalms 103:20, 21

ANGELS KNOW OUR NAME, ADDRESS, & OCCUPATION

3. He [Cornelius] saw in a vision evidently [clearly] about the ninth hour of the day an angel of God coming in to him, and saying unto him, Cornelius.
4. And when he looked on him, he was afraid, and said, What is it, Lord? and he said unto him, Thy prayers and thine alm are come up for a memorial before God.
5. And now send men to Joppa, and call for one Simon, whose surname is Peter:
6. He lodgeth with one Simon a tanner, whose house is by the sea side: he shall tell thee what thou oughtest to do.
—Acts 10:3-6

ANGELS INSTRUCT GOD'S PEOPLE

3. And the angel of the LORD appeared unto the woman, and said unto her, Behold now, thou art barren, and bearest not: but thou shalt conceive, and bear a son.
4. Now therefore beware, I pray thee, and drink not wine nor strong drink, and eat not any unclean thing:
5. For, lo, thou shalt conceive, and bear a son; and no razor shall come on his head: for the child shall be a Nazarite unto God from the womb: and he shall begin to deliver Israel out of the hand of the Philistines.
—Judges 13:3-5

ANGELS HELP GOD'S PEOPLE PREACH THE GOSPEL

17. . . . the high priest . . . and Sadducees . . .
18. . . . laid their hands on the apostles, and put them in the common prison.
19. But the angel of the Lord by night opened the prison doors, and brought them [Peter and another apostle] forth, and said,
20. Go, stand and speak in the temple to the people all the words of this life.
21. And when they heard that, they entered into the temple early in the morning, and taught . . .
—Acts 5:17-21
26. And the angel of the Lord spake unto Philip, saying, Arise, and go toward the south unto the way that goeth down from Jerusalem unto Gaza, which is desert.
—Acts 8:26
6. And I saw another angel fly in the midst of heaven, having the everlasting gospel to preach unto them that dwell on the earth, and to every nation, and kindred, and tongue, and people,
—Revelation 14:6

GOD USES ANGELS AS MINISTERS OF JUSTICE

31. Then the LORD opened the eyes of Balaam, and he saw the angel of the LORD standing in the way, and his sword drawn in his hand: and he bowed down his head, and fell flat on his face.
—Numbers 22:31
(Read Also: Numbers 22:22-35)
35. And it came to pass that night, that the angel of the LORD went out, and smote in the camp of the Assyrians an hundred fourscore and five thousand: and when they arose early in the morning behold, they were all dead corpses.

—2 Kings 19:35

13. . . . A watcher and a holy one [angel] came down from heaven;

16. Let his heart be changed from man's, and let a beast's heart be given unto him; and let seven times pass over him.

17. This matter is by the decree of the watchers [angels], and the demand by the word of the holy ones . . .
—Daniel 4:13,16-17
(Read Also: Daniel 4:31-33.)

1. And I saw another sign in heaven, great and marvelous, seven angels having the seven last plagues; for in them is filled up the wrath of God.
—Revelation 15:1

1. And I heard a great voice out of the temple saying to the seven angels, Go your ways, and put out the vials of the wrath of God upon the earth.
—Revelation 16:1
(Read Also: Revelation 16:2-21)

ANGELS GUIDE, DIRECT, PROTECT, AND PROVIDE

5. And as he [Elijah] lay and slept under a juniper tree, behold, then an angel touched him, and said unto him, arise and eat.

6. And he looked, and, behold, there was a cake baken on the coals, and a cruse of water at his head. And he did eat and drink, and laid him down again.

7. And the angel of the LORD came again the second time, and touched him, and said, Arise and eat; because the journey is too great for thee.
—1 Kings 19:5-7

3. But the angel of the LORD said to Elijah the Tishbite, Arise, go up to meet the messengers of the King of Samaria, and say unto them, Is it not because there is not a God in Israel, that ye go to inquire of Baalzebub the God of Ekron?

15. And the angel of the LORD said unto Elijah, Go down

with him: be not afraid of him. And he arose, and went down with him unto the king.
—2 Kings 1:3, 15
7. The angel of the LORD encampeth round about them that fear him, and delivereth them.
—Psalm 34:7
11. For He shall give His angels charge over thee, to keep thee in all thy ways.
—Psalms 91:11
23. For there stood by me this night the angel of God, whose I am, and whom I serve,
—Acts 27:23
16. And he [Elisha] answered, Fear not: for they that be with us are more than they that be with them.
17. And Elisha prayed, and said. Lord. I pray thee, open his eyes, that he may see. And the LORD opened the eyes of the young man; and he saw and, behold, the mountains was full of horses and chariots of fire round about Elisha.
—2 Kings 6:16, 17

ANGELS INTERVENE IN WORLD AFFAIRS, HOLD BACK DESTRUCTIVE FORCES, RESTRAIN TYRANTS, AND PUNISH EVIL

11. And he [the angel] said unto me, O Daniel, a man greatly beloved, understand the words that I speak unto thee . . .
14. Now I am come to make thee understand what shall befall thy people in the latter days . . .
—Daniel 10:11, 14
(Read Also: Daniel 10:10, 13)
21. And upon a set day Harod, arrayed in royal apparel, sat upon his throne, and made an oration unto them.
22. And the people gave a shout, saying, It is the voice of a god, and not of a man.
23. And immediately the angel of the Lord smote him, because he gave not God the glory: and he was eaten of worms, and gave up the ghost.

—Acts 12:23
(Read Also: Acts 12:21-23)

1. And after these things I saw four angels standing on the four corners of the earth, holding the four winds of the earth, that the wind should not blow on the earth, nor on the sea, nor on any tree.
2. And I saw another angel ascending from the east, having the seal of the living God: and he cried with a loud voice to the four angels, to whom it was given to hurt the earth and the sea,
3. Saying, Hurt not the earth, neither the sea, nor the trees, till we have sealed the servants of our God in their foreheads.
—Revelation 7:1-3

ANGELS WITNESS GOD'S JUDGMENT

9. I beheld till the thrones were cast down [placed], and the Ancient of days did sit [in judgment] . . .
10. . . . thousand thousand [angels] ministered unto Him, and ten thousand times ten thousand stood before Him: the judgment was set, and the books were opened.
—Daniel 7:9, 10
(Read Also: Daniel 7:11)
11. And I beheld, and I heard the voice of many angels round about the throne and the beasts (living creatures) and the elders: and the number of them was ten thousand times ten thousand, and thousand of thousands;
—Revelation 5:11
(Read Also: Revelation 5:8-14)

ANGELS REFUSE WORSHIP, BUT WORSHIP GOD

10. And I fell at his [the angels] feet to worship him, and he said unto me, See thou do it not: . . .
—Revelation 19:10
8. . . . I fell down to worship before the feet of the angel which showed me these things.

9. Then saith he unto me, See thou do it not: for I am thy fellowservant . . .
—Revelation 22:8, 9
6. And again, when He [God] bringeth in the first begotten [Son] in the world, He saith, and let all the angels of God worship Him.
—Hebrews 1:6

ANGELS WILL ACCOMPANY CHRIST AT HIS RETURN

39. The enemy that sowed them [tares] is the devil; the harvest is the end of the world; and the reapers are the angels.
49. So shall it be at the end of the world: the angels shall come forth, and sever the wicked from among the just,
—Matthew 13:39, 49
30. And then shall appear the sign of the Son of man in heaven: and then shall all the tribes of the earth mourn, and they shall see the Son of man coming in the clouds of heaven with power and great glory.
31. And He shall send His angels with a great sound of a trumpet, and they shall gather together His elect from the four winds, from one end of heaven to the other.
—Matthew 24:30-31
31. When the Son of Man shall come in His glory, and all the holy angels with Him, then shall He sit upon the throne of His glory:
—Matthew 25:31

ANGELS—OUR COMPANIONS IN HEAVEN

7. Thus saith the LORD of hosts; If thou wilt . . . keep my charge [law] then thou shalt also judge my house, and shalt also keep my courts, and I will give thee places to walk among these [angels] that stand by.
—Zechariah 3:7

CHAPTER 14

CREATION

CREATION

11. For in six days the LORD made heaven and earth, the sea, and all that in them is, and rested the seventh day: Wherefore the LORD blessed the Sabbath day, and hallowed it.
—Exodus 20:11
(Read Also: Genesis Chapters 1, 2)

6. By the word of the LORD were the heavens made; and all the host of them by the breath of His mouth.
9. For He spake, and it was done; He commanded, and it stood fast.
—Psalms 33:6, 9

3. Through faith we understand that the worlds were framed by the word of God, so that things which are seen were not made of things which do appear.
—Hebrews 11:3

1. . . . In the day that God created man, in the likeness of God made He him;
2. Male and female created He them; and blessed them, and called their name Adam, in the day when they were created.
—Genesis 5:1, 2

Creation

1. In the beginning was the Word, and the Word was with God, and the Word was God.
2. The same was in the beginning with God.
3. All things were made my Him; and without Him was not any things made that was made.
   —John 1:1-3
14. And the Word was made flesh, and dwelt among us, (and we beheld His glory, the glory as of the only begotten of the Father,) full of grace and truth.
    —John 1:14
9. And to make all men see what is the fellowship of the mystery, which from the beginning of the world hath been hid in God, created all things by Jesus Christ:
   —Ephesians 3:9
2. Hath in these last days spoken unto us by His Son, whom He hath appointed heir of all things, by whom also He made the worlds;
   —Hebrews 1:2
1. The heavens declare the glory of God; and the firmament showeth His handiwork.
2. Day unto day uttereth speech, and night unto night showeth knowledge.
3. There is no speech nor language where their voice is not heard.
4. Their line is gone out through all the earth, and their words to the end of the world. In them hath He set a tabernacle for the sun . . .
   —Psalms 19:1-4
20. For the invisible things of Him from the creation of the world are clearly seen, being understood by the things that are made, even His eternal power and Godhead; so that they are without excuse:
    —Romans 1:20
8. Drop down, ye heavens, from above, and let the skies pour down righteousness: let the earth open, and let them

bring forth salvation, and let righteousness spring up together; I the LORD have created it.
—Isaiah 45:8

9. Neither was the man created for the women; but the woman for the man.
—1 Corinthians 11:9

24. Declare His glory among the heaven; His marvelous works among all nations.

25. For great is the LORD, and greatly to be praised: He also is to be feared above all gods.

26. For all the gods of the people are idols: but the LORD made the heavens.

27. Glory and honour are in His presence; strength and gladness are in His place.
—1 Chronicles 16:24-27
(Read Also: Psalms 96:5, 6; Isaiah 40:18-26; and Isaiah chapter 44)

6. O come, let us worship and bow down: let us kneel before the LORD our maker.
—Psalm 95:6

7. Saying with a loud voice, Fear God, and give glory to Him; for the hour of His judgment is come: and worship Him that made heaven, and earth and the sea, and the fountains of water.
—Revelation 14:7

10. Have we not all one father? hath not one God created us? . . .
—Malachi 2:10

8. And the LORD God planted a garden eastward in Eden; and there He put the man whom He had formed.
—Genesis 2:8

28. And God blessed them, and God said unto them, Be fruitful, and multiply, and replenish the earth, and subdue it: and have dominion over the fish of the sea, and over the fowl of the air, and over every living thing that moveth upon the earth.
—Genesis 1:28

15. And the LORD God took the man, and put him into the garden of Eden to dress it and to keep it.
—Genesis 2:15

THE WORTH OF THE PHYSICAL UNIVERSE

10. And God called the dry land earth; and the gathering together of the waters called He Seas: and God saw that is was good.
12. And the earth brought forth grass, and herb yielding seed after his kind, and the tree yielding fruit, whose seed was in itself, after his kind: and God saw that it was good.
—Genesis 1:10, 12
17. And God set them in the firmament of the heaven to give light upon the earth,
21. And God created great whales, and every living creature that moveth, which the waters brought forth abundantly, after their kind, and every winged fowl after his kind: and God saw that it was good.
25. And God made the beast of the earth after his kind, and cattle after their kind, and every thing that creepeth upon the earth after his kind: and God saw that it was good.
—Genesis 1:17, 21, 25
31. And God saw every thing that He had made, and, behold, it was very good. . . .
—Genesis 1:31

THE SACREDNESS OF LIFE

13. For thou hast possessed my reins [formed my inward parts]: Thou hast covered me [knit me together] in my mother's womb.
14. I will praise thee; for I am fearfully and wonderfully made: marvelous are thy works; and that my soul knoweth right well.
15. My substance was not hid from thee, when I was made in secret, and curiously wrought [skillfully woven together] in the lowest parts of the earth.
16. Thine eyes did see my substance, yet being unperfect;

and in thy book all my members were written, which in continuance were fashioned, when as yet there was none of them.
—Psalms 139:13-16
24. Thus saith the LORD, thy redeemer, and He that formed thee from the womb, I am the LORD that maketh all things; that stretcheth forth the heavens alone; that spreadeth abroad the earth by myself;
—Isaiah 44:24

HAS GOD FINISHED HIS CREATION

1. Thus the heavens and the earth were finished, and all the host of them.
2. And on the Seventh day God ended His work which He had made; and He rested on the seventh day from all His work which He had made.
3. And God blessed the seventh day, and sanctified it: because that in it He had rested from all His work which God created and made.
—Genesis 2:1-3
3. For we which have believed do enter into rest, as He said, as I have sworn in My wrath, if they shall enter into My rest: although the works were finished from the foundation of the world.
4. For He spake in a certain place of the seventh day on this wise, and God did rest the seventh day from all His works.
—Hebrews 4:3, 4

CHRIST AND HIS CREATIVE WORD TODAY

8. Who covereth the heaven with clouds, who prepareth rain for the earth, who maketh grass to grow upon the mountains.
9. He giveth to the beast his food and to the young ravens which cry.
—Psalms 147:8, 9

7. He stretcheth out the north over the empty place, and hangeth the earth upon nothing.
   —Job 26:7
   (Read Also: Job 26:8-14)
17. And He is before all things, and by Him all things consist (in Him all things hold together).
   —Colossians 1:17
3. Who being the brightness of His glory, and the express image of His person, and upholding all things by the word of His power, when He had by Himself purged our sins, sat down on the right hand of the Majesty on high;
   —Hebrews 1:3
28. For in Him we live, and move, and have our being; as certain also of your own poets have said, For we are also His offspring.
   —Acts 17:28
24. Thus saith the LORD, thy redeemer, and He that formed thee from the womb, I am the LORD that maketh all things; that stretcheth forth the heavens alone; that spreadeth abroad the earth by Myself:
   —Isaiah 44:24
10. Create in me a clean heart, O God; and renew a right spirit within me.
   —Psalms 51:10
10. For we are His workmanship, created in Christ Jesus unto good works, which God hath before ordained that we should walk in them.
   —Ephesians 2:10
17. Therefore if any man be in Christ, he is a new creature: old things are passed away; behold, all things are become new.
   —2 Corinthians 5:17
17. For, behold, I created new heavens and a new earth: and the former shall not be remembered, nor come into mind.
   —Isaiah 65:17
   (Read Also: Revelation Chapters 21, 22)

CHRIST RE-CREATED WHILE ON EARTH

14. And the Word was made flesh, and dwelt among us . . .
—John 1:14

HE GAVE SIGHT TO THE BLIND.

30. And, behold, two blind men sitting by the way side, when they heard that Jesus passed by, cried out, saying, Have mercy on us, O Lord, thou son of David.
32. And Jesus stood still, and called them, and said, what will ye that I shall do unto you?
33. They say unto Him, Lord, that our eyes may be opened.
34. So Jesus had compassion on them, and touched their eyes: and immediately their eyes received sight, and they followed Him.
—Matthew 20:30-34
(Read Also: John 9:6-41; Matthew 9:27-31; Mark 8:22-25; 10:46-52; Luke 4:18, 19; 18:35-43)

HE GAVE SPEECH TO THE DUMB.

32. As they went out, behold, they brought to him a dumb man possessed with a devil.
33. And when the devil was cast out, the dumb spake: and the multitudes marvelled, saying, It was never so seen in Israel.
—Matthew 9:32, 33

HE OPENED DEAF EARS.

32. And they bring unto him one that was deaf, and had an impediment in his speech; and they beseech him to put his hand upon him.
33. And he took him aside from the multitude, and put his fingers into his ears, and he spit, and touched his tongue;
34. And looking up to heaven, he sighed, and saith unto him, Ephphatha, that is, Be opened.

35. And straightway his ears were opened, and the string of his tongue was loosed, and he spake plain.
36. And he charged them that they should tell no man: but the more he charged them, so much the more a great deal they published it;
37. And were beyond measure astonished, saying, He hath done all things well: he maketh both the deaf to hear, and the dumb to speak.
—Mark 7:32-37

HE HEALED LEPERS.

12. And as he entered into a certain village, there met him ten men that were lepers, which stood afar off:
13. And they lifted up their voices, and said, Jesus, Master, have mercy on us.
14. And when he saw them, he said unto them, Go shew yourselves unto the priests. And it came to pass, that, as they went, they were cleansed.
15. And one of them, when he saw that he was healed, turned back, and with a loud voice glorified God,
16. And fell down on his face at his feet, giving him thanks: and he was a Samaritan.
17. And Jesus answering said, Were there not ten cleansed? but where are the nine?
18. There are not found that returned to give glory to God, save this stranger.
19. And he said unto him, Arise, go thy way: thy faith hath made thee whole.
—Luke 17:12-19

2. And, behold, there came a leper and worshipped him, saying, Lord, if thou wilt, thou canst make me clean.
3. And Jesus put forth his hand, and touched him, saying, I will; be thou clean. And immediately his leprosy was cleansed.
—Matthew 8:2, 3

HE RAISED THE DEAD.

1. Then Jesus six days before the passover came to Bethany, where Lazarus was, which had been dead, whom he raised from the dead.
2. There they made him a supper; and Martha served: but Lazarus was one of them that sat at the table with him.
—John 12:1, 2
(Read Also: John 11:14-45)
12. Now when he came nigh to the gate of the city, behold, there was a dead man carried out, the only son of his mother, and she was a widow: and much people of the city was with her.
13. And when the Lord saw her, he had compassion on her, and said unto her, Weep not.
14. And he came and touched the bier: and they that bare him stood still. And he said, Young man, I say unto thee, Arise.
15. And he that was dead sat up, and began to speak. And he delivered him to his mother.
—Luke 7:12-15
(Read Also: Mark 5:22-24, 35-43; Matthew 11:5)

*Christ rested on the seventh day, both after creation. (*Genesis 2:2) *and after his act of redemption of mankind on the cross.* (John 19:30)

CHAPTER 15
THE WORD OF GOD

DIVINE REVELATION, GENERAL:

1. The heavens declare the glory of God; and the firmament showeth His handiwork.
—Psalms 19:1
20. For the invisible things of Him from the creation of the world are clearly seen, being understood by the things that are made, even His eternal power and Godhead; so that they are without excuse:
—Romans 1:20

SPECIAL REVELATION:

1. God, who at sundry times and in divers manners spake in times past unto the fathers by the prophets,
2. Hath in these last days spoken unto us by His Son, whom He hath appointed heir of all things, by whom also He made the worlds;
—Hebrews 1:1, 2
3. And this is life eternal, that they might know thee the only true God, and Jesus Christ, whom thou hast sent.
—John 17:3

AUTHORSHIP OF THE SCRIPTURES:

21. For the prophecy came not in old times by the will of man: but holy men of God spake as they were moved by the Holy Ghost.
—2 Peters 1:21

2. The Spirit of the LORD spake by me [David], and His word was in my tongue.
—2 Samuel 23:2

2. And the Spirit entered into me [Ezekiel] when He spake unto me, and set me upon my feet, that I heard Him that spake unto me.
—Ezekiel 2:2
(Read Also: Jeremiah 38:21)

1. Now the Spirit speaketh expressly, that in the latter times some shall depart from the faith . . .
—1 Timothy 4:1

10. I was in the SPIRIT on the Lord's day, and heard behind me a great voice, as of a trumpet,
—Revelation 1:10

2. Until the day in which He was taken up, after that He through the HOLY GHOST had given commandments unto the apostles whom He had chosen:
—Acts 1:2

INSPIRATION OF THE SCRIPTURES

16. All scripture is given by inspiration of God, and is profitable for doctrine, for reproof, for correction, for instruction in righteousness:
—2 Timothy 3:16

14. And the Word was made flesh, and dwelt among us, (and we beheld His glory, the glory as of the only begotten of the Father,) full of grace and truth.
—John 1:14

WRITERS SOMETIMES PERPLEXED OVER MESSAGE:

27. And I Daniel fainted, and was sick certain days; afterwards I rose up, and did the King's business; and I was astonished at the vision, but none understood it.
—Daniel 8:27

4. And I wept much, because no man was found worthy to open and to read the book, neither to look thereon.
—Revelation 5:4

10. Of which salvation the prophets have inquired and searched diligently, who prophesied of the grace that should come unto you:
—1 Peter 1:10

THE METHODS AND CONTENT OF REVELATION

6. And He said, Hear now My words: If there be a prophet among you, I the LORD will make Myself known unto him in a vision, and will speak unto him is a dream.
—Numbers 12:6

15. Now the LORD had told Samuel in his ear a day before Saul came . . .
—1 Samuel 9:15

4. How that he [Paul] was caught up into paradise, and heard unspeakable words, which it is not lawful for a man to utter.
—2 Corinthians 12:4

1. After this I looked, and, behold, a door was opened in heaven: and the first voice which I heard was as it were of a trumpet talking with me; which said, come up hither, and I will show thee things which must be hereafter.
—Revelation 4:1
(Read Also: Revelation 4; 5; 10; Ezekiel 8; Daniel 2; 7; 8; 12)

INSPIRATION AND HISTORY

15. And that from a child thou hast known the holy scriptures, which are able to make thee wise unto salvation through faith which is in Christ Jesus.
—*2* Timothy 3:15

1. These are the journeys of the children of Israel, which went forth out of the land of Egypt with their armies under the hand of Moses and Aaron.
2. And Moses wrote their going out according to their Journeys by the commandment of the LORD . . .
—Numbers 33:1, 2

11. Now all these things happened unto them for ensamples: and they are written for our admonition, upon whom the ends of the world are come.
—1 Corinthians 10:11

4. For whatsoever things were written aforetime were written for our learning, that we through patience and comfort of the scriptures might have hope.
—Romans 15:4

6. And turning the cities of Sodom and Gomorrah into ashes condemned them with an overthrow, making them an ensample unto those that after should live ungodly;
—2 Peters 2:6
(Read Also: Joshua 24:25, 26; Ezekiel 24:2; Romans 4:1-25; James 2:14-22; 1 Corinthians 9:8, 9)

4. That thou mightest know the certainty of those things, wherein thou hast been instructed.
—Luke 1:4

31. But these are written, that ye might believe that Jesus is the Christ, the Son of God; and that believing ye might have life through His name.
—John 20:31
(Read Also: Matthew 12:39-41; 19:4-6; 24:37-39.)

THE CLAIMS OF THE SCRIPTURES

9. Then the LORD put forth His hand, and touched my mouth. And the LORD said unto me, Behold, I have put My words in thy mouth.
—Jeremiah 1:9

3. The word of the LORD came expressly unto Ezekiel the priest, the son of Buzi, in the land of the Chaldeans by the river Chebar; and the hand of the LORD was there upon him.
—Ezekiel 1:3
(Read Also: Hosea 1:1; Joel 1:1; Jonah 1:1)

13. Then spake Haggai the LORD's messenger in the LORD's message unto the people, saying, I am with you, saith the LORD.
—Haggai 1:13

4. For they are impudent children and stiffhearted. I do send thee unto them; and thou shalt say unto them, Thus saith the Lord GOD,
—Ezekiel 2:4
(Read Also: 2 Chronicles 36:16)

7. Thus saith the Lord GOD, It shall not stand, neither shall it come to pass.
—Isaiah 7:7

22. Now all this was done, that it might be fulfilled which was spoken of the Lord by the prophet . . .
—Matthew 1:22

15. And account that the longsuffering of our Lord is salvation; even as our beloved brother Paul also according to the wisdom given unto him hath written unto you;
—2 Peter 3:15

12. For I neither received it of man, neither was I taught it, but by the revelation of Jesus Christ.
—Galatians 1:12

JESUS AND THE AUTHORITY OF SCRIPTURE

4. But He answered and said, It is written, Man shall not live by bread alone, but by every word that proceedeth out of the mouth of God.

7. Jesus said unto him [Satan], It is written again, Thou shalt not tempt the Lord thy God.

10. Then saith Jesus unto him, Get thee hence, Satan: for it is written, Thou shalt worship the Lord thy God, and Him only shalt thou serve.
—Matthew 4:4, 7, 10

26. He said unto him, What is written in the law? How readest thou?
—Luke 10:26

7. Howbeit in vain do they worship Me, teaching for doctrines the commandments of men.

9. . . . Full well ye reject the commandment of God, that ye may keep your own tradition.
—Mark 7:7, 9

42. Jesus saith unto them, Did ye never read in the scriptures, The stone which the builders rejected the same is become the head of the corner: this is the Lord's doing, and it is marvelous in our eyes?
—Matthew 21:42
(Read Also: Luke 20:17)

39. Search the scriptures; for in them ye think ye have eternal life: and they which testify of me.

46. For had ye believed Moses, ye would have believed me: for he wrote of me.
—John 5:39, 46

25. Then He said unto them, O fools, and slow of heart to believe all that the prophets have spoken:

26. Ought not Christ to have suffered these things, and to enter into His glory?

27. And beginning at Moses and all the prophets, He expounded unto them in all the scriptures the things concerning Himself.
—Luke 24:25-27

THE HOLY SPIRIT AND THE AUTHORITY OF SCRIPTURE

13. When Jesus came into the coast of Caesarea Philippi, He asked His disciples, saying, Who do men say that I the Son of Man am?
14. And they said, Some say thou art John the Baptist: some Elias; and others, Jeremias, or one of the prophets.
15. He saith unto them, But whom say ye that I am?
16. And Simon Peter answered and said, Thou art the Christ, the Son of the living God.
17. And Jesus answered and said unto him, Blessed art thou, Simon Barjona: for flesh and blood hath not revealed it unto thee, but My Father which is in heaven.
 —Matthew 16:13-17
3. Wherefore I give you to understand, that no man speaking by the Spirit of God calleth Jesus accursed: and that no man can say that Jesus is the Lord, but by the Holy Ghost.
 —1 Corinthians 12:3
18. For the preaching of the cross is to them that perish foolishness; but unto us which are saved it is the power of God.
 —1 Corinthians 1:18
 (Read Also: 1 Corinthians 2:11, 14)
10. But God hath revealed them unto us by His Spirit: for the Spirit searcheth all things, yea, the deep things of God.
 —1 Corinthians 2:10
12. Now we have received, not the spirit of the world, but the spirit which is of God; that we might know the things that are freely given to us of God.
 —1 Corinthians 2:12

THE SCOPE OF SPIRITUAL AUTHORITY

20. To the law and to the testimony: if they speak not according to this word, it is because there is no light in them.
 —Isaiah 8:20
 (Read Also: 1 Corinthians 12; Ephesians 4:7-16)

CHAPTER 16

THE NATURE OF MAN

THE NATURE OF MAN

7. And the LORD God formed man of the dust of the ground, and breathed into his nostrils the breath of life; and man became a living soul.
—Genesis 2:7
26. And God said, Let us make man in our image, after our likeness: and let them have dominion over the fish of the sea, and over the fowl of the air, and over the cattle, and over all the earth and over every creeping thing that creepeth upon the earth.
—Genesis 1:26

GOD CREATED WOMAN FROM MAN

18. And the LORD God said, It is not good that the man should be alone; I will make him an help meet for him.
21. And the LORD God caused a deep sleep to fall upon Adam, and he slept: and He took one of his ribs, and closed up the flesh instead thereof;
22. And the rib, which the LORD God had taken from man, made He a woman, and brought her unto the man.
—Genesis 2:18, 21, 22

MAN BECAME SUBJECT TO DEATH

8. And the LORD God planted a garden eastward in Eden; and there He put the man whom He had formed.
9. And out of the ground made the Lord God to grow every tree that is pleasant to the sight, and good for food; the tree of life also in the midst of the garden, and the tree of knowledge of good and evil.
—Genesis 2:8, 9
17. But of the tree of the knowledge of good and evil, thou shalt not eat of it: for in the day that thou eatest thereof thou shalt surely die.
—Genesis 2:17

MAN CREATED AFTER A DIVINE TYPE

38. Which was the son of Enos, which was the son of Seth, which was the son of Adam, which was the son of God.
—Luke 3:38

MAN TO RULE OTHER CREATURES

28. And God blessed them, and God said unto them, Be fruitful, and multiply, and replenish (fill up) the earth, and subdue it: and have dominion over the fish of the sea, and over the fowl of the air, and over every living thing that moveth upon the earth.
—Genesis 1:28
4. What is man, that thou art mindful of him? and the son of man that thou visitest him?
5. For thou hast made him a little lower than the angels, and hast crowned him with glory and honour.
6. Thou madest him to have dominion over the works of thy hands; thou hast put all things under his feet:
7. All sheep and oxen, yea, and the beast of the field;
8. The fowl of the air, and the fish of the sea, and whatsoever passeth through the paths of the sea.
—Psalms 8:4-8

THE UNITY OF THE HUMAN RACE

26. And hath made of one blood all nations of men for to dwell on all the face of the earth, and hath determined the times before appointed, and the bounds of their habitation:
—Acts 17:26
12. Wherefore, as by one man sin entered into the world, and death by sin; and so death passed upon all men, for that all have sinned:
19. For as by one man's disobedience many were made sinners, so by the obedience of one shall many be made righteous.
—Romans 5:12, 19

THE BREATH OF LIFE

7. And the LORD God formed man of the dust of the ground, and breathed into his nostrils the breath of life; and man became a living soul.
—Genesis 2:7
4. The spirit of God hath made me, and the breath of the Almighty hath given me life.
—Job 33:4

MAN, A LIVING SOUL

(earth's elements + the breath of life = a living being, or living soul.)

15. And they went in unto Noah in the ark, two and two of all flesh, wherein is the *breath of life*.
22. All in whose nostrils was the *breath of life*, of all that was in the dry land, died.
—Genesis 7:15, 22
13. Say, I pray thee, thou art my sister: that it may be well with me for thy sake: and *my soul* shall live because of thee.
—Genesis 12:13

The Nature of Man

2. Many there be which say of *my [nephesh] soul*, There is no help for him in God.
—Psalms 3:2

THE SOUL, AN INDIVISIBLE UNITY

Hebrew word (*nephesh*) is found in the O. T. 755 times, translated many ways.

NEPHESH TRANSLATED AS PERSON OR SELF

22. The fathers went down into Egypt with threescore and ten [*nephesh*] persons; and now the LORD thy God hath made thee as the stars of heaven for multitude.
—Deuteronomy 10:22
(Read Also: Numbers 5:6; Genesis 14:21; Leviticus 11:43; 1 Kings 19:4; Isaiah 46:2)

100 TIMES NEPHESH TRANSLATED LIFE

13. For I have heard the slander of many: fear was on every side: while they took counsel to take away my [*nephesh*] life.
—Psalms 31:13
(Read Also: Genesis 9:4, 5; 1 Samuel 19:5; Job 2:4, 6)

NEPHESH REFERS TO DESIRES, APPETITE, PASSIONS OR SEAT OF AFFECTIONS

7. All the labour of man is for his mouth, and yet the (*nephesh*) appetite is not filled.
—Ecclesiastes 6:7
(Read Also: Genesis 34:3; Deuteronomy 23:24; Proverbs 23:2; Song of Solomon 1:7)

NEPHESH (SOUL) DOES NOT LIVE FOREVER NEPHESH DIES, IS KILLED, IS A CORPSE

7. And those men said unto him, We are defiled by the [*nephesh*] dead body of a man:
—Numbers 9:7

28. Ye shall not make any cuttings in your flesh for the [*nephesh*] dead, nor print any marks upon you: I am the LORD.
—Leviticus 19:28
(Read Also: Judges 16:30; Numbers 5:2)

THE GREEK WORD "PSUCHE" IN THE N. T. IS USED SIMILARLY. IT IS USED OF ANIMALS AS WELL AS HUMANS. IN THE K. J. V. IT IS TRANSLATED FORTY TIMES AS LIFE OR LIVES.

25. For whosoever will save his [*psuche*] life shall lose it: and whosoever will lose his [*psuche*] life for my sake shall find it.
—Matthew 16:25
(Read Also: Matthew 2:20; 6:25)

SOMETIMES USED TO MEAN "PEOPLE"

37. And we were in all in the ship two hundred three score and sixteen souls [people].
—Acts 27:37
(Read Also: Acts 7:14; Romans 13:1; 1 Peter 3:20)

SOMETIMES IT REFERS TO THE EMOTIONS, MIND OR HEART

6. Not with eyeservice, as menpleasers; but as the servants of Christ, doing the will of God from the [*psuche*] heart;
—Ephesians 6:6
(Read Also: Mark 14:34; Luke 2:35. Acts 14:2; Philippians 1:27)

PSUCHE IS SUBJECT TO DEATH

3. And the second angel poured out his vial upon the sea; and it became as the blood of a dead man: and every living [*psuche*] soul died in the sea.
—Revelation 16:3
(Read Also: Matthew 10:28)

THE BIBLICAL MEANING OF SPIRIT
RUACH OCCURS 377 TIMES IN THE O. T.
USUALLY TRANSLATED SPIRIT, WIND, OR BREATH

1. And God remembered Noah, and every living thing, and all the cattle that was with him in the ark: and God made a [*rauch*] wind to pass over the earth, and the waters asswaged [subsided];
—Genesis 8:1

RAUCH (BREATH) LEAVES BODY AT DEATH

4. His [*rauch*] breath goes forth, he returneth to the earth; in that very day his thoughts perish.
—Psalms 146:4
19. For that which befalleth the sons of men befalleth beasts; even one thing befalleth them: as the one dieth, so dieth the other; yea, they have all one [*rauch*] breath . . .
—Ecclesiastes 3:19
(Read Also: Ecclesiastes 12:7; Job 34:14)

IN N. T. THE GREEK PNEUMA IS USED
IT IS YIELDED TO THE LORD AT DEATH

46. And when Jesus had cried with a loud voice, He said, Father, into thy hands I commend My [*pneuma*] spirit . . .
—Luke 23:46
(Read Also: Acts 7:59)

UNITY OF BODY, SOUL, AND SPIRIT

23. . . . I pray God your whole [*pneuma*] spirit and whole body be preserved blameless unto the coming of our Lord Jesus Christ.
—1 Thessalonians 5:23
(Read Also: Luke 1:46, 47; Matthew 10:28; 1 Corinthians 7:34)

MAN CREATED IN THE IMAGE OF GOD

27. So God created man in His own image in the image of God created He him; male and female created He them.
—Genesis 1:27

7. Thou madest him a little lower than the angels; thou crownedst him with glory and honour, and didst set him over the works of thy hands:
—Hebrews 2:7

THE FALL OF MAN, GOD DIDN'T CAUSE SIN

13. Let no man say when he is tempted, I am tempted of God: for God cannot be tempted with evil, neither tempteth He any man:
14. But every man is tempted, when he is drawn away of his own lust, and enticed.
—James 1:13, 14

THE AUTHOR OF SIN

12. How art thou fallen from heaven, O Lucifer, son of the morning! how art thou cut down to the ground, which didst weaken the nations!
13. For thou hast said in thine heart, I will ascend into heaven, I will exalt my throne above the stars of God: I will sit also upon the mount of the congregation, in the sides of the north:
14. I will ascend above the heights of the clouds; I will be like the Most High.
—Isaiah 14:12-14

THE ORIGIN OF SIN IN THE HUMAN RACE

4. And the serpent [Lucifer] said unto the woman, Ye shall not surely die:
5. For God doth know that in the day ye eat thereof, then your eyes shall be opened, and ye shall be as gods, knowing good and evil.

6. And when the woman saw that the tree was good for food, and that it was pleasant to the eyes, and a tree to be desired to make one wise, she took of the fruit thereof, and did eat, and gave also unto her husband with her; and he did eat.
—Genesis 3:4-6

IMPACT OF SIN, IMMEDIATE CONSEQUENCES

7. And the eyes of them both were opened, and they knew that they were naked; and they sewed fig leaves together, and made themselves aprons.
8. And they heard the voice of the LORD God walking in the garden in the cool of the day: and Adam and his wife hid themselves from the presence of the LORD God amongst the trees of the garden.
9. And the LORD God called unto Adam, and said unto him, Where art thou?
10. And he said, I heard thy voice in the garden, and I was afraid, because I was naked; and I hid myself.
11. And He said, Who told thee that thou wast naked? Hast thou eaten of the tree, Whereof I commanded thee that thou shouldest not eat?
12. And the man said, The woman whom Thou gavest to be with me, she gave me of the tree, and I did eat.
13. And the LORD God said unto the woman, What is this that thou hast done? And the woman said, The serpent beguiled me, and I did eat.
—Genesis 3:7-13

THE DEFINITION OF SIN

4. Whosoever committeth sin transgresseth also the law: for sin is the transgression of the law.
—1 John 3:4
17. Therefore to him that knoweth to do good, and doeth it not, to him it is sin.
—James 4:17

23. . . . for whatsoever is not of faith is sin.
 —Romans 14:23
10. For whosoever shall keep the whole law, and yet offend in one point, he is guilty of all.
 —James 2:10

SIN CAUSES GUILT

19. . . . under the law . . . all the world may become guilty before God.
 —Romans 3:19
23. For all have sinned and come short of the glory of God;
 —Romans 3:23

THE CONTROL CENTER OF SIN

23. Keep thy heart with all diligence; for out of it are the issues of life.
 —Proverbs 4:23
9. The heart is deceitful above all things, and desperately wicked: who can know it?
 —Jeremiah 17:9

THE UNIVERSAL SINFULNESS OF MAN

3. . . . they are all together become filthy: there is none that doeth good, no, not one.
 —Psalms 14:3
20. For there is not a just man upon earth, that doeth good, and sinneth not.
 —Ecclesiastes 7:20
8. If we say that we have no sin, we deceive ourselves, and the truth is not in us.
 —1 John 1:8

IS SIN INHERITED OR ACQUIRED

12. Wherefore, as by one man [Adam] sin entered into the world, and death by sin; and so death passed upon all men, for that all have sinned:
—Romans 5:12

5. Behold, I was shapen in iniquity; and in sin did my mother conceive me.
—Psalms 51:5

THE ERADICATION OF SINFUL BEHAVIOR

36. If the Son therefore shall make you free, ye shall be free indeed.
—John 8:36

8. For by grace are ye saved through faith; and that not of yourselves: it is the gift of God:
9. Not of works, lest any man should boast.
—Ephesians 2:8, 9

17. Therefore if any man be in Christ, he is a new creature: old things are passed away; behold, all things are become new.
—2 Corinthians 5:17

1. My little children, these things write I unto you, that ye sin not. And if any man sin, we have an advocate with the Father, Jesus Christ the righteous:
2. And He is the propitiation for our sins: and not for ours only, but also for the sins of the whole world.
—1 John 2:1, 2

THE BIBLE VIEW OF EVOLUTION

29. Lo, this only have I found, that God hath made man upright; but they have sought out many inventions.
—Ecclesiastes 7:29

4. . . . Have ye not read, that He which made them at the beginning made them male and female,
—Matthew 19:4

4. And the serpent [devil] said unto the woman, Ye shall not surely die:
—Genesis 3:4

44. Ye are of your father the devil, and the lust of your father ye will do. He was a murderer from the beginning, and abode not in the truth, because there is no truth in him, when he speaketh a lie, he speaketh of his own: for he is a liar, and the father of it.
—John 8:44

9. And the great dragon was cast out, that old serpent, called the Devil, and Satan, which deceiveth the whole world: he was cast out into the earth, and his angels were cast out with him.
—Revelation 12:9

THE ORIGINAL PLAN FOR MAN

5. For thou hast made him a little lower than the angels, and hast crowned him with glory and honour.
6. Thou madest him to have dominion over the works of thy hands; thou hast put all things under his feet:
—Psalms 8:5, 6
(Read Also: Hebrews 2:7)

THE COVENANT GIVEN AT THE FALL

15. And I [God] will put enmity [hatred] between thee [satan] and the woman [Mary], and between thy seed [wicked people] and her seed [Christ]; it shall bruise thy head [fatal], and thou [satan] shall bruise His [Christ's] heel [non fatal].
—Genesis 3:15

THE COVENANT ESTABLISHED BEFORE CREATION

4. According as He hath chosen us in Him before the foundation of the world, that we should be holy and without blame before Him in love:

5. Having predestinated us unto the adoption of children by Jesus Christ to Himself, according to the good pleasure of His will,
—Ephesians 1:4, 5
9. Who hath saved us, and called us with a holy calling, not according to our works, but according to His own purpose and grace which was given us in Christ Jesus before the world began.
—2 Timothy 1:9
20. Who verily was foreordained before the foundation of the world, but was manifest in these last times for you,
—1 Peter 1:20
40. And this is the will of Him who sent Me, that every one which seeth the Son, and believeth on Him, may have everlasting life: and I will raise him up at the last day.
—John 6:40

THE COVENANT RENEWAL THROUGH ABRAHAM

18. Seeing that Abraham shall surely become a great and mighty nation, and all the nations of the earth shall be blessed in him?
—Genesis 18:18
2. And I will make my covenant between me and thee and will multiply thee exceedingly.
—Genesis 17:2
3. And I will bless them that bless thee, and curse him that curseth thee: and in thee shall all families of the earth be blessed.
—Genesis 12:3
(Read Also: Genesis 22:18)
23. And the Scripture was fulfilled which saith, Abraham believed God, and it was imputed unto him for righteousness: and he was called the friend of God.
—James 2:23
29. And if ye be Christ's, then are ye Abraham's seed, and heirs according to the promise.
—Galatians 3:29

THE NEW COVENANT

6. But now hath He obtained a more excellent ministry, by how much also He is the mediator of a better covenant, which was established upon better promises.
7. For if that first covenant had been faultless, then should no place have been sought for the second.
8. For finding fault with them, He saith, Behold, the days come, saith the Lord, When I will make a new covenant with the house of Israel and with the house of Judah:
9. Not according to the covenant that I made with their fathers in the day when I took them by the hand to lead them out of the land of Egypt; because they continued not in my covenant, and I regarded them not, saith the Lord.
10. For this is the covenant that I will make with the house of Israel after those days, saith the Lord; I will put my laws into their mind, and write them in their hearts: and I will be to them a God, and they shall be to me a people:
11. And they shall not teach every man his neighbour, and every man his brother, saying, Know the Lord: for all shall know me, from the least to the greatest.
12. For I will be merciful to their unrighteousness, and their sins and their iniquities will I remember no more.
13. In that He saith, A new covenant, He hath made the first old. Now that which decayeth and waxeth old is ready to vanish away.
—Hebrews 8:6-13
33. But this shall be the covenant that I will make with the house of Israel; After those days, saith the LORD, I will put my law in their inward parts, and write it in their hearts; and will be their God, and they shall be my people.
—Jeremiah 31:33

CHAPTER 17

THE GREAT CONTROVERSY A BATTLE BETWEEN CHRIST AND SATAN

ANGELS A HIGHER ORDER THAN HUMANS

5. For thou hast made him [mankind] a little lower than the *angel*s, and hast crowned him with glory and honour.
—Psalms 8:5
1. The Revelation of Jesus Christ, which God gave unto Him, to show unto His servants things which must shortly come to pass; and He sent and signified it by His *angels* unto His servant John:
—Revelation 1:1
5. He that overcometh, the same shall be clothed in white raiment; and I will not blot out his name out of the book of life, but I will confess his name before my Father, and before His angels.
—Revelation 3:5
11. And I beheld, and I heard the voice of many *angels* round about the throne and the beasts [living creatures] and the elders: and the number of them was ten thousand times ten thousand;
—Revelation 5:11
20. Bless the LORD, ye His *angels*, that excel in strength,

that do his commandments, hearkening unto the voice of His word;
—Psalms 103:20

14. Are they not all ministering spirits, sent forth to minister for them who shall be heirs of salvation:
—Hebrews 1:14

2. Be not forgetful to entertain strangers: for thereby some have entertained *ANGELS* unawares.
—Hebrews 13:2
Angels sometimes appear in human form.
(Read Also: Genesis chapters 18 and 19)

THE ORIGIN OF THE CONTROVERSY

12. How art thou fallen from heaven, O Lucifer, son of the morning! how art thou cut down to the ground, which didst weaken the nations!
—Isaiah 14:12

14. Thou art the anointed cherub that covereth; and I have set thee so: thou wast upon the holy mountain of God; thou hast walked up and down in the midst of the stones of fire.

15. Thou wast perfect in thy ways from the day that thou wast created, till iniquity was found in thee.
—Ezekiel 28:14, 15

17. Thine heart was lifted up because of thy beauty, thou hast corrupted thy wisdom by reason of thy brightness . . .
—Ezekiel 28:17

4. And his tail drew the third part of the stars [angels] of heaven, and did cast them to the earth: and he stood before the woman [Mary] which was ready to be delivered, for to devour her child as soon as it was born.

7. And there was war in heaven: Michael [Christ] and His angels fought against the dragon [Satan]; and the dragon fought and his angels,

9. And the great dragon was cast out, that old serpent, called the Devil, and Satan, which deceiveth the whole world:

he was cast out into the earth, and his angels were cast out with him.
—Revelation 12:4, 7, 9

HOW DID HUMAN BEINGS BECOME INVOLVED?

5. For God doth know that in the day ye eat thereof, then your eyes shall be opened, and ye shall be as gods, knowing good and evil.
—Genesis 3:5
(Read Also: Genesis Chapter 3)

THE INPACT ON THE HUMAN RACE

15. And I will put enmity between thee [Satan] and the woman [Mary], and between thy seed and her seed; it shall bruise thy head, and thou shalt bruise His heel.
—Genesis 3:15
(See study on: THE NATURE OF MAN)

8. And Cain talked with Able his brother: and it came to pass, when they were in the field, that Cain rose up against Abel his brother and slew him.
—Genesis 4:8

5. And God saw that the wickedness of man was great in the earth, and that every imagination of the thoughts of his heart was only evil continually.
—Genesis 6:5

17. And the flood was forty days upon the earth; and the waters increased, and bare up the ark, and it was lift up above the earth.
—Genesis 7:17

21. And all flesh died that moved upon the earth, . . . and every man:

22. And in whose nostrils was the breath of life, of all that was in the dry land, died.
—Genesis 7:21, 22

EARTH, THE THEATER OF THE UNIVERSE

9. . . . for we are made a spectacle unto the world, and to angels, and to men.
—1 Corinthians 4:9

15. If ye love me, keep my commandment.
—John 14:15

3. And the LORD said unto Satan, Hast thou considered my servant job, that there is none like him in the earth, a perfect and an upright man, one that feareth God, and escheweth evil? and still he holdeth fast his integrity, although thou movest me against him without cause.

4. And Satan answered the LORD and said, Skin for skin, yea, all that a man hath will he give for his life.

5. But put forth thine hand now, and touch his bone and his flesh, and he will curse thee to thy face.

6. And the LORD said unto Satan, Behold, he is in thine hand; but save his life.

7. So went Satan forth from the presence of the LORD, and smote Job with sore boils from the sole of his foot unto his crown.

9. Then said his wife unto him, Doest thou still retain thine integrity? Curse God, and die.

10. But he said unto her, Thou speakest as one of the foolish women speaketh. What: shall we receive good at the hand of God, and shall we not receive evil? In all this did not Job sin with his lips.
—Job 2:3-7, 9, 10
(Read Also: Job Chapters 1 and 2)

THE COSMIC ISSUE, GOD'S GOVERNMENT AND LAW

4. Whosoever committeth sin transgresseth also the law: for sin is the transgression of the law.
—1 John 3:4

CHRIST AND THE ISSUE OF OBEDIENCE

17. Wherefore in all things it behoved Him to be made like unto His brethren, that He might be a merciful and faithful high priest in things pertaining to God, to make reconciliation for the sins of the people.
—Hebrews 2:17

3. And when the tempter [Satan] came to Him [Christ], he said, If thou be the Son of God, command that these stones be made bread.
4. But He answered and said, It is written, Man shall not live by bread alone, but by every word that proceedeth out of the mouth of God.
—Matthew 4:3, 4
(Read Also: Matthew 4:1-11)

SHOWDOWN AT CALVARY

49. And one of them, named Caiaphas, being the high priest that same year, said unto them, Ye know nothing at all,
50. Nor consider that it is expedient for us, that one man should die for the people, and that the whole nation perish not.
53. Then from that day forth they took counsel together for to put Him to death.
—John 11:49, 50, 53
(Read Also: John 11:45-54)

63. . . . And the high priest answered and said unto Him, I adjure thee by the living God, that thou tell us whether thou be the Christ, the Son of God.
64. Jesus saith unto him, Thou has said: nevertheless I say unto you, Hereafter shall ye see the Son of man sitting on the right hand of power and coming in the clouds of heaven.
—Matthew 26:63, 64

7. The Jews answered him [Pilate], We have a law, and by our law He ought to die, because He made Himself the Son of God.
—John 19:7

31. Now is the judgment of this world: now shall the prince of the world (Satan) be cast out.
—John 12:31
(Read Also: John 16:11)

THE MOST CRUCIAL QUESTION

13. When Jesus came into the coast of Caesarea Philippi, He asked His desciples, saying, Whom do men say that I the Son of man am?
14. And they said, Some say that thou art John the Baptist: some, Elias; and others, Jeremias, or one of the prophets.
15. He saith unto them, But who say ye that I am?
16. And Simon Peter answered and said, Thou art the Christ, the Son of the living God.
17. And Jesus answered and said unto him, Blessed art thou, Simon Bar jona: for flesh and blood hath not revealed it unto thee, but my Father which is in heaven.
—Matthew 16:13-17

THE CENTER OF BIBLE DOCTRINES

5. Thomas saith unto Him, Lord, we know not whither thou goest; and how can we know the *way*?
6. Jesus saith unto him, I AM the *way*, the *truth*, and the *life*: no man cometh unto the Father, but by ME.
—John 14:5, 6
(Read Also: Ephesians 4:21)
12. For we wrestle not against flesh and blood, but against principalities, against powers, against the rulers of the darkness of this world, against spiritual wickedness in high places.
—Ephesians 6:12
(Read Also: Ephesians 6:13-18)
37. Nay, all these things we are more than conquerors through Him that loved us.
—Romans 8:37

EVIL DID NOT ORIGINATE WITH GOD

9. Thou hast loved righteousness, and hated iniquity; therefore God, even thy God, hath anointed thee with the oil of gladness above thy fellows.
—Hebrews 1:9

UPON CHRIST'S RETURN TO HEAVEN HE PROVIDED FOR US IN THE FOLLOWING WAYS:

BY THE HOLY SPIRIT

16. And He shall give you another comforter, that He may abide with you for ever:
—John 14:16

TEACHERS

20. Teaching them to observe all things whatsoever I have commanded you: and, lo, I am with you alway, even unto the end of the world.
—Matthew 28:20

ANGELS

14. Are they not all ministering spirits [Angels], sent forth to minister for them who shall be heirs of salvation.
—Hebrews 1:14

CHAPTER 18

THE LIFE, DEATH, AND RESURRECTION OF CHRIST

ONLY CHRIST LIVED THE PERFECT LIFE

2. And I saw a strong angel proclaiming with a loud voice, Who is worthy to open the book, and to loose the seals thereof?

5. And one of the elders saith unto me, Weep not: behold, the Lion of the tribe of Juda, the Root of David, [Christ] hath prevailed to open the book, and to loose the seven seals thereof.

9. And they sung a new song, saying, Thou art worthy to take the book, and to open the seals thereof: for thou wast slain, and hast redeemed us to God by thy blood out of every kindred, and tongue, and people, and nation:

10. And hast made us unto our God kings and priests: and we shall reign on the earth.

13. And every creature which is in heaven, and on the earth, and under the earth, and such as are in the sea, and all that are in them, heard I saying, Blessing, and honour, and glory, and power, be unto Him that sitteth upon the throne, and unto the Lamb [Christ] for ever and ever.
—Revelation 5:2, 5, 9, 10, 13

7. Then said I, Lo, I come: in the volume of the book it is written of Me [Christ].

The Life, Death, and Resurrection of Christ

8. I delight to do Thy will, O my God: yea, Thy law is within My heart.
—Psalms 40:7, 8

GOD'S SAVING GRACE

8. He that loveth not knoweth not God; for God is love.
—1 John 4:8
3. The LORD hath appeared of old unto me, saying, Yea, I have loved thee with an everlasting love: therefore with loving kindness have I drawn thee.
—Jeremiah 31:3
20. Behold, I stand at the door, and knock: if any man hear my voice, and open the door, I will come in to him, and will sup with him, and he with Me.
21. To him that overcometh will I grant to sit with Me in My throne, even as I also overcame, and Am set down with My Father in His throne.
—Revelation 3:20, 21

THE DIVINE INITIATIVE

15. And I [God] will put enmity between thee [Satan] and the woman [Mary], and between thy seed [the wicked] and her seed [Christ]; it shall bruise thy [Satan's] head [deadly], and thou shalt bruise His [Christ's] heel [temporary].
—Genesis 3:15
8. But God commandeth His love toward us, in that, while we were yet sinners, Christ died for us.
—Romans 5:8

A BLEND OF GRACE AND JUSTICE

6. And the LORD passed by before him, and proclaimed, the LORD, the LORD God, merciful and gracious, long-suffering, and abundant in goodness and truth,
7. Keeping mercy for thousands, forgiving iniquity and transgression and sin, and that will by no means clear the guilty; visiting the iniquity of the fathers upon the chil-

dren, and upon the children's children, unto the third and to the fourth generation.
—Exodus 34:6, 7

A GOD OF FORGIVENESS

7. Let the wicked forsake his way, and the unrighteous man his thoughts: and let him return unto the LORD, and he will have mercy upon him; and to our God, for He will abundantly pardon.
—Isaiah 55:7
22. Look unto Me, and be ye saved, all the ends of the earth: for I Am God, and there is none else.
—Isaiah 45:22

GOD'S WRATH IS AGAINST SIN NOT PEOPLE

21. And you, that were sometime alienated and enemies in your mind by wicked works, yet now hath He reconciled.
—Colossians 1:21
23. For all have sinned, and come short of the glory of God;
—Romans 3:23
3. Among whom also we all had our conversation in times past in the lust of our flesh, fulfilling the desires of the flesh and of the mind; and were by nature the children of wrath, even as others.
—Ephesians 2:3
16. And they left all the commandments of the LORD their God, and made them molten images, even two calves, and made a grove, and worshipped all the host of heaven, and served Baal.
17. And they caused their sons and their daughters to pass through the fire, and used divination and enchantments, and sold themselves to do evil in the sight of the LORD, to provoke Him to anger.
18. Therefore the LORD was very angry with Israel, and removed them out of His sight: there was none left but the tribe of Judah only.
—2 Kings 17:16-18

16. But they mocked the messengers of God, and despised His words, and misused His prophets, until the wrath of the LORD arose against His people till there was no remedy.
—2 Chronicles 36:16
6. Let no man deceive you with vain words: for because of these things cometh the wrath of God upon the children of disobedience.
—Ephesians 5:6
29. For our God is a consuming fire.
—Hebrews 12:29
18. For the wrath of God is revealed from heaven against all ungodliness and unrighteousness of men, who hold the truth in unrighteousness;
—Romans 1:18
23. For the wages of sin is death; but the gift of God is eternal life through Jesus Christ our Lord.
—Romans 6:23

THE HUMAN RESPONSE

7. That in the ages to come He might show the exceeding riches of His grace in His kindness toward us through Christ Jesus.
—Ephesians 2:7
4. In Him was life; and the life was the light of men.
—John 1:4
30. But of Him are ye in Christ Jesus, who of God is made unto us wisdom, and righteousness, and sanctification, and redemption:
31. That, according as it is written, He that glorieth, let him glory in the Lord.
—1 Corinthians 1:30, 31
4. Or despisest thou the riches of His goodness and forbearance and longsuffering; not knowing that the goodness of God leadeth thee to repentance?
—Romans 2:4

3. For I say, through the grace given unto me, to every man that is amoung you, not to think of himself more highly than he ought to think; but to think soberly, according as God hath dealt to every man the measure of faith.
—Romans 12:3

31. Him hath God exalted with His right hand to be a Prince and a Saviour, for to give repentance to Israel, and forgiveness of sins.
—Acts 5:31

19. We love Him, because He first loved us.
—1 John 4:19

6. But we are all as an unclean thing, and all our righteousness are as filthy rags; and we all do fade as a leaf; and our iniquities, like the wind, have taken us away.
—Isaiah 64:6

4. But God, who is rich in mercy, for His great love wherewith He loved us,

5. Even when we were dead in sins, hath quickened us together with Christ . . .

8. For by grace are ye saved through faith; and that not of yourselves: it is the gift of God:

9. Not of works, lest any man should boast.
—Ephesians 2:4, 5, 8, 9

CHRIST'S MINISTRY OF RECONCILIATION

19. To wit, that God was in Christ, *reconciling* the world unto himself, not imputing their trespasses unto them; and hath committed unto us the word of *reconciliation*.
—2 Corinthians 5:19

10. For if when we were enemies, we were *reconciled* to God by the death of His Son, much more, being *reconciled*, we shall be saved by His life.

11. And not only so, but we also joy in God through our Lord Jesus Christ, by whom we have now received the *atonement*.
—Romans 5:10, 11

CHRIST'S DEATH A NECESSITY

36. He that believeth on the Son hath everlasting life: and he that believeth not the Son shall not see life; but the wrath of God abideth on him.
—John 3:36
26. To declare, I say, at this time His righteousness: that He might be just, and the justifier of him which believeth in Jesus.
—Romans 3:26

WHAT DOES THE ATONING SACRIFICE ACCOMPLISH?

25. Whom God hath set forth to be a propitiation through faith in His blood, to declare His righteousness of sins that are past, through the forbearance of God;
—Romans 3:25
2. And walk in love, as Christ also hath loved us, and hath given himself for us an offering and a sacrifice to God for a sweetsmelling savour.
—Ephesians 5:2

CHRIST THE VICARIOUS SIN-BEARER

5. But He was wounded for our transgressions, He was bruised for our iniquities: the chastisement of our peace was upon Him; and with His stripes we are healed.
6. All we like sheep have gone astray; we have turned every one to his own way; and the LORD hath laid on Him the iniquity of us all.
10. Yet it pleased the LORD to bruise Him; He hath put Him to grief: when thou shalt make His soul an offering for sin, He shall see His seed, He shall prolong His days, and the pleasure of the LORD shall prosper in His hand.
12. Therefore will I divide Him portion with the great, and He shall divide the spoil with the strong; because He hath poured out His soul unto death: and He was numbered

with the transgressors; and He bare the sin of many, and made intercession for the transgressors.
—Isaiah 53:5, 6, 10, 12

4. Who gave Himself for our sins, that He might deliver us from this present evil world, according to the will of God and our Father:
—Galatians 1:4

3. For I delivered unto you first of all that which I also received, how that Christ died for our sins according to the scriptures:
—1 Corinthians 15:3

WHAT IS THE ROLE OF THE BLOOD

11. For the life of the flesh is in the *blood*: and I have given it to you upon the alter to make an atonement for your souls: for it is the *blood* that maketh an atonement for the soul.
—Leviticus 17:11

14. How much more shall the *blood* of Christ, who through the eternal Spirit offered Himself without spot to God, purge your conscience from dead works to serve the living God?
—Hebrews 9:14

25. Whom, God hath set forth to be a propitiation through faith in His *blood*, to declare His righteousness for the remission of sins that are past, through the forbearance of God;
—Romans 3:25

10. Herein is love, not that we loved God, but that He loved us, and sent His Son to be the propitiation for our sins.
—1 John 4:10

CHRIST THE RANSOM

4. Therefore we are buried with Him by baptism into death: that like as Christ was *raised* up from the dead by the glory of the Father, even so we also should walk in newness of life.
—Romans 6:4

14. I will *ransom* them from the power of the grave; I will *redeem* them from death: O death, I will be thy plagues; O grave, I will be thy destruction:
—Hosea 13:14
28. Even as the Son of Man came not to be ministered unto, but to minister, and to give His life a *ransom* for many.
—Matthew 20:28
6. Who gave Himself a *ransom* for all, to be testified in due time.
—1 Timothy 2:6
28. Take heed therefore unto yourselves, and to all the flock, over the which the Holy Ghost hath made you overseers, to feed the church of God, which He hath *purchased* with His own blood.
—Acts 20:28
7. In whom we have *redemption* through His blood, the forgiveness of sins, according to the riches of His grace.
—Ephesians 1:7
24. Being justified freely by His grace through the *redemption* that is in Christ Jesus:
—Romans 3:24
14. Who gave Himself for us, that He might *redeem* us from all iniquity, and purify unto Himself a peculiar [special] people, zealous of good works.
—Titus 2:14

WHAT DID THE RANSOM ACCOMPLISH?

19. What? know ye not that your body is the temple of the Holy Ghost which is in you, which ye have of God, and ye are not your own?
20. For ye are *bought* with a price: therefore glorify God in your body, and in your spirit, which are God's
—1 Corinthians 6:19, 20
23. Ye are *bought* with a price; be not ye the servants of men.
—1 Corinthians 7:23
18. For as much as ye know that ye were not *redeemed* with corruptible things, as silver and gold, from your vain con-

versation [behavior] received by tradition from your fathers;
19. But with the precious *blood* of Christ, as of a lamb without blemish and without spot:
—1 Peter 1:18, 19
22. But now being made free from sin, and become servants to God, ye have your fruit unto holiness, and the end everlasting life.
—Romans 6:22
9. And they sung a new song, saying, Thou art worthy to take the book, and to open the seals thereof: for Thou was slain, and hast *redeemed* us to God by Thy blood out of every kindred, and tongue, and people, and nation;
10. And hast made us unto our God Kings and priest: and we shall reign on the earth.
—Revelation 5:9, 10

CHRIST THE REPRESENTATIVE OF HUMANITY

45. And so it is written, The first man Adam was made a living soul; the last Adam was made a quickening spirit.
47. The first man is of the earth, earthly: the second man is the Lord from heaven.
—1 Corinthians 15:45, 47
22. For as in Adam all die, even so in Christ shall all be made alive.
—1 Corinthians 15:22
21. For he hath made Him to be sin for us, Who knew no sin; that we might be made the righteousness of God in Him.
—2 Corinthians 5:21
23. For the wages of sin is death: but the gift of God is eternal life through Jesus Christ our Lord.
—Romans 6:23
18. For Christ also hath once suffered for sins, the just for the unjust, that He might bring us to God, being put to death in the flesh, but quickened by the Spirit:
—1 Peter 3:18

9. But we see Jesus, who was made a little lower than the angels for the suffering of death, crowned with glory and honour; that He by the grace of God should taste death for every man.
—Hebrews 2:9

12. Wherefore, as by one man sin entered into the world, and death by sin; and so death passed upon all men, for that all have sinned:
—Romans 5:12

6. Blessed and holy is he that hath part in the first resurrection: on such the second death hath no power, but they shall be priests of God and of Christ, and shall reign with Him a thousand years.
—Revelation 20:6

CHRIST'S PERFECT LIFE OUR SALVATION

10. For if, when we were enemies, we were *reconciled* to God by the death of His Son, much more being *reconciled*, we shall be saved by his life.
—Romans 5:10

10. I will greatly rejoice in the LORD, my soul shall be joyful in my God; for He hath clothed me with the garments of Salvation, He hath covered me with the robe of righteousness, . . .
—Isaiah 61:10

THE INSPIRATION OF CHRIST'S LIFE

21. For even hereunto were ye called: because Christ also suffered for us, leaving us an example, that ye should follow His steps:
22. Who did no sin, neither was guile found in His mouth:
23. Who, when He was reviled, reviled not again; when He suffered, He threatened not; but committed himself to Him that judgeth righteously:
—1 Peter 2:21-23

13. I can do all things through Christ which strengtheneth me.
    —Philippians 4:13

CHRIST'S RESURRECTION AND SALVATION

29. And when they had fulfilled all that was written of Him, they took Him down from the tree, and laid Him in a sepulcher.
30. But God raised Him from the dead:
31. And He was seen many days of them which came up with Him from Galilee to Jerusalem, who are His witnesses unto the people.
    —Acts 13:29-31
9. That if thou shalt confess with thy mouth the Lord Jesus, and shalt believe in thine heart that God hath raised him from the dead, thou shalt be saved.
    —Romans 10:9
17. And if Christ be not raised, you faith is vain; ye are yet in your sins.
    —1 Corinthians 15:17

RECONCILIATION THROUGHOUT THE UNIVERSE

10. To the intent that now unto the principalities and powers in *heavenly* places might be known by the church the manifold wisdom of God,
    —Ephesians 3:10
20. And, having made peace through the blood of His cross, by Him to *reconcile* all things unto himself; by Him, I say, whether they be things in earth, or things in heaven.
    —Colossians 1:20
10. That at the name of Jesus every knee should bow, of things in *heaven*, and things in earth, and things under the earth;
11. and that *every* tongue should confess that Jesus Christ is Lord, to the glory of God the Father.
    —Philippians 2:10, 11

THE VINDICATION OF GOD'S LAW

3. For what the LAW could not do, in that it was weak through the flesh, God sending His own Son in the likeness of sinful flesh, and for sin, condemned sin in the flesh:
4. That the righteousness of the law might be fulfilled in us, who walk not after the flesh, but after the Spirit.
—Romans 8:3, 4

JUSTIFICATION

1. Therefore being *justified* by faith, we have peace, with God through our Lord Jesus Christ:
—Romans 5:1
7. That being *justified* by His grace, we should be made heirs according to the hope of eternal life.
—Titus 3:7
9. Much more then, being now *justified* by His [Christ's] blood, we shall be saved from wrath through Him.
—Romans 5:9
20. Therefore by the deeds of the law there shall no flesh by *justified* in His sight: for by the law is [only] the knowledge of sin.
—Romans 3:20

SALVATION COMES THROUGH RIGHT CONNECTIONS

1. I Am the true vine, and My Father is the husbandman.
2. Every branch in Me that beareth not fruit He taketh away: and every branch that beareth fruit, He purgeth it, that it may bring forth more fruit.
3. Now ye are clean through the word which I have spoken unto you.
4. Abide in Me, and I in you. As the branch cannot bear fruit of itself, except it abide in the vine; no more can ye, except ye abide in Me.

5. I Am the vine, ye are the branches: He that abideth in me, and I in him, the same bringeth forth much fruit: for without Me ye can do nothing.
6. If a man abide not in Me, he is cast forth as a branch, and is withered; and men gather them, and cast them into the fire, and they are burned.
7. If ye abide in Me, and My words abide in you, ye shall ask what ye will, and it shall be done unto you.
8. Herein is My Father glorified, that ye bear much fruit; so shall ye be My disciples.
9. As the Father hath loved me, so have I loved you: continue ye in My love.
10. If ye keep My commandments, ye shall abide in My love; even as I have kept My Father's commandments, and abide in His love.
—John 15:1-10

THE MOTIVATION FOR MISSION

20. Now then we are ambassadors for Christ, as though God did beseech you by us: we pray you in Christ's stead, be ye reconciled to God.
21. For He hath made Him to be sin for us, Who knew no sin: that we might be made the righteousness of God in Him.
—2 Corinthians 5:20, 21

CHAPTER 19

REPENTANCE/CONFESSION AND FORGIVENESS

FIRST: REPENTANCE

32. I came not to call the righteous, but sinners to *repentance*.
—Luke 5:32
47. And that *repentance* and remission of sins should be preached in His name among all nations . . .
—Luke 24:47
20. . . . By the law is the knowledge of sin.
—Romans 3:20
9. . . . We have before proved both Jews and Gentiles, that they are all under sin;
—Romans 3:9
6. Let no man deceive you with vain words: for because of these things cometh the wrath of God upon the children of disobedience.
—Ephesians 5:6
8. And when He [the Comforter] is come, He will reprove [convince, Margin] the world of sin . . .
—John 16:8
37. . . . Men and brethren, what shall we do?
38. . . . *repent*, and be baptized every one of you in the name of Jesus Christ for the *remission* of sins . . .
—Acts 2:37, 38
30. . . . Sirs, what must I do to be saved?

31. Believe on the Lord Jesus Christ, and thou shalt be saved, . . .
—Acts 16:30, 31
18. For I will *declare* mine iniquity; I will be sorry for my sin.
—Psalms 38:18
10. Godly sorrow brings *repentance* that leads to salvation and leaves no regret, but worldly sorrow brings death.
11. See what this godly sorrow has produced in you: what earnestness, what eagerness to clear yourselves, what indignation, what alarm, what longing, what concern, what readiness to see justice done . . .
—2 Corinthians 7:10, 11 NIV
7. . . . O generation of vipers, who hath warned you to flee from the wrath to come?
8. Bring forth therefore fruits meet for *repentance*:
—Matthew 3:7, 8

(NOTE: THERE CAN BE NO REPENTANCE WITHOUT REFORMATION. REPENTANCE IS A CHANGE OF MIND; REFORMATION IS A CHANGE OF LIFE.)

10. And God saw their works, that they turned from their evil way; and God *repented* of the evil that He had said that He would do unto them; and He did it not.
—Jonah 3:10
4. Or despisest thou the riches of His goodness and forbearance and long-suffering; not knowing that the goodness of God leadeth thee to *repentance*?
—Romans 2:4
17. I came not to call the righteous, but sinners to *repentance*.
—Mark 2:17
7. I say unto you, that likewise joy shall be in heaven over one sinner that repenteth, more than over ninety and nine just person, which need no *repentance*.

—Luke 15:7

SECOND: CONFESSION AND FORGIVENESS

6. Speak unto the children of Israel, When a man or woman shall commit any sin that men commit, to do a trespass against the LORD, and that person be guilty;
7. then shall they *confess* their sin which they have done . . .
—Numbers 5:6, 7
23. But if ye will not do so, behold, ye have sinned against the LORD: and be sure your sin will find you out.
—Numbers 32:23
8. Thou hast set our iniquities before Thee, our secret sins in the light of Thy countenance.
—Psalm 90:8
13. . . . All things are naked and opened unto the eyes of Him with whom we have to do.
—Hebrews 4:13
9. If we *confess* our sins, He is faithful and just to forgive us our sins, and to cleanse us from all unrighteousness.
—1 John 1:9
13. He that covereth his sins shall not proper: but whoso *confesseth* and forsaketh them shall have mercy.
—Proverbs 28:13
5. And it shall be, when he shall be guilty in one of these things, that he shall *confess* that he hath sinned in that thing:
—Leviticus 5:5

(Note: "True confession is always of a specific character, and acknowledges particular sins. They may be of such a nature as to be brought before God only; they may be wrongs that should be confessed to individuals who have suffered injury through them; or they may be of a public character, and should then be as publicly confessed. But all confession should be

definite and to the point, acknowledging the very sins of which you are guilty."
—*Steps to Christ; E. G. White, Page 43*)

19. And all the people said unto Samuel, Pray for thy servants unto the LORD thy God, that we die not: for we have added unto all our sins this evil, to ask us a king.
—1 Samuel 12:19

5. I acknowledged my sin unto Thee, and mine iniquity have I not hid. I said, I will *confess* my transgressions unto the LORD; and Thou *forgavest* the iniquity of my sin.
—Psalms 32:5

1. Have mercy upon me, O God, according to Thy loving kindness: according unto the multitude of Thy tender mercies blot out my transgressions.
—Psalms 51:1

5. For Thou, Lord, art good, and ready to *forgive*; and plenteous in mercy unto all them that call upon Thee.
—Psalms 86:5

11. For as the heaven is high above the earth, so great is His mercy toward them that fear Him.
—Psalms 103:11

7. Let the wicked forsake his way, and the unrighteous man his thoughts: and let him return unto the LORD, and He will have mercy upon him; and to our God, for He will *abundantly pardon*.
—Isaiah 55:7

18. Who is a God like unto Thee, that *pardoneth* iniquity, and passeth by the transgression of the remnant of His heritage?
—Micah 7:18

38. But He, being full of compassion, *forgave* their iniquity, and destroyed them not: yea, many a time turned He His anger away, and did not stir up all His wrath.
—Psalms 78:38

9. The Lord is not slack concerning His promise, as some

men count slackness; but is long-suffering to us ward, not willing that any should perish, but that all should come to *repentance*.
—2 Peter 3:9

MOSES' PRAYER TO GOD

19. *Pardon*, I beseech Thee, the iniquity of this people according unto the greatness of Thy mercy, and as Thou hast *forgiven* this people, from Egypt even until now.
—Numbers 14:19

THE LORD'S IMMEDIATE REPLY

20. And the LORD said, I have *pardoned* according to thy word:
—Numbers 14:20
20. . . . But when he was yet a great way off, his father saw him, and had *compassion*, and ran, and fell on his neck, and kissed him.
—Luke 15:20
22. But the father said to the servants, Bring forth the best robe, and put it on him; and put a ring on his hand, and shoes on his feet:
23. And bring hither the fatted calf, and kill it; and let us eat, and be merry:
24. For this my son was dead, and is alive again; he was lost, and is found . . .
—Luke 15:22-24
10. Likewise, I say unto you, there is joy in the presence of the angels of God over one sinner that *repenteth*.
—Luke 15:10
17. Behold, for peace I had great bitterness: but Thou hast in love to my soul delivered it from the pit of corruption: for Thou hast cast all my sins behind Thy back.
—Isaiah 38:17
19. . . . Thou wilt cast all their sins into the depth of the sea.
—Micah 7:19

12. As far as the east is from the west, so far hath He removed our transgressions from us.
—Psalms 103:12
5. Then went out to him Jerusalem, and all Judea, and all the region round about Jordan,
6. And were baptized of him [John the Baptist] in Jordan, *confessing* their sins.
—Matthew 3:5, 6
18. And many that believed came, and *confessed*, and showed their deeds.
19. Many of them also which used curious arts brought their books together, and burned them before all men: and they counted the price of them, and found it fifty thousand pieces of silver.
—Acts 19:18, 19
30. The God of our fathers raised up Jesus, whom ye slew and hanged on a tree.
31. Him hath God exalted with His right hand to be a Prince and a Saviour, for to give *repentance* to Israel, and *forgiveness* of sins.
—Acts 5:30, 31
31. Wherefore I say unto you, All manner of sin and blasphemy shall be *forgiven* unto men; but the blasphemy against the Holy Ghost shall not be *forgiven* unto men.
32. And whosoever speaketh a word against the Son of man, it shall be *forgiven* of him: but whosoever speaketh against the Holy Ghost, it shall not be *forgiven* him, neither in this world, neither in the world to come.
—Matthew 12:31, 32
12. And *forgive* us our debts, as we *forgive* our debtors.
—Matthew 6:12
14. For if ye *forgive* men their trespasses, your Heavenly Father will also *forgive* you:
15. but if ye *forgive* not men their trespasses, neither will your Father *forgive* your trespasses.
—Matthew 6:14, 15
32. And be ye kind one to another, tenderhearted, *forgiving*

one another, even as God for Christ's sake hath *forgiven* you.
—Ephesians 4:32

25. And when ye stand praying, *forgive*, if ye have ought against any: that your Father also which is in heaven may *forgive* you your trespasses.
26. But if ye do not *forgive*, neither will your Father which is in heaven *forgive* your trespasses.
—Mark 11:25, 26

4. And if he trespass against thee seven times in a day, and seven times in a day turn again to thee, saying, I repent; thou shalt *forgive* him.
—Luke 17:4

15. And the prayer of faith shall save the sick, and the Lord shall raise him up; and if ye have committed sins, they shall be *forgiven* him.
16. *Confess* your faults one to another, and pray one for another, that ye may be healed. The effectual fervent prayer of a righteous man availeth much.
—James 5:15, 16

1. Blessed is he whose transgression is *forgiven*, whose sin is covered.
2. Blessed is the man unto whom the LORD imputeth not iniquity, and in whose spirit there is no guile.
—Psalms 32:1, 2

CHAPTER 20
JUSTIFICATION AND SANCTIFICATION

JUSTIFICATION BY FAITH

7. That being *justified* by His grace, we should be made heirs according to the hope of eternal life.
   —Titus 3:7
9. Much more then, being now *justified* by His [Christ's] blood, we shall be saved from wrath through Him.
   —Romans 5:9
28. Therefore we conclude that a man is *justified* by faith without the deeds of the law.
    —Romans 3:28
16. Knowing that a man is not *justified* by the works of the law, but by the faith of Jesus Christ, even we have believed in Jesus Christ, that we might be *justified* by the faith of Christ, and not by the works of the law: for by the works of the law shall no flesh be *justified*.
    —Galatians 2:16
5. And he brought him [Abraham] forth abroad, and said, Look now toward heaven, and tell the stars, if thou be able to number them: and He said unto him, So shall thy seed be.
6. And he believed in the LORD; and He counted it to him for righteousness.
   —Genesis 15:5, 6

Justification and Sanctification

9. And be found in Him, not having thine own righteousness, which is of the law, but that which is through the faith of Christ, the righteousness which is of God by faith.
—Philippians 3:9

16. And not as it was by one that sinned, so is the gift: for the judgment was by one to condemnation, but the free gifts is of many offenses unto *justification*.
—Romans 5:16

4. Now to him that worketh is the reward not reckoned of grace, but of debt.

5. But to him that worketh not, but believeth on Him that justifieth the ungodly, his faith is counted for righteousness.
—Romans 4:4, 5

6. And if by grace, then is it no more of works: otherwise grace is no more grace. But if it be of works, then is it no more grace: otherwise work is no more work.
—Romans 11:6

29. Is He the God of the Jews only? Is He not also of the Gentiles? Yes, of the Gentiles also:

30. Seeing it is one God, which shall JUSTIFY the circumcision by faith, and uncircumcision through faith.
—Romans 3:29, 30

20. He staggered not at the promise of God through unbelief; but was strong in faith, giving glory to God;

21. And being fully persuaded that, what He had promised, He was able also to perform.

22. And therefore it was imputed to him for righteousness.

23. Now it was not written for his sake alone, that it was imputed to him;

24. But for us also, to whom it shall be imputed, if we believe on Him that raised up Jesus our Lord from the dead:

25. Who was delivered for our offenses, and was raised again for our *justification*.
—Romans 4:20-25

38. Be it known unto therefore, men and brethern, that through this man is preached unto you the forgiveness of sins:

39. And by Him all that believe are *justified* from all things, from which you could not be *justified* by the law of Moses.
—Acts 13:38, 39

19. For as by one man's disobedience many were made sinners, so by the obedience of one shall many be made righteous.
—Romans 5:19

25. In the LORD shall all the seed of Israel be *justified*, and shall glory.
—Isaiah 45:25

11. ... By His knowledge shall My righteous servant *justify* many; for He shall bear their iniquities.
—Isaiah 53:11

26. To declare, I say, at this time His righteousness: that He might be *just*, and the *justifier* of him which believeth in Jesus.
—Romans 3:26

5. Behold, the days come, saith the LORD, that I will raise unto David a righteous Branch, and a King shall reign and prosper, and shall execute judgment and *justice* in the earth.

6. In His days Judah shall be saved, and Israel shall dwell safely: and this is His name whereby He shall be called, *the LORD our righteousness.*
—Jeremiah 23:5, 6

1. Therefore being *justified* by faith, we have peace with God through our Lord Jesus Christ:
—Romans 5:1

14. For He is our peace, who hath made both one, and hath broken down the middle wall of partition between us;
—Ephesians 2:14

20. Therefore by the deeds of the law there shall no flesh be *justified* in His sight: for by the law is the knowledge of sin.
—Romans 3:20

21. I do not frustrate the grace of God: for if righteousness come by the law, then Christ is dead in vain.
—Galatians 2:21
4. Christ is become of no effect unto you, whosoever of you are *justified* by the law; ye are fallen from grace.
—Galatians 5:4
31. But Israel, which followed after the law of righteousness, hath not attained to the law of righteousness.
32. Wherefore? Because they sought it not by faith, but as it were by the works of the law. For they stumbled at that stumblingstone,
—Romans 9:31, 32
20. . . . By the law is knowledge of sin.
21. But now the righteousness of God without the law is manifested, being witnessed by the law and the prophets;
—Romans 3:20, 21
31. Do we then make void the law through faith? God forbid: yea, we established the law.
—Romans 3:31
1. What shall we say then? Shall we continue in sin, that grace may abound?
2. God forbid. How shall we, that are dead to sin, live any longer therein?
—Romans 6:1, 2
20. But wilt thou know, O vain man, that faith without works is dead?
—James 2:20
18. . . . Shew me thy faith without thy works, and I will show thee my faith by my works.
—James 2:18
24. Ye see then how that by works a man is *justified*, and not by faith only.
—James 2:24
21. For He hath made Him to be sin for us, who knew no sin; that we might be made the righteousness of God in Him.
—2 Corinthians 5:21

BIBLE SANCTIFICATION

23. And the very God of peace *sanctify* you wholly; and I pray God your whole spirit and soul and body be preserved blameless unto the coming of our Lord Jesus Christ.
—1 Thessalonians 5:23

14. Follow after peace with all men, and the *sanctification* without which no man shall see the Lord.
—Hebrews 12:14, R.V.

3. For this is the will of God, even your *sanctification* . . .
—1 Thessalonians 4:3

25. Husband, love you wives, even as Christ also loved the church, and gave Himself for it;
26. That He might *sanctify* and cleanse it with the washing of water by the word.
27. That He might present it to Himself a glorious church, not having spot, or wrinkle, or any such thing; but that it should be holy and without blemish.
—Ephesians 5:25-27

13. . . . God hath from the beginning chosen you to salvation through *sanctification* of the Spirit and belief of the truth.
—2 Thessalonians 2:13

18. But grow in grace, and in the knowledge of our Lord and Saviour Jesus Christ
—2 Peter 3:18

13. Brethren, I count not myself to have apprehended: but this one thing I do, forgetting those things which are behind, and reaching forth unto those things which are before,
14. I press toward the mark for the prize of the high calling of God in Christ Jesus.
—Philippians 3:13, 14

13. For if the blood of bulls and of goats, and the ashes of an heifer sprinkling the unclean, *sanctifieth* to the purifying of the flesh:
14. How much more shall the blood of Christ, who through

the eternal Spirit offered Himself without spot to God, purge your conscience from dead works to serve the living God?
—Hebrews 9:13, 14

2. And be not conformed to this world: but be ye transformed by the renewing of your mind, that ye may prove what is that good, and acceptable, perfect, will of God.
—Romans 12:2

8. If we say that we have no sin, we deceive ourselves, and the truth is not in us.
—1 John 1:8

3. Seek ye the LORD, all ye meek of the earth, which have wrought His judgment; seek righteousness, seek meekness: it may be ye shall be hid in the day of the LORD's anger.
—Zephaniah 2:3

17. And whatsoever ye do in word or deed, do all in the name of the Lord Jesus
—Colossians 3:17

31. Whether therefore ye eat, or drink, or whatsoever ye do, do all to the glory of God.
—1 Corinthians 10:31

5. Be sure of this, that no immoral or impure man, or one who is covetous [that is, an idolater], has any inheritance in the kingdom of Christ and of God.
—Ephesians 5:5, R.S.V.

9. Do you know that the unrighteous will not inherit the Kingdom of God? Do not be deceived; neither the immoral, nor idolaters, nor adulterers, nor homosexuals,

10. nor thieves, nor the greedy, nor drunkards, nor revilers, nor robbers will inherit the kingdom of God.
—1 Corinthians 6:9, 10, R.S.V.

5. Put to death therefore what is earthly to you: immorality, impurity, passion, evil desire, and covetousness, which is idolatry.

6. On account of these the wrath of God is coming.

—Colossians 3:5, 6, R.S.V.
21. If a man therefore purge himself from these, he shall be a vessel unto honour, *sanctified*, and meet for the Master's use and prepared unto every good work.
—2 Timothy 2:21

[Sanctification is the work of the Holy Spirit upon the character of those who are justified, in order that we may be glorified.]

30. ... Whom He justified, them He also glorified.
—Romans 8:30

[The grace of God is given to make us holy, to fit us for God's presence in eternity:]

14. ... for without holiness no man shall see the Lord.
—Hebrews 12:14

CHAPTER 21
GRACE

GRACE

(From Webster's Third International Dictionary, Unabridged)
grace 1a: beneficence or generosity shown by God to man . . . divine favor unmerited by man: the mercy of God as distinguished from His justice.
Synonym: = mercy
mercy 1a: compassion or forbearance shown to an offender or subject: clemency or kindness extended to someone instead of strictness or severity.

2a: blessing regarded as an act of divine favor or compassion.
   Synonym: = clemency, lenity, charity, GRACE.
 2. *Grace* be to you, and *peace*, from God our Father, and from the Lord Jesus Christ.
 6. To the praise of the Glory of His *grace*, wherein He hath made us accepted in the beloved.
   —Ephesians 1:2, 6
24. *Grace* be with all them that love our Lord Jesus Christ in sincerity.
   —Ephesians 6:24

GRACE IS A GIFT

 9. Who hath saved us, and called us with an holy calling, not according to our works, but according to His own pur-

pose and *grace*, which was given us in Christ Jesus before the world began.
—2 Timothy 1:9

16. Let us therefore come boldly unto the throne of *grace*, that we *may obtain mercy*, and find *grace* to help in time of need.
—Hebrews 4:16

5. . . . be clothed with humility: for God resisteth the proud, and *giveth grace* to the humble.
—1 Peter 5:5

1. We then, as workers together with Him, beseech you also that *ye receive* not the *grace* of God in vain.
—2 Corinthians 6:1

9. And He said unto me, *My grace* is sufficient for thee: for my strength is made perfect in weakness. Most gladly therefore will I rather glory in my infirmities, that the power of Christ may rest upon me.
—2 Corinthians 12:9

4. I thank my God always on your behalf, for the *grace* of God which is *given* you by Jesus Christ:
—1 Corinthians 1:4

15. But not as the offence, so also is the *free gift*, For if through the offence of one [Adam] many be dead, much more the *grace* of God, and the *gift* by *grace*, which is by one man, Jesus Christ, hath abounded [overflowed] unto many.
—Romans 5:15

17. For if by one man's offence death reigned by one; much more they which *receive* abundance of *grace* and of the *gift* of righteousness shall reign in life by one Jesus Christ.

20. Moreover the law entered, that the offence might abound [be magnified]. But where sin abounded *grace* did much more abound [overflow]:

21. That as sin hath reigned unto death even so might *grace* reign through righteousness unto eternal life by Jesus Christ our Lord.
—Romans 5:17, 20, 21

7. Whereof I was made a minister, according to the *gift* of the *grace* of God *given* unto me by the effectual working of His power.
—Ephesians 3:7

SALVATION BY GRACE ALONE

7. In whom we have *redemption* through His blood, the forgiveness of sins, according to the riches of His *grace*;
—Ephesians 1:7

11. For the *grace* of God that *bringeth salvation* hath appeared to all men,
—Titus 2:11

7. That being *justified* by *His grace*, we should be made heirs according to the hope of eternal life.
—Titus 3:7

6. And if by *grace*, then is it no more of works: otherwise *grace* is no more *grace*. But if it be of works, then is it no more *grace*: otherwise work is no more work.
—Romans 11:6

7. That in the ages to come He might show the exceeding riches of His *grace* in His kindness toward us through Christ Jesus.
—Ephesians 2:7

GOD WAS A GOD OF GRACE ALSO IN THE O. T.

(From Bible Dictionary:)
Hebrew word "chen" and Greek word "charis" means favor or kindness, undeserved. ex: "If I have found favour [or *grace*] in thine eyes"
—Genesis 30:27

26. And the child Samuel grew on, and was in favour [found *grace*] both with the LORD, and also with men.
—1 Samuel 2:26

Hebrew word "chesed" translated "lovingkindness" in KJV and "steadfast love" in the RSV.
(Read Also: Psalms 17:7; 26:3; 36:7)

6. And the LORD passed by before him, and proclaimed, The LORD, the LORD God, *merciful* and *gracious*, longsuffering, and abundant in goodness and truth,
7. Keeping *mercy* for thousands, forgiving iniquity and transgression and sin . . .
—Exodus 34:6, 7

15. But thou, O Lord, art a God full of compassion, and *gracious*, longsuffering, and plenteous in *mercy* and truth.
—Psalms 86:15

1. Have *mercy* upon me, O God, according to thy loving kindness: according unto the multitude of thy tender *mercies* blot out my transgressions.
—Psalm 51:1

34. O give thanks unto the LORD; for He is good; for His *mercy [grace]* endureth forever.
—1 Chronicles 16:34

5. For the LORD is good; His *mercy [grace]* is everlasting; and His truth endureth to all generations.
—Psalm 100:5

13. And rend your heart, and not your garments, and turn unto the LORD your God: for He is *gracious* and *merciful*, slow to anger, and of great kindness, and repenteth Him of the evil.
—Joel 2:13

2. And He [Jonah] prayed unto the LORD, and said, I pray Thee, O Lord, was not this my saying, when I was yet in my country? Therefore I fled before [hastened to flee] unto Tarshish: for I knew that Thou art a *gracious God, and Merciful*, slow to anger, and of great kindness, and repentest thee of the evil.
—Jonah 4:2

GRACE = MERCY ALSO IN THE NEW TESTAMENT

4. To Titus, mine own son after the common faith: *grace, mercy*, and peace, from God the Father and the Lord Jesus Christ our Saviour.
—Titus 1:4

11. But we believe that through the *grace [mercy]* of the Lord Jesus Christ we shall be saved, even as they.
—Acts 15:11

5. Having predestinated us unto the adoption of children by Jesus Christ to Himself, according to the good pleasure of His will,
6. To the praise of the glory of His grace, wherein He hath *made us accepted* in the beloved.
7. In whom we have *redemption* through His blood, the forgiveness of sins, according to the riches of His *grace*.
—Ephesians 1:5-7

4. But God, who is rich in *mercy*, for His great love wherewith He loved us,
5. Even when we were dead in sins, hath quickened us together with Christ, *(by grace ye are saved;)*
6. And hath raised us up together, and made us sit together in heavenly places in Christ Jesus:
7. That in the ages to come He might show the exceeding riches of His *grace in His kindness* toward us through Christ Jesus.
8. For by *grace are ye saved* through faith: and that not of yourselves: it is the gift of God:
9. Not of works, lest any man should boast.
10. For we are His workmanship, created in Christ Jesus unto good works, which God hath before ordained that we should walk in them.
—Ephesians 2:4-10

20. Moreover the law entered, that the offence might abound. But where sin abounded, *grace* did much more abound:
—Romans 5:20

9. For ye know that *grace* of our Lord Jesus Christ, that, though He was rich, yet for your sakes He became poor, that ye through His poverty *might be rich*.
—2 Corinthians 8:9

GRACE AND OBEDIENCE

5. By whom we have received *grace* and apostleship, for obedience to the faith among all nations, for His name.
—Romans 1:5
11. For the *grace* of God that *bringeth salvation* hath appeared to all men,
—Titus 2:11
10. Of which salvation the prophets have inquired and searched diligently, who prophesied of the *grace* that should come unto you:
13. Wherefore gird of the loins of your mind, be sober, and hope to the end for the *grace* that is to be brought unto you at the revelation of Jesus Christ;
—1 Peter 1:10, 13
18. But grow in *grace*, and in the knowledge of our Lord and Saviour Jesus Christ.
—2 Peter 3:18
28. Wherefore we receiving a kingdom which cannot be moved, let us have *grace*, whereby we may serve God acceptably with reverence and godly fear:
—Hebrews 12:28

THE LIMITS OF GRACE

14. For sin shall not have dominion over you: for ye are not under the law, but under *grace*.
15. What then? Shall we sin, because we are not under the law, but under *grace*? God forbid.
—Romans 6:14, 15
7. That being *justified* by His *grace*, we should be made heirs according to the hope of eternal life.
—Titus 3:7
24. Being *justified freely* by His *grace* through the redemption that is in Christ Jesus:
25. Whom God hath set forth to be a propitiation through faith in His blood, to declare His righteousness for the

remission of sins that are past, through the forbearance of God;
—Romans 3:24, 25

14. And by their prayer for you, which long after you for the exceeding *grace* of God in you.
—2 Corinthians 9:14

1. What shall we say them? Shall we continue in sin, that *grace* may abound?
2. God, forbid. How shall we, that are dead to sin, live any longer therein?
—Romans 6:1, 2

10. But by the *grace* of God I [Paul] am what I am: And His *grace* which was bestowed upon me was not in vain; but I laboured more abundantly than they all: yet not I, but the *grace* of God which was in me.
—1 Corinthians 15:10

14. And the *grace* of our Lord was exceeding abundant with faith and love which is in Christ Jesus.
—1 Timothy 1:14

14. The *grace* of the Lord Jesus Christ, and the love of God, and the communion of the Holy Ghost, be with you all. Amen.
—2 Corinthians 13:14

CHAPTER 22
FAITH

FAITH

1. *Faith* is the substance of things hoped for, the evidence of things not seen.
   —Hebrews 11:1
6. Without *faith* it is impossible to please Him. For he that cometh to God must believe that He is, and that He is a rewarder of them that diligently seek Him.
   —Hebrews 11:6
3. ... God hath dealt to every man the measure of *faith*.
   —Romans 12:3
2. Looking unto Jesus the author and finisher of our *faith*; ...
   —Hebrews 12:2
17. So then *faith* cometh by hearing, and hearing by the word of God.
    —Romans 10:17
3. Through *faith* we understand that the worlds were framed by the word of God ...
   —Hebrews 11:3
6. In Jesus Christ neither circumcision availeth anything, nor uncircumcision; but *faith* which worketh by love.
   —Galatians 5:6
22. But the fruit of the Spirit is love, joy, peace, long-suffering, gentleness, goodness, *faith*,
    —Galatians 5:22

3. Remembering without ceasing your work of *faith*, and labor of love . . .
   —1 Thessalonians 1:3
2. For unto us was the gospel preached, as well as unto them: but the word preached did not profit them, not being mixed with *faith* in them that heard it.
   —Hebrews 4:2
19. Thou believest that there is one God; thou doest well: the devils also believe, and tremble.
    —James 2:19
23. . . . Whatsoever is not of *faith* is sin.
    —Romans 14:23
2. But wilt thou know, O vain man, that *faith* without works is dead?
   —James 2:20
8. By *faith* Abraham, when he was called to go out into a place which he should after receive for an inheritance, obeyed; and he went out, not knowing whither he went.
   —Hebrews 11:8
   (Read also: Hebrews Chapter 11.)
22. Seest thou how *faith* wrought with his works, and by works was *faith* made perfect?
    —James 2:22
    (Faith first, works follow.)
25. Whom God hath set forth to be a propitiation through faith in His blood, to declare His righteousness for the remission of sins that are past, through the forbearance of God.
    —Romans 3:25
5. to him that worketh not, but believeth on Him that justifieth the ungodly, his *faith* is counted for righteousness.
   —Romans 4:5
   (Only *faith* will save us but good works will follow.)
1. Therefore being justified by *faith*, we have peace with God through our Lord Jesus Christ:

2. By whom also we have access by *faith* into this grace wherein we stand, and rejoice in hope of the glory of God.
—Romans 5:1, 2

8. For by grace are ye saved through *faith*; and that not of yourselves: it is the gift of God.
—Ephesians 2:8

20. I am crucified with Christ: nevertheless I live; yet not I, but Christ liveth in me: and the life which I now live in the flesh I live by the *faith* of the Son of God, who loved me, and gave Himself for me.
—Galatians 2:20

3. Knowing this, that the trying of your *faith* worketh patience.
—James 1:3

12. That ye be not slothful, but followers of them who through *faith* and patience inherit the promises.
—Hebrews 6:12

12. Here is the patience of the saints: here are they that keep the commandments of God, and the *faith* of Jesus.
—Revelation 14:12

26. For ye are all the children of God by *faith* in Christ Jesus.
—Galatians 3:26

7. (For we walk by FAITH, not by sight:)
—2 Corinthians 5:7

28. Then Jesus answered and said unto her, O woman, great is thy *faith*: be it unto thee even as thou wilt. And her daughter was made whole from that very hour.
—Matthew 15:28
(Read also: Matthew 15:21-28)

6. But let him ask in *faith*, nothing wavering. For he that wavereth is like a wave of the sea driven with the wind and tossed.
—James 1:6

8. . . . Putting on the breastplate of *faith* and love;
—1 Thessalonians 5:8

16. Above all, taking the shield of *faith*, wherewith ye shall be able to quench all the fiery darts of the wicked.
—Ephesians 6:16

12. Fight the good fight of *faith*, lay hold on eternal life, . . .
    —1 Timothy 6:12
38. Now the just shall live by *faith*: but if any man draw back, my soul shall have no pleasure in Him.
    —Hebrews 10:38
22. Let us draw near with a true heart in full assurance of *faith*, having our hearts sprinkled from an evil conscience, and our bodies washed with pure water.
23. Let us hold fast the profession of our *faith* without wavering; (for He is *faithful* that promised;)
    —Hebrews 10:22, 23
17. That Christ may dwell in you hearts by *faith*; that ye, being rooted and grounded in love.
    —Ephesians 3:17
5. And so were the churches established in the *faith*, and increased in number daily.
    —Acts 16:5
15. And the prayer of *faith* shall save the sick, and the Lord shall raise him up; and if he have committed sins, they shall be forgiven him.
    —James 5:15
4. . . . This is the victory that overcometh the world, even our *faith*.
    —1 John 5:4
9. Receiving the end of your *faith*, even the salvation of your souls.
    —1 Peter 1:9

CHAPTER 23
HOPE

HOPE

1. Now faith is the substance of things *hoped* for, the evidence of things not seen.
—Hebrews 11:1
4. For whatsoever things were written aforetime were written for our learning, that we through patience and comfort of the Scriptures might have *hope*.
—Romans 15:4
15. But sanctify the Lord God in your hearts: and be ready always to give an answer to every man that asketh you a reason of the *hope* that is in you with meekness and fear:
—1 Peter 3:15
4. We will not hide them from their children, showing to the generation to come the praises of the LORD, and His strength, and His wonderful works that He hath done.
7. That they might set their *hope* in God, and not forget the works of God, but keep His commandments:
—Psalms 78:4, 7
7. That being justified by His grace, we should be made heirs according to the *hope* of eternal life.
—Titus 3:7
11. Wherefore remember, that ye being in time past Gentiles in the flesh . . .
12. That at that time ye were without Christ, being aliens from the commonwealth of Israel, and strangers from the

covenants of promise, having no *hope*, and without God in the world:
—Ephesians 2:11, 12

27. To whom God would make known what is the riches of the glory of this mystery among the Gentiles; which is Christ in you, the *hope* of glory:
—Colossians 1:27

19. For the law made nothing perfect, but the bringing in of a better *hope* did; by the which we draw nigh unto God.
—Hebrews 7:19

19. Which *hope* we have as an anchor of the soul, both sure and steadfast, and which entereth into that within the veil;
—Hebrews 6:19

32. The wicked is driven away in his wickedness: but the righteous hath *hope* in his death.
—Proverbs 14:32

13. But I would not have you to be ignorant, brethren, concerning them which are asleep, that ye sorrow not, even as others which have no *hope*.
—1 Thessalonians 4:13

3. Blessed be the God and Father of our Lord Jesus Christ, which according to His abundant mercy hath begotten us again unto a lively *hope* by the resurrection of Jesus Christ from the dead,
—1 Peter 1:3

13. Looking for that blessed *hope*, and the glorious appearing of the great God and our Saviour Jesus Christ;
—Titus 2:13

8. Henceforth there is a laid up for me a crown of righteousness, which the Lord, the righteous Judge, shall give me at that day: and not to me only, but unto all them also that love His appearing.
—2 Timothy 4:8

3. And every man that hath this *hope* in him purifieth himself, even as He [Christ] is pure.
—1 John 3:3

24. For we are saved by *hope*: but *hope* that is seen is not *hope*: for what a man seeth, why doth he yet *hope* for?
25. But if we *hope* for that we see not, then do we with patience wait for it.
—Romans 8:24, 25
24. The LORD is my portion, saith my soul; therefore will I *hope* in Him.
26. It is good that a man should both *hope* and quietly wait for the salvation of the LORD.
—Lamentations 3:24, 26
13. So are the paths of all that forget God; and the hypocrit's *hope* shall perish:
14. Whose *hope* shall be cut off, and whose trust shall be a spider's web.
—Job 8:13, 14
22. Let thy mercy, O LORD, be upon us, according as we *hope* in Thee.
—Psalms 33:22
18. Behold, the eye of the LORD is upon them that fear Him, upon them that *hope* in His mercy;
—Psalms 33:18
11. The LORD taketh pleasure in them that fear Him, in those that *hope* in His mercy.
—Psalms 147:11
5. Happy is he that hath the God of Jacob for his help, whose *hope* is in the LORD his God:
—Psalms 146:5
7. Blessed is the man that trusteth in the LORD, and whose *hope* the LORD is.
—Jeremiah 17:7
13. Now the God of *hope* fill you with all joy and peace in believing, that ye may abound in *hope*, through the power of the Holy Ghost.
—Romans 15:13
2. By whom also we have access by faith into the grace wherein we stand, and rejoice in *hope* of the glory of God.
—Romans 5:2

5. And *hope* maketh not ashamed; because the love of God is shed abroad in our hearts by the Holy Ghost which is given unto us.
—Romans 5:5

16. The LORD also shall roar out of Zion, and utter His voice from Jerusalem; and the heavens and the earth shall shake: but the LORD will be the *hope* of His people, and the strength of the children of Israel.
—Joel 3:16

24. Be of good courage, and He shall strengthen your heart, all ye that *hope* in the LORD.
—Psalms 31:24

13. Wherefore gird up the loins of your mind, be sober, and *hope* to the end for the grace that is to be brought unto you at the revelation of Jesus Christ;
—1 Peter 1:13

11. And we desire that every one of you do show the same diligence to the full assurance of *hope* unto the end.
—Hebrews 6:11

CHAPTER 24
THE CHURCH

THE CHURCH

8. Take the rod, and gather thou the *assembly [church]* together, thou [Moses], and Aaron thy brother, and speak ye unto the *rock* before their eyes; and it shall give forth His water, and thou shalt bring forth to them water out of the *rock*; so thou shalt give the *congregation* and their beasts drink.
—Numbers 20:8
(Read Also: Numbers 20:7-12)

CHURCH BUILT UPON CHRIST THE ROCK

3. Because I will publish the name of the LORD: ascribe ye greatness unto our God.
4. He is the *rock*, His work is perfect: for all His ways are judgment: a God of truth and without iniquity, just and right is He.
—Deuteronomy 32:3, 4

7. In God is my salvation and my glory: the *rock* of my strength, and my refuge, is in God.
—Psalms 62:7

4. To whom coming, as unto a living *stone*, disallowed indeed of men, but chosen of God, and precious,
—1 Peter 2:4

4. And did all drink the same spiritual drink: for they drank of that spiritual *rock* that followed them: and that *rock* was Christ.
—1 Corinthians 10:4
(Read Also: Matthews 16:18)

THE CHURCH EXISTED BEFORE N. T. TIMES

9. The LORD shall establish thee an holy people unto Himself, as He hath sworn unto thee, if thou shalt keep the commandments of the LORD thy God, and walk in His way.
—Deuteronomy 28:9
12. And I will walk among you, and will be your God, and ye shall be My people.
—Leviticus 26:12
38. This is he [Moses], that was in the church in the wilderness with the angel which spake to him in the mount Sina, and with our fathers: who received the lively oracles to give unto us:
—Acts 7:38

CHRIST CALLED HIS PEOPLE A CHURCH WHILE HE WAS ON EARTH AS A MAN.

17. And if he shall neglect to hear them, tell it unto the church: but if he neglect to hear the church, let him be unto thee as an heathen man and a publican.
—Matthew 18:17

THE MISSION OF THE CHURCH

19. Go ye therefore, and teach all nations, baptizing them in the name of the Father, and the Son, and of the Holy Ghost:
—Matthew 28:19

THE CHURCH AS A BODY

13. For by one Spirit are we all baptized into one body, whether we be Jews or Gentiles, whether we be bond or fee; and have been all made to drink into one Spirit.
—1 Corinthians 12:13
18. And He [Christ] is the head of the body, the church: who is the beginning, the firstborn from the dead; that in all things He might have the preeminence.
—Colossians 1:18
23. For the husband is the head of the wife, even as Christ is the head of the church: and He is the saviour of the body.
—Ephesians 5:23

THE CHURCH AS A TEMPLE

16. Know ye not that ye are the *temple* of God, and that the Spirit of God dwelleth in you?
—1 Corinthians 3:16
20. And are built upon the foundation of the apostles and prophets, Jesus Christ Himself being the chief corner *stone*;
—Ephesians 2:20
4. To whom coming, as unto a living stone, disallowed indeed of men, but chosen of God, and precious,
5. Ye also, as lively [living] stones, are build up a spiritual house, an holy priesthood, to offer up spiritual sacrifices, acceptable to God by Jesus Christ.
6. Wherefore also it is contained in the scripture, Behold, I lay in Sion a chief corner *stone*, elect, precious: and he that believeth on Him shall not be confounded.
—1 Peter 2:4-6
(Read Also: 1 Corinthians 3:12, 13)
22. In whom ye also are builded together for an habitation of God through the Spirit.
—Ephesians 2:22
17. If any man defile the *temple* of God, Him shall God destroy: for the *temple* of God is holy, which *temple* ye are.
—1 Corinthians 3:17

16. And what agreement hath the *temple* of God with idols? for ye are the *temple* of the living God; as God hath said, I will dwell in them, and walk in them; and I will be their God, and they shall be my people.
—2 Corinthians 6:16

THE CHURCH AS A BRIDE

14. Turn, O backsliding children, saith the LORD; for I Am *married* unto you: and I will take you one of a city, and two of a family, and I will bring you to Zion:
—Jeremiah 3:14
2. For I am jealous over you with godly jealousy: for I have espoused *[betrothed]* you to one husband, that I may present you as a chaste virgin to Christ.
—2 Corinthians 11:2
15. *Husband* love your *wives*, even as Christ also loved the church, and gave Himself for it;
—Ephesians 5:25

THE CHURCH AS "JERSUALEM ABOVE"

2. Beautiful for situation, the joy of the whole earth, is *mount zion*, on the sides of the north, the city of the great King.
—Psalms 48:2
20. For our conversation is in *heaven*, from whence also we look for the Saviour, the Lord Jesus Christ:
—Philippians 3:20
22. But ye are come unto mount Sion, and unto the city of the living God, the heavenly Jerusalem, and to an innumerable company of angels,
23. To the general assembly and church of the firstborn, which are written in heaven, and to God the judge of all, and to the spirits of just men made perfect,
—Hebrews 12:22, 23

THE CHURCH AS A FAMILY

14. . . . I bow my knees unto the Father of our Lord Jesus Christ,
15. Of whom the whole family in heaven and earth is named,
—Ephesians 3:14, 15
4. According as He hath chosen us in Him before the foundation of the world, that we should be holy and without blame before Him in love:
5. Having predestinated us unto the adoption of children by Jesus Christ to Himself, according to the good pleasure of His will,
6. To the praise of the glory of His grace, wherein He hath made us accepted in the beloved.
—Ephesians 1:4-6
29. And if ye be Christ's them are ye Abraham's seed, and heirs according to the promise.
—Galatians 3:29
4. But when the fulness of time was come, God sent forth His Son, made of a woman, made under the law,
5. To redeem them that were under the law, that we might receive the adoption of sons.
6. And because ye are sons, God hath sent forth the Spirit of His Son into your hearts, crying, Abba, Father.
—Galatians 4:4-6
10. As we have therefore opportunity, let us do good unto all men, especially unto them who are of the household of faith.
—Galatians 6:10

THE CHURCH A PILLAR AND FOUNDATION OF TRUTH

15. But if I tarry long, that thou mayest know how thou oughtest to behave thyself in the house of God, which is the church of the living God, the pillar and ground of the truth.
—1 Timothy 3:15

20. To the law and to the testimony: if they speak not according to this word, it is because there is no light in them.
—Isaiah 8:20
14. Where no counsel is, the people fall: but in the multitude of counselors there is safety.
—Proverbs 11:14
13. Ye are the salt of the earth: but if the salt have lost his savour, wherewith shall it be salted? it is thence forth good for nothing, but to be cast out, and to be trodden under foot of men.
14. Ye are the light of the world. A city that is set on an hill cannot be hid.
15. Neither do men light a candle, and put it under a bushel, but on a candlestick; and it giveth light unto all that are in the house.
—Matthew 5:13-15

THE CHURCH AN ARMY, MILITANT AND TRIUMPHANT

12. For we wrestle not against flesh and blood, but against principalities, against powers, against the rulers of the darkness of this world, against spiritual wickedness in high places.
13. Wherefore take unto you the whole armour of God, that ye may be able to withstand in the evil day, and having done all, to stand.
—Ephesians 6:12, 13
29. For I know this, that after my departing shall grievous wolves enter in among you, not sparing the flock.
30. Also of your own selves shall men arise, speaking perverse things, to draw away disciples after them.
—Acts 20:29, 30
1. Now the Spirit speaketh expressly, that in the latter times some shall depart from the faith, giving heed to seducing spirits, and doctrines of devils;
—1 Timothy 4:1

24. Another parable put He forth unto them, saying, The kingdom of heaven is likened unto a man which sowed good seed in his field:
25. But while men slept, his enemy came and sowed tares among the wheat, and went his way.
—Matthew 13:24, 25
12. Therefore rejoice, ye heavens, and ye that dwell in them, Woe to the inhabiters of the earth and of the sea! for the devil is come down unto you, having great wrath, because he knoweth that he hath but a short time.
17. And the dragon was wrath with the woman, and went to make war with the remnant of her seed, which keep the commandments of God,, and have the testimony of Jesus Christ.
—Revelation 12:12, 17
1. And at that time shall Michael [Christ] stand up, the great prince which standeth for the children of thy people: and there shall be a time of trouble, such as never was since there was a nation even to that same time: and at that time thy people shall be delivered, every one that shall be found written in the book.
—Daniel 12:1
13. But he that shall endure unto the end, the same shall be saved.
—Matthew 24:13

THE VISIBLE CHURCH

18. And Jesus came and spake unto them, saying, All power is given unto me in heaven and in earth.
19. Go ye therefore, and teach all nations, baptizing them in the name of the Father, and of the son, and of the Holy Ghost:
—Matthew 28:18, 19
23. And the very God of peace sanctify you wholly; and I pray God your whole spirit and soul and body be preserved blameless unto the coming of our Lord Jesus Christ.
—1 Thessalonians 5:23

27. That He might present it to Himself a glorious church, not having spot, or wrinkle, or any such thing; but that it should be holy and without blemish.
—Ephesians 5:27
18. The Spirit of the Lord is upon Me, because He hath anointed Me to preach the gospel to the poor; He hath sent Me to heal the brokenhearted, to preach deliverance to the captives, and recovering of sight to the blind, to set at liberty them that are bruised,
19. To preach the acceptable year of the Lord.
—Luke 4:18, 19

THE INVISIBLE CHURCH

9. That was the true light, which lighteth every man that cometh into the world.
—John 1:9
14. For when the Gentiles, which have not the law, do by nature the things contained in the law, these, having not the law, are a law unto themselves:
15. Which shew the work of the law written in their hearts, their conscience also bearing witness, and their thoughts the mean while accusing or else excusing one another;
—Romans 2:14, 15
23. But the hour cometh, and now is, when the true worshippers shall worship the Father in spirit and in truth: for the Father seeketh such to worship Him.
—John 4:23
16. And other sheep I have, which are not of this fold: them also I must bring, and they shall hear My voice; and there shall be one fold, and one shepherd.
—John 10:16
4. And I heard another voice from heaven, saying, Come out of her, my people, that ye be not partakers of her sins, and that ye receive not of her plagues.
—Revelation 18:4

14. And this gospel of the kingdom shall be preached in all the world for a witness unto all nations; and then shall the end come.
—Matthew 24:14

THE ORGANIZATION OF THE CHURCH

33. For God is not the author of confusion, but of peace, as in all churches of the saints.
40. Let all things be done decently and in order.
—1 Corinthians 14:33, 40

MEMBERSHIP QUALIFICATIONS

36. Therefore let all the house of Israel know assuredly, that God hath made that same Jesus, whom ye have crucified, both Lord and Christ.
37. Now when they heard this, they were pricked in their heart, and said unto Peter and to the rest of the apostles, Men and brethren, what shall we do?
38. Then Peter said unto them, Repent, and be baptized every one of you in the name of Jesus Christ for the remission of sins, and ye shall receive the gift of the Holy Ghost.
39. For the promise is unto you, and to your children, and to all that are afar off, even as many as the Lord our God shall call.
40. And with many other words did he testify and exhort, saying, Save yourselves from this untoward (crooked) generation.
41. Then they that gladly received his word were baptized: and the same day there were added unto them about three thousand souls.
—Acts 2:36-41
20. Teaching them to observe all things whatsoever I have commanded you: and, lo, I am with you alway, even unto the end of the world.
—Matthew 28:20

The Church

EQUALITY AND SERVICE

8. But be not ye called Rabbi: for one is your Master, even Christ; and all ye are brethren.
11. But he that is greatest among you shall be your servant.
—Matthew 23:8, 11

PRIESTHOOD OF ALL BELIEVERS

5. Ye also, as lively [living] stones, are built up a spiritual house, an holy priesthood, to offer up spiritual sacrifices, acceptable to God by Jesus Christ.
9. But ye are a chosen generation [race], a royal priesthood, an holy nation, a peculiar [special] people; that ye should show forth the praises of Him who hath called you out of darkness into His marvelous light:
—1 Peter 2:5, 9

ALLEGIANCE TO GOD AND STATE

4. For he [the ruler] is the minister of God to thee for good. But if thou do that which is evil, be afraid; for he beareth not the sword in vain: for he is the minister of God, a revenger to execute wrath upon him that doeth evil.
7. Render therefore to all their dues: tribute to whom tribute is due; custom to whom custom; fear to whom fear; honour to whom honour.
—Romans 13:4, 7
21. They say unto Him, Caesar's. Then saith he [Christ] unto them, Render therefore unto Caesar the things which are Caesar's; and unto God the things that are God's .
—Matthew 22:21

WORSHIP AND EXHORTATION

25. Not forsaking the assembling of ourselves together, as the manner of some is; but exhorting one another: and so much the more, as ye see the day approaching.
—Hebrews 10:25

CHRISTIAN FELLOWSHIP

3. That which we have seen and heard declare we unto you, that ye also may have *fellowship* with us: and truly our *fellowship* is with the Father, and with His Son Jesus Christ.
6. If we say that we have *fellowship* with Him, and walk in darkness, we lie, and do not the truth:
7. But if we walk in the light, as he is in the light, we have *fellowship* one with another, and the blood of Jesus Christ His Son cleanseth us from all sin.
—1 John 1:3, 6, 7

INSTRUCTION IN THE SCRIPTURE

63. It is the spirit that quickeneth; the flesh profiteth nothing: the words that I speak unto you, they are spirit, and they are life.
68. Then Simon Peter answered Him, Lord, to whom shall we go? thou hast the words of eternal life.
—John 6:63, 68
4. But He [Christ] answered and said, It is written, Man shall not live by bread alone, but by every word that proceedeth out of the mouth of God.
—Matthew 4:4

WORLDWIDE PROCLAMATION OF THE GOSPEL

14. And this gospel of the kingdom shall be preached in all the world for a witness unto all nations; and then shall the end come.
—Matthew 24:14
6. And I saw another angel fly in the midst of heaven, having the everlasting gospel to preach unto them that dwell on the earth, and to every nation, kindred, and tongue, and people,
7. Saying with a loud voice, Fear God, and give glory to him; for the hour of his judgment is come: and worship him

that made heaven, and earth, and the sea, and the fountains of waters;
8. And there followed another angel, saying, Babylon is fallen, is fallen, that great city, because she made all nations drink of the wine of the wrath of her fornication.
9. And the third angel followed them, saying with a loud voice, If any man worship the beast and his image, and receive his mark in his forehead, or in his hand,
10. The same shall drink of the wine of the wrath of God, which is poured out without mixture into the cup of his indignation; and he shall be tormented with fire and brimstone in the presence of the holy angels, and in the presence of the lamb:
11. And the smoke of their torment ascendeth up for ever and ever: and they have no rest day nor night, who worship the beast and his image, and whosoever receiveth the mark of his name.
12. Here is the patience of the saints: here are they that keep the commandments of God, and the faith of Jesus.
—Revelation 14:6-12
4. And I heard another voice from heaven, saying, Come out of her, my people, that ye be not partakers of her sins, and that ye receive not of her plagues.
—Revelation 18:4

THE GOVERNMENT OF THE CHURCH

3. Wherefore, brethren, look ye out among you seven men of honest report, full of the Holy Ghost and wisdom, whom we may appoint [deacons] over this business.
6. Whom they set before the apostles: and when thy had prayed, they laid their hands on them.
—Acts 6:3, 6
23. And when they had ordained them elders in every church, and had prayed with fasting, they commended them to the Lord, on whom they believed.
—Acts 14:23

4. And when they were come to Jerusalem, they were received of the church, and of the apostle and elders, and they declared all things that God had done with them.
—Acts 15:4
(Read Also: Acts 15:22, 23)

CHRIST IS HEAD OF THE CHURCH

18. And Jesus came and spake unto them, saying, All power is given unto Me in heaven and in earth.
—Matthew 28:18
22. And hath put all things under His feet, and gave him to be the head over all things to the church,
23. Which is His body, the fulness of Him that filleth all in all.
—Ephesians 1:22, 23
10. That at the name of Jesus every knee should bow, of things in heaven, and things in earth, and things under the earth;
11. And that every tongue should confess that Jesus Christ is Lord, to the glory of God the Father.
—Philippians 2:10, 11
18. And He is the head of the body, the church: who is the beginning, the firstborn from the dead; that in all things He might have the preeminence.
—Colossians 1:18
30. For we are members of His body, of His flesh, and of His bones.
—Ephesians 5:30
19. And not holding the Head, from which all the body by joints and bands having nourishment ministered, and knit together, increaseth with the increase of God.
—Colossians 2:19

CHRIST IS THE SOURCE OF ALL ITS AUTHORITY

18. And I say also unto thee, That thou art Peter, and upon

this rock [Christ] I will build My church; and the gates of hell shall not prevail against it.
—Matthew 16:18
21. Then said Jesus to them again, Peace be unto you: as My Father hath sent Me, even so send I you.
22. And when He had said this, He breathed on them, and saith unto them, Receive ye the Holy Ghost:
—John 20:21, 22
13. Howbeit when He, the Spirit of truth, is come, He will guide you into all truth: for He shall not speak of Himself; but whatsoever He shall hear, that shall He speak: and He will show you things to come.
14. He shall glorify Me: for He shall receive of Mine, and shall show it unto you.
15. All things that the Father hath are mine: therefore said I, that He shall take of Mine, and shall show it unto you.
—John 16:13-15
11. And He gave some, apostles; and some, prophets; and some, evangelists; and some, pastors and teachers;
12. For the perfecting of the saints, for the work of the ministry, for the edifying of the body of Christ:
13. Till we all come in the unity of the faith, and of the knowledge of the Son of God, unto a perfect man, unto the measure of the stature of the fulness of Christ:
—Ephesians 4:11-13

THE SCRIPTURES CARRY CHRIST'S AUTHORITY

15. And that from a child thou hast known the holy scriptures, which are able to make thee wise unto salvation through faith which is in Christ Jesus.
16. All scripture is given by inspiration of God, and is profitable for doctrine, for reproof, for correction, for instruction in righteousness:
17. That the man of God may be perfect, thoroughly furnished unto all good works.
—2 Timothy 3:15-17

THE NEW TESTAMENT OFFICERS OF THE CHURCH

"Elder" from Greek word presbuteros.
"Bishop" from Greek episkopos—"overseer".
(Paul used the three words interchangeably.)

17. And from Miletus he sent to Ephesus, and called the *elders* of the church.
28. Take heed therefore unto yourselves, and to all the flock, over the which the Holy Ghost hath made you overseers, to feed the church of God, which He hath purchased with His own blood.
—Acts 20:17, 28

1. The *elders* which are among you I exhort, who am also an elder, and a witness of the sufferings of Christ, and also partaker of the glory that shall be revealed:
—1 Peter 5:1
1. The elder unto the elect lady and her children, whom I love in the truth; and not I only, but also all they that have known the truth;
—2 John 1:1
(Read Also: 3 John 1)

QUALIFICATIONS OF AN ELDER

1. This is a true saying, If a man desire the office of a bishop, he desireth a good work.
2. A bishop then must be blameless, the husband of one wife, vigilant, sober, of good behaviour, given to hospitality, apt to teach;
3. Not given to wine, no striker, not greedy of filthy lucre [gain]; but patient, not a brawler, not covetous;
4. One that ruleth well his own house, having his children in subjection with all gravity;
5. (For if a man know not how to rule his own house, how shall he take care of the church of God?)
6. Not a novice, lest being lifted up with pride he fall into the condemnation of the devil.

The Church

7. Moreover he must have a good report of them which are without; lest he fall into reproach and the snare of the devil.
   —1 Timothy 3:1-7
   (Read Also: Titus 1:5-9.)
22. Lay hands suddenly [hastily] on no man, neither be partaker of other men's sins: keep thyself pure.
    —1 Timothy 5:22

ELDERS RESPONSIBILTY AND AUTHORITY

28. Take heed therefore unto yourselves, and to all the flock, over the which the Holy Ghost hath made you overseers, to feed the church of God, which He hath purchased with His own blood.
29. For I know this, that after my departing shall grievous wolves enter in among you not sparing the flock.
30. Also of your own selves shall men arise, speaking perverse things, to draw away disciples after them.
31. Therefore watch, and remember, . . .
35. I have shewed you all things, how that so labouring ye ought to support the weak, and to remember the words of the Lord Jesus, how he said, It is more blessed to give than to receive.
    —Acts 20:28-31, 35
3. Neither as being lords over God's heritage, but being ensamples to the flock.
   —1 Peter 5:3

THE ATTITUDE TOWARD THE ELDERS

12. And we beseech you, brethren, to know them which labour among you, and over you in the Lord, and admonish you;
13. And to esteem them very highly in love for their work's sake. And be at peace among yourselves.
    —1 Thessalonians 5:12, 13
17. Let the elders that rule well be counted worthy of double

honour, especially they who laboured in the word and doctrine.
19. Against an elder receive not an accusation, but before two or three witnesses.
—1 Timothy 5:17, 19
17. Obey them that have the watch for the your souls, as they that must give account, that they may do it with joy, and not with grief: for that is unprofitable for you.
—Hebrews 13:17
5. Likewise, ye younger, submit your selves unto the elder. Yea, all of you be subject one to another, and be clothed with humility: for God resisteth the proud, and giveth grace to the humble.
—1 Peter 5:5

THE DEACONS AND DEACONESS

8. Likewise must the deacons be grave, not doubletongued, not given to much wine, not greedy of filthy lucre [gain];
9. Holding the mystery of the faith in a pure conscience.
10. and let these also first be proved; then let them use the office of a deacon, being found blameless.
11. Even so must their wives be grave, not slanderers, sober, faithful in all things.
12. Let the deacons be the husbands of one wife, ruling their children and their own houses well.
13. For they that have used the office of a deacon well purchase to themselves a good degree [good standing], and great boldness in the faith which is in Christ Jesus.
—1 Timothy 3:8-13

DEALING WITH PRIVATE OFFENSES

15. Moreover if thy brother shall trespass against thee, go and tell him his fault between thee and him alone: if he shall hear thee, thou hast gained thy brother.
16. But if he will not hear thee, then take with thee one or two more, that in the mouth of two or three witnesses every word may be established.

17. And if he shall neglect to hear them, tell it unto the church: but if he neglect to hear the church, let him be unto thee as an heathen man and a publican.
—Matthew 18:15-17

DEALING WITH PUBLIC OFFENSES

4. In the name of our Lord Jesus Christ, when ye are gathered together, and my spirit, with the power of our Lord Jesus Christ,
5. To deliver such an one unto Satan for the destruction of the flesh, that the spirit may be saved in the day of the Lord Jesus.
7. Purge out therefore the old leaven, that ye may be a new lump, as ye are unleavened. For even Christ our passover is sacrificed for us:
11. But now I have written unto you not to keep company, if any man that is called a brother be a fornicator, or covetous, or an idolater, or a railer, or a drunkard, or an extortioner; with such an one no not to eat.
13. But them that are without God judgeth. Therefore put away from among yourselves that wicked person.
—1 Corinthians 5:4, 5, 7, 11, 13

DEALING WITH DIVISIVE PERSONS

17. Now I beseech you, brethren, mark them which cause division and offences contrary to the doctrine which ye have learned; and avoid them.
—Romans 16:17
6. Now we command you brethren, in the name of our Lord Jesus Christ, that ye withdraw yourselves from every brother that walketh disorderly, and not after the tradition which he received of us.
14. And if any man obey not our word by this epistle, note that man, and have no company with him, that he may be ashamed.

15. Yet count him not as an enemy, but admonish him as a brother.
—2 Thessalonians 3:6, 14, 15
10. A man that is an heretick after the first and second admonition reject;
11. Knowing that he that is such subverted, and sinneth, being condemned of himself.
—Titus 3:10, 11

RESTORATION OF OFFENDERS

6. Sufficient to such a man is this punishment, which was inflicted of many.
7. So that contrariwise ye ought rather to forgive him, and comfort him, lest perhaps such a one should be swallowed up with overmuch sorrow.
8. Wherefore I beseech you that ye would confirm your love toward him.
9. For to this end also did I write, that I might know the proof of you, whether ye be obedient in all things.
10. To whom ye forgive any thing, I forgive also: for if I forgave any thing . . . for your sakes forgave I it in the person of Christ;
—2 Corinthians 2:6-10
20. Behold, I stand at the door, and knock: if any man hear my voice, and open the door, I will come into him, and will sup with him, and he with me.
—Revelation 3:20

CHAPTER 25
UNITY IN THE BODY OF CHRIST AND SPIRITUAL GIFTS AND MINISTRIES

FIRST: UNITY

34. A new commandment I give unto you, That ye love one another; as I have loved you, that ye also love one another.
35. By this shall all men know that ye are My disciples, if ye have love one to another.
—John 13:34, 35
1. Behold, how good and how pleasant it is for brethren to dwell together in UNITY!
—Psalms 133:1
20. Neither pray I for these alone, but for them also which shall believe on Me through their word;
21. That they all may be one; as thou, Father, art in Me, as I in thee, that they also may be one in Us: that the world may believe that thou hast sent Me.
22. And the glory which thou gavest Me I have given them; that they may be one, even as We are one:
23. I in them, and thou in Me, that they may be made perfect in one; and that the world may know that thou hast sent Me, and hast loved them, as thou hast loved Me.
24. Father, I will that they also, whom thou hast given Me, be with Me where I Am; that they may behold My glory, which thou hast given Me: for thou lovedst Me before the foundation of the world.
—John 17:20-24

UNITY OF THE SPIRIT

13. For by one Spirit are we all baptized into one body, whether we be Jews or Gentiles, whether we be bond or free; and have been all made to drink into one Spirit.
—1 Corinthians 12:13

3. Endeavouring to keep the unity of the Spirit in the bond of peace.
4. There is one body, and one Spirit, even as ye are called in one hope of your calling;
5. One Lord, one faith, one baptism,
6. One God and Father of all, who is above all, and through all, and in you all.
—Ephesians 4:3-6

3. For what if some did not believe? shall their unbelief make the faith of God without effect?
4. God forbid: yea, let God be true, but every man a liar; as it is written, That thou mightest be justified in thy sayings, and mightest overcome when thou art judged.
5. But if our unrighteousness command the righteousness of God, what shall we say? Is God unrighteous who taketh vengeance? (I speak as a man)
6. God forbid: for then how shall God Judge the world?
—Romans 3:3-6

4. Now there are diversities of gifts, but the same Spirit.
5. And there are differences of administrations, but the same Lord.
6. And there are diversities of operations, but it is the same God which worketh all in all.
—1 Corinthians 12:4-6

UNITY IN DIVERSITY

11. But all these worketh that one and the selfsame Spirit, dividing to every man severally as he will.
—1 Corinthians 12:11

1. I Am the true vine, and My Father is the husbandman.
2. Every branch in Me that beareth not fruit He taketh away:

and every branch that beareth fruit, He purgeth [prunes] it, that it may bring forth more fruit.
3. Now ye are clean through the word which I have spoken unto you.
4. Abide in Me, and I in you. As the branch cannot bear fruit of itself, except it abide in the vine; no more can ye, except ye abide in Me.
5. I am the vine, ye are the branches: He that abideth in Me, and I in him, the same bringeth forth much fruit: for without Me ye can do nothing.
6. If a man abide not in Me, he is cast forth as a branch, and is withered; and men gather them, and cast them into the fire, and they are burned.
—John 15:1-6
6. And there are diversities of operations, but it is the same God which worketh all in all.
—1 Corinthians 12:6

UNITY OF FAITH

12. Here is the patience of the saints: here are they that keep the commandments of God, and the faith of Jesus.
—Revelation 14:12

STRENGTH IN UNITY

9. For we are labourers together with God: ye are God's husbandry [field], ye are God's building.
—1 Corinthians 3:9

UNITY TRANSCENDS HUMAN DIFFERENCES

26. For ye are all the children of God by faith in Christ Jesus.
27. For as many of you as have been baptized into Christ have put on Christ.
28. There is neither Jew nor Greek, there is neither bond nor free, there is neither male nor female: for ye are all one in Jesus Christ.
—Galatians 3:26-28

UNITY THROUGH DIFFERENT GIFTS

3. Endeavouring to keep the unity of the Spirit in the bond of peace.
11. And He gave some, apostles; and some, prophets; and some, evangelists; and some, pastors and teachers;
12. For the perfecting of the saints, for the work of the ministry, for the edifying of the body of Christ:
13. Till we all come in the unity of the faith, and of the knowledge of the Son of God, unto a perfect man, unto the measure of the stature of the fulness of Christ:
14. That we henceforth be no more children, tossed to and fro, and carried about with every wind of doctrine, by the sleight [deceitfulness] of men, and cunning craftiness, whereby they lie in wait to deceive;
15. But speaking the truth in love, may grow up into Him in all things, which is the head, even Christ:
16. From whom the whole body fitly joined together and compacted [knit together] by that which every joint supplieth, according to the effectual working in the measure of every part, maketh increase of the body unto the edifying of itself in love.
—Ephesians 4:3, 11-16

UNITY AT THE CROSS

32. And I, if I be lifted up from the earth, will draw all men unto Me.
—John 12:32
2. Bear ye one another's burdens, and so fulfil the law of Christ.
—Galatians 6:2

AVOID ATTITUDES OF DIVISIVENESS

9. In this was manifested the love of God toward us, because that God sent His only begotten Son into the world, that we might live through Him.

10. Herein is love, not that we loved God, but that He loved us, and sent His Son to be the propitiation for our sins.
11. Beloved, if God so loved us, we ought also to love one another.
    —1 John 4:9-11
16. This I say then, Walk in the Spirit, and ye shall not fulfil the lust of the flesh.
22. But the fruit of the Spirit is love, joy, peace, longsuffering, gentleness, goodness, faith,
23. Meekness, temperance: against such there is no law.
    —Galatians 5:16, 22, 23
9. But if ye have respect to persons [external appearance], ye commit sin, and are convinced [convicted] of the law as transgressors.
    —James 2:9
34. Then Peter opened his mouth, and said, Of a truth I perceive that God is no respecter of persons:
    —Acts 10:34
40. And the King shall answer and say unto them, Verily I say unto you, Inasmuch as ye have done it unto one of the least of these my brethren, ye have done it unto me.
    —Matthew 25:40

SECONDLY: SPIRITUAL GIFTS AND MINISTRIES

15. And He said unto them, Go ye into all the world, and preach the gospel to every creature.
    —Mark 16:15
4. And, being assembled together with them, commanded them that they should not depart from Jerusalem, but wait for the promise of the Father, which, saith He, ye have heard of Me.
8. But ye shall receive power, after that the Holy Ghost is come upon you: and ye both in Jerusalem, and in all Judaea, and in Samaria, and unto the uttermost part of the earth.
    —Acts 1:4, 8

THE GIFTS OF THE HOLY SPIRIT

38. How God anointed Jesus of Nazareth with the Holy Ghost and with power: who went about doing good, and healing all that were oppressed of the devil; for God was with Him.
—Acts 10:38

5. For John truly baptized with water; but ye shall be baptized with the Holy Ghost not many days hence.
—Acts 1:5

41. Then they that gladly received his word were baptized: and the same day there were added unto them about three thousand souls.
—Acts 2:41

14. For the kingdom of heaven is as a man traveling into a far country, who called his own servants, and delivered unto them his goods.

15. And unto one he gave five talents, to another two, and to another one; to every man according to his several ability; and straightway took his journey.
—Matthew 25:14, 15

34. For the Son of Man is as a man taking a far journey, who left his house, and gave authority to his servants, and to every man his work, and commanded the porter to watch.
—Mark 13:34

8. Wherefore He saith, When He ascended up on high, He led captivity captive, and gave gifts unto men.

7. But unto every one of us is given grace according to the measure of the gift of Christ.
—Ephesians 4:8, 7

11. But all these worketh that one and the selfsame Spirit, dividing to every man severally as He will.
—1 Corinthians 12:11

HARMONY WITHIN THE CHURCH

4. I thank my God always on your behalf, for the grace of God which is given you by Jesus Christ;

Unity In the Body of Christ and Spiritual Gifts

7. So that ye come behind in no gift; waiting for the coming of our Lord Jesus Christ:
   —1 Corinthians 1:4, 7
4. Now there are diversities of gifts, but the same Spirit.
5. And there are differences of administrations, but the same Lord.
6. And there are diversities of operations, but it is the same God which worketh all in all.
11. But all these worketh that one and the selfsame Spirit, dividing to every man severally as he will.
18. But now hath God set the members every one of them in the body, as it hath pleased him.
21. And the eye cannot say unto the hand, I have no need of thee: nor again the head to the feet, I have no need of you.
22. May, much more those members of the body, which seem to be more feeble, are necessary:
23. And those members of the body which we think to be less honourable, upon these we bestow more abundant honour; and our uncomely parts have more abundant comeliness.
24. For our comely parts have no need but God hath tempered the body together having given more abundant honour to that part which lacked:
25. That there should be no schism in the body; but that the members should have the same care one for another.
26. And whether one member suffer, all the members suffer with it; or one member be honoured, all the members rejoice with it.
28. And God hath set some in the church, first apostles, secondarily prophets, thirdly teachers, after that miracles, then gifts of healings, helps, governments, diversities of tongues.
31. But covet [desire] earnestly the best gifts: and yet show I unto you a more excellent way.
    —1 Corinthians 12:4-6, 11, 18, 21-26, 28, 31

11. And He gave some, apostles; and some, prophets; and some, evangelists; and some, pastors and teachers;
—Ephesians 4:11

THE INDISPENSABLE DIMENSION

22. But the fruit of the Spirit is love, joy, peace, longsuffering, gentleness, goodness, faith,
23. Meekness, temperance: against such there is no law.
—Galatians 5:22, 23
9. (For the fruit of the Spirit is in all goodness and righteousness and truth;)
—Ephesians 5:9
4. Charity suffereth long, and is kind; charity envieth not; charity vaunteth not itself, is not puffed up,
8. Charity never faileth: but whether there be prophecies, they shall fail; whether there be tongues, they shall cease; whether there be knowledge, it shall vanish away.
—1 Corinthians 13:4, 8
1. Follow after charity, and desire spiritual gifts, but rather that ye may prophesy.
—1 Corinthians 14:1

LIVING IN GOD'S GLORY

36. For of Him, and through Him, and to Him, are all things: to whom be glory for ever.
—Romans 11:36
1. I beseech you therefore, brethren, by the mercies of God, that ye present your bodies a living sacrifice, holy, acceptable unto God, which is your reasonable service.
2. And be not conformed to this world: but be ye transformed by the renewing of your mind, that ye may prove what is that good, and acceptable, and perfect, will of God.
3. For I say, through the grace given unto me, to every man that is among you, not to think of himself more highly than he ought to think; but to think soberly, according as God hath dealt to every man the measure of faith.

4. For as we have many members in one body, and all members have not the same office:
5. So we, being many, are one body in Christ, and every one members one of another.
6. Having then gifts differing according to the grace that is given to us, whether prophecy, let us prophesy according to the proportion of faith;
7. Or ministry, let us wait on our ministering: or he that teacheth, on teaching;
8. Or he that exhorteth, on exhortation: he that giveth, let him do it with simplicity; he that ruleth, with diligence; he that showeth mercy, with cheerfulness.
9. Let love be without dissimulation. Abhor that which is evil; cleave to that which is good.
10. Be kindly affectioned one to another with brotherly love; in honour preferring one another;
11. Not slothful in business; fervent in spirit; serving the Lord;
—Romans 12:1-11

THE GROWTH OF THE CHURCH

1. I therefore, the prisoner of the Lord, beseech you that ye walk worthy of the vocation wherewith ye are called,
2. With all lowliness and meekness, with longsuffering, forbearing one another in love;
3. Endeavouring to keep the unity of the Spirit in the bond of peace.
16. From whom the whole body fitly joined together and compacted [knit together] by that which every joint supplieth, according to the effectual working in the measure on every part, maketh increase of the body unto the edifying of itself in love.
—Ephesians 4:1-3, 16

A COMMON MINISTRY

9. But ye are a chosen generation [race], a royal priesthood, an holy nation, a peculiar [special] people; that ye should show forth the praises of Him who hath called you out of darkness into His marvellous light:
—1 Peter 2:9

18. And Jesus came and spake unto them, saying, All power is given unto Me in heaven and in earth.
19. Go ye therefore, and teach all nations, baptizing them in the name of the Father, and of the Son, and of the Holy Ghost:
20. Teaching them to observe all things whatsoever I have commanded you: and, lo, I Am with you always, even unto the end of the world.
—Matthew 28:18-20

6. And I saw another angel fly in the midst of heaven, having the everlasting gospel to peach unto them that dwell on the earth, and to every nation, and kindred, and tongue, and people.
7. Saying with a loud voice, Fear God, and give glory to Him; for the hour of His judgment is come: and worship Him that made heaven, and earth, and the sea, and the fountains of waters.
8. And there followed another angel, saying, Babylon is fallen, is fallen, that great city, because she made all nations drink of the wine of the wrath of her fornication.
9. And the third angel followed them, saying with a loud voice, If any man worship the beast and his image, and receive his mark in his forehead, or in his hand,
10. The same shall drink of the wine of the wrath of God, which is poured out without mixture into the cup of His indignation; and he shall be tormented with fire and brimstone in the presence of the holy angels, and in the presence of the Lamb:
11. And the smoke of their torment ascendeth up for ever and ever: and they have no rest day nor night, who worship

the beast and his image, and whosoever receiveth the mark of his name.
12. Here is the patience of the saints: here are they that keep the commandments of God, and the faith of Jesus.
—Revelation 14:6-12

THE FAILURE TO USE SPIRITUAL GIFTS

26. His lord answered and said unto him, Thou wicked and slothful servant, thou knowest that I reap where I sowed not, and gather where I have not strawed [winnowed]:
27. Thou oughtest therefore to have put my money to the exchangers, and then at my coming I should have received mine own with usury.
28. Take therefore the talent from him, and give it unto him which hath ten talents.
29. For unto every one that hath shall be given, and he shall have abundance: but from him that hath not shall be taken away even that which he hath.
30. And cast ye the unprofitable servant into outer darkness: there shall be weeping and gnashing of teeth.
—Matthew 25:26-30

SPIRITUAL PREPARATION AND GUIDANCE

5. If any of you lack wisdom, let him ask of God, that giveth to all men liberally, and upbraideth not; and it shall be given him. —James 1:5
13. For it is God which worketh in you both to will and to do of His good pleasure.
—Philippians 2:13

CHAPTER 26
BAPTISM

BAPTISM—PART OF OUR CHRISTIAN CONFESSION

16. He that believeth and is baptized shall be saved; but he that believeth not shall be damned.
—Mark 16:16
37. Now when they heard this, they were pricked in their heart, and said unto Peter and the rest of the apostles, Men and brethren, what shall we do?
38. Then Peter said unto them, Repent, and be baptized every one of you in the name of Jesus Christ for the remission of sins and ye shall receive the gift of the Holy Ghost.
—Acts 2:37, 38

JESUS BAPTIZED BY IMMERSION IN THE JORDAN RIVER.

9. And it came to pass in those days, that Jesus came from Nazareth of Galilee, and was baptized of John in Jordan.
10. And straightway coming up out of the water, He saw the heavens opened, and the Spirit like a dove descending upon Him:
11. And there came a voice from heaven, saying, Thou art my beloved Son, in whom I am well pleased.
—Mark 1:9-11

THE ONLY DESCRIPTION WE HAVE OF HOW THE APOSTLES BAPTIZED PEOPLE IS BY IMMERSION.

36. And as they went on their way, they came unto a certain water: and the eunuch said, See, here is water; what doth hinder me to be baptized?
37. And Philip said, If thou believest with all thine heart, thou mayest, and he answered and said, I believe that Jesus Christ is the Son of God.
38. And he commanded the chariot to stand still: and *they went down both into the water*, both Philip and the eunuch; and he baptized him.
39. And when they were come up out of the water, the Spirit of the Lord caught away Philip, that the eunuch saw him no more: and he went on his way rejoicing.
—Acts 8:36-39

NO RECORD IN BIBLE OF INFANT BAPTISM

12. But when they believed Philip preaching the things concerning the Kingdom of God, and the name of Jesus Christ, they were baptized, both men and women.
—Acts 8:12

WE ARE TO BE BURIED (COVERED OVER) WITH CHRIST IN BAPTISM.

12. [We are] Buried with Him in baptism wherein also ye are risen with Him through the faith of the operation of God, who hath raised Him from the dead.
—Colossians 2:12

BEFORE BAPTISM A PERSON MUST BE TAUGHT ALL THINGS A CHRISTIAN MUST FOLLOW.

19. Go ye therefore, and teach all nations, baptizing them in the name of the Father, and of the Son, and of the Holy Ghost:

20. Teaching them to observe all things whatsoever I have commanded you: and, lo, I am with you always, even unto the end of the world.
—Matthew 28:19, 20

WHEN A PERSON RECEIVES THE FULL CHRISTIAN MESSAGE IT IS WELL TO BE RE-BAPTIZED.

1. . . . Paul having passed through the upper coasts came to Ephesus: and finding certain disciples,
2. He said unto them, Have ye received the Holy Ghost since ye believed? And they said unto him, We have not so much as heard whether there be any Holy Ghost.
3. And he said unto them, Unto what then were ye baptized? And they said, Unto John's baptism.
4. Then said Paul, John verily baptized with the baptism of repentance, saying unto the people, that they should believe on Him which should come after him, that is on Christ Jesus.
5. When they heard this, they were baptized in the name of the Lord Jesus.
—Acts 19:1-5

AFTER BAPTISM WE RISE IN NEWNESS OF LIFE.

3. Know ye not, that so many of us as were baptized into Jesus Christ were baptized into His death.
4. Therefore we are buried with Him by baptism into death: that like as Christ was raised up from the dead by the glory of the Father, even so we also should walk in newness of life.
5. For if we have been planted together in the likeness of His death, we shall be also in the likeness of His resurrection:
8. Now if we be dead with Christ, we believe that we shall also live with Him:
—Romans 6:3-5, 8

1. If ye then be risen with Christ, seek those things which are above where Christ sitteth on the right hand of God.
 —Colossians 3:1

THROUGH BAPTISM WE "PUT ON CHRIST".

27. For as many of you as have been baptized into Christ have put on Christ.
 —Galatians 3:27

AFTER BAPTISM WE ARE TO WALK AS DID JESUS.

6. He that saith he abideth in Him ought himself also so to walk, even as He walked.
 —1 John 2:6

THERE IS ONLY ONE BIBLICAL METHOD OF BAPTISM

4. There is one body, and one Spirit, even as ye are called in one hope of your calling;
5. One Lord, one faith, one baptism,
6. One God and Father of all, who is above all, and through all, and in you all.
 —Ephesians 4:4-6

(Baptize from Greek "baptzein" = to dip)
[Note: Sprinkling not accepted as equal to immersion by the European medieval church until 1300 A.D.]

14. Blessed are they that do His commandments, that they may have right to the tree of life, and may enter in through the gates into the city.
 —Revelation 22:14

CHAPTER 27

BORN AGAIN

BORN AGAIN CHRISTIANS

3. Jesus answered and said unto him, Verily, verily, I say unto thee, Except a man be *born again*, he cannot see the kingdom of God.
4. Nicodemus saith unto Him, How can a man be born when he is old? can he enter the second time into his mother's womb, and be born?
5. Jesus answered, Verily, verily, I say unto thee, Except a man be born of water and of the Spirit, he cannot enter into the kingdom of God.
6. That which is *born* of the *flesh* is flesh; and that which is *born* of the *spirit* is *spirit.*
—John 3:3-6
(Read full story: John 3:1-15)

GOD HAS A SPIRITUAL NATURE

23. But the hour cometh, and now is, when the true worshippers shall worship the Father in spirit and in *truth*: for the Father seeketh such to worship Him.
24. God is a Spirit: and they that worship Him must worship Him in *spirit* and in *truth.*
—John 4:23, 24
(Read entire story: John 4:5-42)

[Man cannot truly worship God until he is born again and receives a new Spiritual nature.]

GOD CREATED THE MAN AND WOMAN WITH A SPIRITUAL NATURE.

27. So God created man in His own image, in the image of God created He him: male and female created He them.
—Genesis 1:27

WHEN MAN SINNED THE SPIRITAL NATURE DIED THAT VERY DAY

17. But of the tree of the knowledge of good and evil, thou shalt not eat of it: for in the *day* that thou eatest thereof thou shalt surely die.
—Genesis 2:17

10. And he [Adam] said, I heard Thy voice in the garden, and I was afraid, because I was naked: and I hid myself.

11. And He said, Who told thee that thou wast naked? Hast thou eaten of the tree, whereof I commanded thee that thou shouldest not eat?
—Genesis 3:10, 11

[Adam and Eve were naked because the Spiritual nature covering (glorification) had died.]

ALL THAT WAS LEFT WAS A BODY OF FLESH

24. O wretched man that I am! who shall deliver me from the body of this death?
—Romans 7:24

WHEN BORN AGAIN WE ARE GIVEN BACK OUR SPIRITUAL NATURE THROUGH CHRIST AND THE HOLY SPIRIT.

23. Being born again, not of corruptible seed, but of incorruptible, by the word of God, which liveth and abideth for ever.
—1 Peter 1:23

4. Whereby are given unto us exceeding great and precious promises: that by these ye might be partakers of the divine [Spiritual] nature, having escaped the corruption that is in the world through lust.
—2 Peter 1:4

[We cannot pass on a Spiritual nature to our children, only our fleshly nature. Ever since Eden our children are born already half dead.]

WE CAN GET BACK OUR SPIRITUAL NATURE BY BELIEVEING ON JESUS CHRIST

24. Verily, verily, I say unto you, He that *heareth My word*, and *believeth* on Him that sent Me, hath *everlasting life*, and shall not come into condemnation; but is passed from death unto life.
—John 5:24

30. And brought them out, and said, Sirs, what must I do to be saved?
31. And they said, *believe* on the Lord Jesus Christ, and thou shalt be saved, and thy house.
—Acts 16:30, 31
(Read entire story: Acts 16:16-40)

BELIEF IS THE EXERCISE OF FAITH

50. And He said to the woman, Thy faith hath saved thee; go in peace.
—Luke 7:50

IF YOU HAVE JESUS YOU HAVE EVERY THING. NOW YOU HAVE BOTH A BODY OF FLESH PLUS A SPIRITUAL NATURE (THROUGH CHRIST.)

11. And this is the record, that God hath given to us eternal life, and this life is in His Son.
12. He that hath the Son hath life; and he that hath not the Son of God hath not life.

13. These things have I written unto you that *believe* on the name of the Son of God; that ye may know that ye have eternal life, and that ye may *believe* on the name of the Son of God.
—1 John 5:11-13
3. For we are [of] the circumcision [Israelites by faith], which worship God in the Spirit, and rejoice in Christ Jesus, and have no confidence in the flesh.
—Philippians 3:3

A NEW BORN BABE MUST BE NOURISHED AND INSTRUCTED, TO GROW UP IN CHRIST

17. Therefore if any man be in Christ, he is a new creature: old things are passed away; behold, all things are become new.
—2 Corinthians 5:17

THE OLD MAN OF SIN MUST BE STARVED OUT

22. That ye put off concerning the former conversation [behavior] the old man, which is corrupt according to the deceitful lusts;
—Ephesians 4:22
24. And that ye put on the new man, which after God is created in righteousness and true holiness.
—Ephesians 4:24

THE SPIRITUAL NATURE OF A BORN AGAIN CHRISTIAN DOES NOT SIN BUT IS THE FLESHLY NATURE THAT WARS AGAINST THE SPIRITUAL NATURE THAT SINS

9. Whosoever is born of God doth not commit sin; for his seed remaineth in him: and he cannot sin, because he is born of God.
—1 John 3:9

18. We know that whosoever is born of God sinneth not; but he that is begotten of God keepeth himself, and that wicked one toucheth him not.
—1 John 5:18
1. My little children, these things write I unto you, that ye sin not. And if any man sin, we have an advocate with the Father, Jesus Christ the righteous:
—1 John 2:1
6. And because ye are [born again] sons, God hath sent forth the Spirit of His Son into your hearts, crying, Abba, Father.
—Galatians 4:6

NEW INFANT CHRISTIANS NEED THE SIMPLE MILK OF THE WORD AND NOT HEAVY FOOD.

13. For every one that useth milk is unskilful in the word of righteousness: for he is a babe.
—Hebrews 5:13
2. As newborn babes, desire the sincere [pure] milk of the word, that ye may grow thereby:
—1 Peter 2:2
14. For we know that the law is spiritual: but I am carnal, sold under sin.
15. For that which I do I allow not [understand not] for what I would, that do I not; but what I hate, that do I.
16. If then I do that which I would not, I consent unto the law that it is good.
17. Now then it is no more I that do it, but sin that dwelleth in me.
18. For I know that in me (that is, in my flesh,) dwelleth no good thing: for to will is present with me; but how to perform that which is good I find not.
—Romans 7:14-18
6. Knowing this, that our old man is crucified with Him, that the body of sin might be destroyed, that henceforth we should not serve sin.
—Romans 6:6

IT IS THE WORD OF GOD THAT GIVES US NOURISHMENT AND INSTRUCTION

11. Thy word have I hid in mine heart, that I might not sin against thee.
—Psalms 119:11
105. Thy word is a lamp unto my feet, and a light unto my path.
—Psalms 119:105

TO STAY HEALTHY A PERSON MUST HAVE NOURISHMENT (BIBLE READING), AIR TO BREATHE (PRAYER) AND EXERCISE (WITNESSING).

9. That if thou shalt *confess [witness]* with thy mouth the Lord Jesus, and shalt *believe* in thine heart that God hath raised Him from the dead, thou shalt be saved.
10. For with the heart man *believeth* unto righteousness; and with the mouth *confession [witnessing]* is made unto salvation.
—Romans 10:9, 10

FOCUSING ON CHRIST MAKES US LIKE HIM

18. But we all, with open face beholding as in a glass [mirror] the glory of the Lord, are changed into the same image from glory to glory, even as by the Spirit of the Lord.
—2 Corinthians 3:18

THE FLESHLY NATURE WARS AGAINST THE NEW BORN SPIRITUAL NATURE

29. But as then he that was born after the flesh persecuted him that was born after the Spirit, even so it is now.
—Galatians 4:29
16. This I say then, Walk in the Spirit, and ye shall not fulfil the lust of the flesh.
—Galatians 5:16

3. For though we walk in the flesh, we do not war after the flesh:
4. (For the weapons of our warfare are not carnal [fleshly], but mighty through God [Spiritual] to the pulling down of strong holds;)
5. Casting down imaginations, and every high thing that exalteth itself against the knowledge of God, and bringing into captivity every thought to the obedience of Christ;
—2 Corinthians 10:3-5
16. For which cause we faint not; but though our *outward [fleshly]* man perish, yet the *inward [spiritual]* man is renewed day by day [by reading the Bible, prayer and witness].
—2 Corinthians 4:16
12. Fight the good fight of faith (by staying close to Jesus), lay hold on eternal life, whereunto thou art also called, and hast professed a good profession before many witnesses.
17. Charge them that are rich in this world, that they be not highminded [proud], nor trust in uncertain riches, but in the living God, who giveth us richly all things to enjoy;
—1 Timothy 6:12, 17
4. For whatsoever is *born of God [A born again Christian]* overcometh the world [our fleshly nature]: and this is the victory that overcometh the world, *even our faith.*
—1 John 5:4

CHAPTER 28
THE GIFT OF TONGUES

CHRIST COMMISSIONS THE PREACHING OF THE GOSPEL

15. And he said unto them, Go ye into all the world, and preach the gospel to every creature.
—Mark 16:15

THE LORD WILL PROTECT THOSE WHO FOLLOW THE GOSPEL COMMISSION AS FOLLOWS:

17. And these signs shall follow them that believe; In my name shall they cast out devils; they shall speak with new tongues;
18. They shall take up serpents (Read Also: Acts 28:3-6); and if they drink any deadly thing, it shall not hurt them; they shall lay hands on the sick (many examples), and they shall recover.
20. And they went forth, and preached every where, the Lord working with them, and confirming the word with signs following.
—Mark 16:17, 18, 20

FIRST THEY MUST WAIT FOR THE HOLY SPIRIT

11. I indeed baptize you with water unto repentance: but He that cometh after me is mightier than I, whose shoes I am

not worthy to bear: He shall baptize you with the Holy Ghost, and with fire:
—Matthew 3:11

THE HOLY SPIRIT WILL GIVE POWER TO WITNESS (HOLY GHOST = HOLY SPIRIT)

8. But ye shall receive power, after that the Holy Ghost is come upon you: and ye shall be witnesses unto me both in Jerusalem, and in all Judaea, and in Samaria, and unto the uttermost part of the earth.
—Acts 1:8
1. And when the day of Pentecost was fully come, they were all with one accord in one place.
2. And suddenly there came a sound from heaven as of a rushing mighty wind, and it filled all the house where they were sitting.
3. And there appeared unto them cloven tongues like as of fire, and it sat upon each of them.
4. And they were all filled with the Holy Ghost, and began to speak with other tongues, as the Spirit gave them utterance.
5. And there were dwelling at Jerusalem Jews, devout men, out of every nation under heaven.
6. Now when this was noised abroad, the multitude came together, and were confounded, because that every man *heard [miracle of hearing]* them speak in his own [nation's] language.
7. And they were all amazed and marvelled, saying one to another, Behold, are not all these which speak Galilaeans [who speak only Aramaic]?
8. And how hear we every man in our own [nation's] tongue, wherein we were born?
9. Parthians, and Medes, and Elamites, and the dwellers in Mesopotamia, and in Judaea, and Cappadocia, in Pontus, and Asia,

10. Phrygia, and Pamphylia, in Egypt, and in the parts of Libya about Cyrene, and strangers of Rome, Jews and proselytes,
11. Cretes and Arabians, we do *hear [miracles of hearing]* them speak in our tongues the wonderful works of God.
—Acts 2:1-11

THESE GIFTS WERE THE FORMER RAIN SPOKEN OF BY THE PROPHET JOEL

23. Be glad then, ye children of Zion, and rejoice in the LORD your God: for He hath given you the *former rain* moderately, and He [the Holy Spirit] will cause to come down for you the rain, the former rain . . .
28. And it shall come to pass ofterward, that I will pour out My Spirit upon all flesh, and your sons and your daughters shall prophesy, your old men shall dream dreams, your young men shall see visions:
29. And also upon the servants and upon the handmaids in those days will I pour out My Spirit.
—Joel 2:23, 28, 29
[In the last days it will happen again as the *latter rain*.]
(Read Also: Joel 2:23 and 28-31)

PETER'S FIRST MISSION TRIP TO GENTILES

44. While Peter yet spake these words, the Holy Ghost fell on all them which heard the word.
45. And they of the circumcision which believed were astonished, as many as came with Peter, because that on the Gentiles also was poured out the gift of the Holy Ghost.
46. For they heard them speak with tongues [languages other than their own], and magnify God. Then answered Peter,
47. Can any man forbid water, that these should not be baptized, which have received the Holy Ghost as well as we?
—Acts 10:44-47

GIFT OF PROPHECY MORE IMPORTANT THAN GIFT OF TONGUES

1. Follow after charity, and desire spiritual gifts, but rather that ye may prophecy.
2. For he that speaketh in an unknown tongue [not known by anyone] speaketh not unto men, but unto God: for no man understandeth him; howbeit in the spirit he speaketh mysteries.
3. But he that prophesieth speaketh unto men to edification, and exhortation, and comfort.

EDIFY = ENLIGHTEN, ELEVATE, UPLIFT

4. He that speaketh in an unknown tongue edifieth himself; but he that prophesieth edifieth the church.
5. I would that ye all spake with tongues, but rather that ye prophesied: for greater is he that prophesieth than he that speaketh with tongues, except he interpret, that the church may receive edifying.
6. Now, brethren, if I come unto you speaking with tongues, what shall I profit you, except I shall speak to you either by revelation, or by knowledge, or by prophesying, or by doctrine?
9. So likewise ye, except ye utter by the tongue words easy to be understood, who shall it be known what is spoken? for ye shall speak into the air.
13. Wherefore let him that speaketh in an unknown tongue pray that he may interpret.
14. For if I pray in an unknown tongue, my spirit prayeth, but my understanding is unfruitful [benefits no one].
15. What is it then? I will pray with the spirit, and I will pray with the understanding also: I will sing with the spirit, and I will sing with the understanding also.
16. Else when thou shalt bless with the spirit, how shall he that occupieth the room of the unlearned say Amen at thy giving of thanks, seeing he understandeth not what thou sayest?

The Gift of Tongues

17. For thou verily givest thanks well, but the other is not edified.
18. I thank my God, I speak with tongues more than ye all:
19. Ye in the church I had rather speak five words with my understanding, that by my voice I might teach others also, than ten thousand words in any unknown tongue.
22. Wherefore tongues are for a sign, not to them that believe, but to them that believe not: but prophesying serveth not for them that believe not, but for them which believe.
23. If therefore the whole church become together into one place, and all speak with tongues, and there come in those that are unlearned, or unbelievers, will they not say that ye are mad?
24. But if all prophesy, and there come in one that believeth not, or one unlearned [an outsider], he is convinced of all, he is judged of all:
27. If any man speak in an unknown tongue, let it be by two, or at the most by three, and that by course [one at a time]; and let one interpret.
28. But if there be no interpreter, let him keep silence in the church; and let him speak to himself, and to God.
39. Wherefore, brethren, covet earnestly [desire] to prophesy, and forbid not to speak with tongues.
40. Let all things be done *decently* and in *order*.
   —1 Corinthians 14:1-6, 9, 13-19, 22-24, 27, 28, 39, 40

[There seems to be a perverted use of the gift of tongues in the church at Corinth. This was a gift as a sign to unbelievers but was having the opposite effect at Corinth.]

1. . . . Paul . . . came to Ephesus: and finding certain disciples,
2. He said unto them, Have ye received the Holy Ghost since ye believed? And they said unto him, We have not so much as heard whether there be any Holy Ghost.

3. And he said unto them, Unto what then where ye baptized? And they said, Unto John's baptism.
4. Then said Paul, John verily baptized with the baptism of repentance, saying unto the people, that they should believe on him which should come after him, that is, on Christ Jesus.
5. When they heard this, they were baptized in the name of the Lord Jesus.
6. And when Paul had laid his hands upon them, the Holy Ghost came on them; and they spake with tongues, and prophesied.
7. And all the men were about twelve.
—Acts 19:1-7

THERE ARE MANY GIFTS OF THE SPIRIT SOME HAVE ONE, OTHERS HAVE ANOTHER.

4. Now there are diversities of gifts, but the same Spirit.
5. And there are differences of administrations, but the same Lord.
6. And there are diversities of operations, but it is the same God which worketh all in all.
7. But the manifestation of the Spirit is given to every man to profit withal.
8. For to one is given by the spirit the word of *wisdom*; to another the word of *knowledge* by the same Spirit;
9. To another faith by the same Spirit; to another the gifts of *healing* by the same Spirit;
10. To another the working of *miracles*; to another *prophecy*; to another discerning of spirits; to another divers kinds of *tongues*; to another the *interpretation of tongues*;

[A human cannot manipulate the gifts of the Spirit. The Holy Spirit bestows gifts on people at His own choosing. Christians should stand ready to be used by the Holy Spirit not to try and use the Holy Spirit.]

11. But all these worketh that one and the selfsame Spirit, dividing [bestowing] to every man severally [one or more] as He [the Holy Spirit] will.

12. For as the body is one, and hath many members, and all the members of that one body, being many, and are one body: so also is Christ.
13. For by one Spirit are we all baptized into one body, whether we be Jews or Gentiles, whether we be bond or free; and have been all made to drink into one Spirit.
   —1 Corinthians 12:4-13
27. Now ye are the body of Christ, and members in particular.
28. And God hath set some in the church, first *apostles*, secondarily *prophets*, thirdly *teachers*, after that *miracles*, then gifts of *healing*, *helps*, *governments*, diversities of *tongues*.

[It is not God's wish that everyone have the same gift.]

29. Are all apostles? are all prophets? are all teachers? are all workers of miracles?
30. Have all the gifts of healing? do all speak with tongues? do all interpret?
31. But covet [desire] earnestly the best gifts: and yet show I unto you a more excellent way.
   —1 Corinthians 12:27-31

THE MORE EXCELLENT WAY IS LOVE

1. Though I speak with the tongues of men and of angels, and have not charity [love], I am become as sounding brass, or a tinkling cymbal.
   —1 Corinthians 13:1

[Without love, speaking in tongues is just so much noise for no good purpose.]

HOW LONG WILL THE GIFTS BE NEEDED?

8. Charity never faileth: but whether there be prophecies, they shall fail; whether there be tongues, they shall cease; whether there be knowledge, it shall vanish away.
   —1 Corinthians 13:8

WHEN WILL THE GIFTS OF THE HOLY SPIRIT NO LONGER BE NEEDED?

10. But when that which is perfect is come [Christ], then that which is in part shall be done away.
—1 Corinthians 13:10

[A person does not need to speak in tongues to demonstrate He/she has any other gifts of the Holy Spirit.]

THE FRUIT OF THE SPIRIT IS DIFFERENT THAN THE GIFT OF THE SPIRIT

22. But the fruit of the Spirit is love, *joy, peace, longsuffering, gentleness, goodness, faith,*
23. *meekness, temperance:* against such there is no law.
—Galatians 5:23

[Every Christian should have *all* of the fruits of the Spirit.]

9. (For the fruit of the Spirit is in all *goodness and righteousness and truth;*)
—Ephesians 5:9
17. For the kingdom of God is not meat [food] and drink; but *righteousness, and peace, and joy* in the Holy Ghost.
—Romans 14:17
4. Charity [love] suffereth long, and is kind; charity envieth not; charity vaunteth not itself, is not puffed up,
5. Doth not behave itself unseemly, seeketh not her own, is not easily provoked, thinketh no evil;
—1 Corinthians 13:4, 5
5. . . . add to your faith virtue; and to virtue *knowledge*;
6. And to knowledge *temperance*: and to temperance *patience*; and to patience *godliness*;
7. And to godliness brotherly kindness; and to *brotherly kindness; charity [love]*.
8. For if these things be in you, and abound, they make you that ye shall neither be barren nor unfruitful in the knowledge of our Lord Jesus Christ.
—2 Peter 1:6-8

CHAPTER 29
THE GIFT OF PROPHECY

THE GIFT OF PROPHECY

20. . . . Jehoshaphat stood and said, Hear me, O judah, and ye inhabitants of Jerusalem; Believe in the LORD your God, so shall ye be established; believe His *prophets*, so shall ye prosper.
    —2 Chronicles 20:20

THE PROPHETIC GIFT IN OLD TESTAMENT TIMES

21. For the *prophecy* came not in old time by the will of man: but holy men of God spake as they were moved by the Holy Ghost.
    —2 Peter 1:21

1. God, who at sundry times and in divers manners [various ways] spake in time past unto the fathers by the *prophets.*
    —Hebrews 1:1

13. Yet the LORD testified against Israel, and against Judah, by all the *prophets*, and by all the seers, saying, Turn ye from your evil ways, and keep My commandments and My statutes, according to all the law which I commanded your fathers, and which I sent to you by My servants the *prophets.*
    —2 Kings 17:13

7. (Beforetime in Israel, when a man went to inquire of God,

thus he spake, Come, and let us go to the seer: for he that is now called a *prophet* was beforetime called a Seer.)
—1 Samuel 9:9
11. For when David was up in the morning, the word of the LORD came unto the *prophet* Gad, David's seer, saying,
12. Go and say unto David, Thus saith the Lord . . .
—2 Samuel 24:11, 12
(Read Also: James 5:17, 18)

THE PROPHETIC GIFT IN THE NEW TESTAMENT CHURCH

6. Having then gifts differing according to the grace that is given to us, whether *prophecy*, let us *prophesy* according to the proportion of faith;
—Romans 12:6
28. And God hath set some in the church, first apostles, secondarily *prophets* . . .
—1 Corinthians 12:28
11. And He gave some, apostles; and some, *prophets*; and some evangelists; and some, pastors and teachers;
—Ephesians 4:11
1. Follow after charity, and desire spiritual gifts, but rather that ye may *prophesy*.
—1 Corinthians 14:1
13. And by a *prophet* the LORD brought Israel out of Egypt, and by a *prophet* was he preserved.
—Hosea 12:13

THEY ASSISTED IN THE FOUNDING OF THE CHURCH

20. And are built upon the foundation of the apostles and *prophets*, Jesus Christ Himself being the chief corner stone:
21. In whom all the building fitly framed together groweth unto an holy temple in the Lord:
—Ephesians 2:20, 21

The Gift of Prophecy

7. Surely the Lord God will do nothing, but He revealeth His secret unto His servants the prophets.
—Amos 3:7
1. Now there were in the church that was at Antioch certain *prophets* and teachers; as Barnabas, and simeon that was called Niger, and Lucius of Cyrene, and Manaen, which had been brought up with Herod the tetrarch, and Saul.
2. As they ministered to the Lord, and fasted, the Holy Ghost said, Separate me Barnabas and Saul for the work whereunto I have called them.
—Acts 13:1, 2; 16:9, 10

THEY EDIFIED AND UNITED THE CHURCH

3. But he that *prophesieth* speaketh unto men to edification, and exhortation, and comfort.
4. He that speaketh in an unknown tongue edifieth himself; but he that *prophesith* edifieth the church.
—1 Corinthians 14:3, 4
11. And He gave some, apostles; and some *prophets*; and some, evangelists; and some, pastors and teachers;
12. For the perfecting of the saints, for the work of the ministry, for the edifying of the body of Christ:
13. Till we all come in the unity of the faith, and of the knowledge of the Son of God, unto a perfect man, unto the measure of the stature of the fulness of Christ:
14. That we henceforth be no more children, tossed to and fro, and carried about with every wind of doctrine, by the sleight of men, and cunning craftiness, whereby they lie in wait to deceive;
—Ephesians 4:11-14

THEY WARNED OF FUTURE DIFFICULTIES

27. And in these days came *prophets* from Jerusalem unto Antioch.
28. And there stood up one of them named Agabus, and signified by the Spirit that there should be great dearth

throughout all the world: which came to pass in the days of Claudius Caesar.

29. Then the disciples, every man according to his ability, determine to send relief unto the brethren which dwelt in Judaea:
30. Which also they did, and sent it to the elders by the hands of Barnabas and Saul.
—Acts 11:27-30

10. And as we tarried there many days, there came down from Judaea a certain *prophet,* named Agabus,
11. And when he was come unto us, he took Paul's girdle, and bound his own hands and feet, and said, Thus saint the Holy Ghost, So shall the Jews as Jerusalem bind the man that owneth this girdle, and shall deliver him into the hands of the Gentiles.
—Acts 21:10, 11

32. And Judas and Silas, being *prophets* also themselves, exhorted the brethren with many words, and confirmed them.
—Acts 15:32

CONTINUATION OF SPIRITUAL GIFTS

19. Quench not the Spirit.
20. Despise not *prophesyings*.
—1 Thessalonians 5:19, 20
1. Follow after charity, and desire spiritual gifts, but rather that ye may *prophesy*.
—1 Corinthians 14:1

PROPHETIC GIFT PRIOR TO THE SECOND ADVENT

28. And it shall come to pass afterward, that I will pour out My spirit upon all flesh; and your sons and your daughters shall *prophesy*, your old men shall dream dreams, your young men shall see visions:
29. And also upon the servants and upon the handmaids in those days will I pour My spirit.

30. And I will show wonders in the heavens and in the earth, blood, and fire, and pillars of smoke.
31. The sun shall be turned into darkness, and the moon into blood, before the great and the terrible day of the *lord come*.
—Joel 2:28-31

THE PROPHETIC GIFT IN THE REMNANT CHURCH

17. And the dragon [Satan] was wroth with the woman [church], and went to make war with the *remenant* of her seed, which keep the commandments of God, and have the testimony of Jesus Christ.
—Revelation 12:17
10. And I fell at his feet to worship him. And he said unto me, See thou do it not: I am thy fellowservant, and of thy brethren that have the testimony of Jesus: worship God: for the testimony of Jesus is the spirit of *prophecy*.
—Revelation 19:10
9. Then saith he unto me, See thou do it not: for I am thy fellowservant, and of thy brethren the *prophets*, and of them which keep the sayings of this book: worship God.
—Revelation 22:9
10. And he saith unto me, Seal not the sayings of the *prophecy* of this book: for the time is at hand.
—Revelation 22:9, 10

HELP IN THE FINAL CRISIS

17. And the dragon was wroth with the woman, and went to make war with the *remnant* of her seed, which keep the commandments of God, and have the testimony of Jesus Christ.
—Revelation 12:17
1. And at that time shall Michael stand up, the great prince which standeth for the children of thy people: and there shall be a time of trouble, such as never was since there was a nation even to that same time: and at that time thy

people shall be delivered, every one that shall be found written in the book.
—Daniel 12:1

TESTING THE PROPHETIC GIFT

20. Despise not *prophesyings*.
21. Prove all things; hold fast that which is good.
    —1 Thessalonians 5:20, 21
 1. Beloved, believe not every spirit, but try the spirits whether they are of God: because many *false prophets* are gone out into the world.
    —1 John 4:1
20. To the law and to the testimony: if they speak not according to this word, it is because there is no light in them.
    —Isaiah 8:20
17. Every good gift and every perfect gift is from above, and cometh down from the Father of lights, with whom is no variableness, neither shadow of turning.
    —James 1:17
21. And if thou say in thine heart, How shall we know the word Which the LORD hath not spoken?
22. When a *prophet* speaketh in the name of the LORD, if the thing follow not, nor come to pass, that is the thing which the LORD hath not spoken, but the *prophet* hath spoken it presumptuously: thou shalt not be afraid of him.
    —Deuteronomy 18:21, 22
    (Read Also: Jeremiah 28:9)

IS CHRIST'S INCARNATION RECOGNIZED

 2. Hereby know ye the Spirit of God: every spirit that confesseth that Jesus Christ is come in the flesh is of God:
 3. And every spirit that confesseth not that Jesus Christ is come in the flesh is not of God: and this is that spirit of Antichrist, whereof ye have heard that it should come; and even now already is it in the world.
    —1 John 4:2, 3

DOES THE PROPHET BEAR GOOD OR BAD FRUIT?

16. Ye shall know them by their fruits. Do men gather grapes of thrones, or figs or thistles?
18. A good tree cannot bring forth evil fruit, neither can a corrupt tree bring forth good fruit.
20. Wherefore by their fruits ye shall know them.
    —Matthew 7:16, 18, 20
22. But the fruit of the Spirit is love, joy, peace, longsuffering, gentleness, goodness, faith,
23. Meekness, temperance: against such there is no law.
    —Galatians 5:22, 23
12. For the perfecting of the saints, for the work of the ministry, for the edifying of the body of Christ:
13. Till we all come in the unity of the faith, and of the knowledge of the Son of God, unto a perfect man, unto the measure of the stature of the fulness of Christ:
14. That we henceforth be no more children, tossed to and fro, and carried about with every wind of doctrine, by the sleight of men, and cunning craftiness, whereby they lie in wait to deceive;
15. But speaking the truth in love, may grow up into him in all things, which is the head, even Christ:
    —Ephesians 4:12-15

CHAPTER 30
THE LORD'S SUPPER

THE LORD'S SUPPER

15. And He said unto them, With desire I have desired to eat this passover with you before I suffer:
16. For I say unto you, I will not any more eat thereof, until it be fulfilled in the kingdom of God.
—Luke 22:15, 16

SEEKING ASCENDANCY

24. And there was also a strife among them, which of them should be accounted the greatest.
—Luke 22:24
1. At the same time came the disciples unto Jesus, saying, Who is the greatest in the kingdom of heaven?
—Matthew 18:1
21. And He said unto her, What wilt thou? She saith unto Him, Grant that these my two sons may sit, the one on thy right hand, and the other on the left, in thy kingdom.
—Matthew 20:21
25. And He said unto them, The kings of the Gentiles exercise lordship over them; and they that exercise authority upon them are called benefactors.
26. But ye shall not be so: but he that is greatest among you, let him be as the younger; and he that is chief, as he that doth serve.
27. For whether is greater, he that sitteth at meat, or he that

serveth? is not he that sitteth at meat? but I am among you as he that serveth.
—Luke 22:25-27

THE SUPPER

14. And when the hour was come, He sat down, and the twelve apostles with Him.
17. And He took the cup, and gave thanks, and said, Take this, and divide it among yourselves:
18. For I say unto you, I will not drink of the fruit of the vine, unto the kingdom of God shall come.
19. And He took bread, and gave thanks, and brake it, and gave unto them, saying, This is my body which is given for you: this do in remembrance of Me.
20. Likewise also the cup after supper, saying, This cup is the new testament in my blood, which is shed for you.
—Luke 22:14, 17-20
(Read Also: Matthew 26:26-30)

THE ORDINANCE OF FOOT WASHING

4. He riseth from supper, and laid aside His garments; and took a towel, and girded himself.
5. After that He poureth water into a basin, and began to wash the disciples' feet, and to wipe them with the towel wherewith He was girded.
6. Then cometh He to Simon Peter: and Peter saith unto Him, Lord, doest thou wash my feet?
7. Jesus answered and said unto him, What I do thou knowest not now; but thou shalt know hereafter.
8. Peter saith unto Him, Thou shalt never wash my feet. Jesus answered him, If I wash thee not, thou hast no part with me.
9. Simon Peter saith unto Him, Lord, not my feet only, but also my hands and my head.
10. Jesus saith to him, He that is washed needeth not save to wash his feet, but is clean every whit: and ye are clean, . . .

12. So after He had washed their feet, and had taken His garments, and was set down again, He said unto them, Know ye what I have done to you?
13. Ye call me Master and Lord: and ye say well; for so I AM.
14. If I then, your Lord and Master, have washed your feet; ye also ought to wash one another's feet.
15. For I have given you an example, that ye should do as I have done to you.
—John 13:4-10, 12-15

A MEMORIAL OF CHRIST'S CONDESCENSION

7. But made Himself of no reputation, and took upon Him the form of a servant, and was made in the likeness of men:
—Philippians 2:7
28. Even as the Son of Man came not to be ministered unto, but to minister and to give His life a ransom for many
—Matthew 20:28
13. For, brethren, ye have been called unto liberty; only use not liberty for an occasion to the flesh, but by love serve one another.
—Galatians 5:13
40. And the King shall answer and say unto them, Verily I say unto you, Inasmuch as ye have done it unto one of the least of these my brethren, ye have done it unto me.
—Matthew 25:40

A FELLOWSHIP OF FORGIVENESS

14. For if ye forgive men their trespasses, your heavenly Father will also forgive you:
15. But if ye forgive not men their trespasses, neither will your Father forgive your trespasses.
—Matthew 6:14, 15

A FELLOWSHIP WITH CHRIST AND BELIEVERS

1. Now before the feast of the Passover, when Jesus knew that His hour was come that He should depart out of this world unto the Father, having loved His own which were in the world, He loved them unto the end.
—John 13:1
34. A new commandment I give unto you, That ye love one another; as I have loved you, that ye also love one another.
—John 13:34
3. Let nothing be done through strife or vainglory; but in lowliness of mind let each esteem other better than themselves.
—Philippians 2:3

THE CELEBRATION OF THE LORD'S SUPPER

16. The cup of blessing which we bless, is it not the communion of the blood of Christ? The bread which we break, is it not the communion of the body of Christ?
—1 Corinthians 10:16
24. And when He had given thanks, He break it, and said, Take, eat: this is My body, which is broken for you: this do in remembrance of me.
—1 Corinthians 11:24

COMMEMORATION OF THE DELIVERANCE FROM SIN

54. Whoso eateth My flesh, and drinketh My blood, hath eternal life; and I will raise Him up at the last day.
—John 6:54
4. Surely He hath borne our griefs, and carried our sorrows: yet we did esteem Him stricken, smitten of God, and afflicted.
5. But He was wounded for our transgressions, He was

bruised for our iniquities: the chastisement of our peace was upon Him; and with His stripes we are healed.
6. All we like sheep have gone astray; we have turned every one to his own way; and the LORD hath laid on Him the iniquity of us all.
7. He was oppressed, and He was afflicted, yet He opened not His mouth: He is brought as a lamb to the slaughter, and as a sheep before her shearers is dumb, so He openeth not His mouth.
8. He was taken from prison and from judgment: and who shall declare His generation? for He was cut off out of the land of the living: for the transgression of my people was He stricken.
9. And He made His grave with the wicked, and with the rich in His death; because He had done no violence, neither was any deceit in His mouth.
—Isaiah 53:4-9

THE BREAD AND THE FRUIT OF THE VINE

1. I am the true vine, and My Father is the husbandman.
—John 15:1
(Read Also: Exodus 24:8)
32. Then Jesus said unto them, Verily, verily, I say unto you, Moses gave you not that bread from heaven; but My Father giveth you the true bread from heaven.
33. For the bread of God is He which cometh down from heaven, and giveth life unto the world.
34. Then said they unto Him, Lord, evermore give us this bread.
35. And Jesus said unto them, I am the bread of life: he that cometh to Me shall never hunger; and he that believeth on Me shall never thirst.
—John 6:32-35
50. This is the bread which cometh down from heaven, that a man may eat thereof, and not die.
51. I am the living bread which came down from heaven: if any man eat of this bread, he shall live for ever: and the

The Lord's Supper

bread that I will give is My flesh, which I will give for the life of the world.
52. The Jews therefore strove among themselves, saying, How can this man give us His flesh to eat?
53. Then Jesus said unto them, Verily, verily, I say unto you, Except ye eat the flesh of the Son of Man, and drink His blood, ye have no life in you.
54. Whoso eateth My flesh, and drinketh My blood, hath eternal life; and I will raise him up at the last day.
55. For My flesh is meat [food] indeed, and My blood is drink indeed.
56. He that eateth My flesh, and drinketh My blood, dwelleth in Me, and I in him.
57. As the living Father sent Me, and I live by [because of] the Father: so he that eateth Me, even he shall live by [because of] Me.
58. This is the bread which came down from heaven: not as your fathers did eat manna, and are dead: he that eateth of this bread shall live for ever.
—John 6:50-58
16. The cup of blessing which we bless, is it not the communion of the blood of Christ? The bread which we break, is it not the communion of the body of Christ?
—1 Corinthians 10:16

ANTICIPATION OF THE SECOND ADVENT

26. For as often as ye eat this bread, and drink this cup, ye do show the Lord's death till He come.
—1 Corinthians 11:26
29. But I say unto you, I will not drink henceforth of this fruit of the vine, until that day when I drink it new with you in my Father's kingdom.
—Matthew 26:29
9. And He saith unto me, Write, Blessed are they which are called unto the marriage supper of the Lamb. And he saith unto me, These are the true sayings of God.
—Revelation 19:9

37. Blessed are those servants, whom the lord when he cometh shall find watching: verily I say unto you, that he shall gird himself, and make them to sit down to meat [food], and will come forth and serve them.
—Luke 12:37

QUALIFICATIONS FOR PARTICIPATION

28. But let a man examine himself, and so let him eat of that bread, and drink of that cup.
29. For he that eateth and drinketh unworthily, eateth and drinketh damnation [condemnation] to himself, not discerning the Lord's body.
—1 Corinthians 11:28, 29

CHAPTER 31
CHRISTIAN BEHAVIOR

CHRISTIAN BEHAVIOR

1. I beseech you therefore, brethren, by the mercies of God, that ye present your bodies a living sacrifice, holy, acceptable unto God, which is your reasonable service.
2. And be not conformed to this world: but be ye transformed by the renewing of your mind, that ye may prove what is that good, and acceptable, and perfect, will of God.
—Romans 12:1, 2
15. I pray not that thou shouldest take them out of the world, but that thou shouldest keep them from the evil.
16. They are not of the world, even as I am not of the world.
—John 17:15, 16

BEHAVIOR AND SALVATION

4. Christ is become of no effect unto you, whosoever of you are justified by the law; ye are fallen from grace.
1. For, brethren, ye have been called unto liberty; only use not liberty for an occasion to the flesh, but by love serve one another.
—Galatians 5:4, 13
1. Brethren, if a man be overtaken in a fault, ye which are spiritual, restore such an one in the spirit of meekness; considering thyself, lest thou also be tempted.

2. Bear ye one another's burdens, and so fulfil the law of Christ.
—Galatians 6:1, 2

THE BLESSING OF PHYSICAL WORK

5. And every plant of the field before if was in the earth, and every herb of the field before it grew: for the LORD God had not caused it to rain upon the earth, and there was not a man to till the ground.
15. And the LORD God took the man, and put him into the garden of Eden to dress it and to keep it.
—Genesis 2:5, 15
19. In the sweat of thy face shalt thou eat bread, till thou return unto the ground; for out of it wast thou taken: for dust thou art, and unto dust shalt thou return.
—Genesis 3:19
6. Go to the ant, thou sluggard; consider her ways, and be wise:
7. Which having no guide, overseer, or ruler,
8. Provideth her meat in the summer, and gathereth her food in the harvest.
9. How wilt thou sleep, O sluggard? when wilt thou arise out of thy sleep?
10. Yet a little sleep, a little slumber, a little folding of the hands to sleep:
11. So shall thy poverty come as one that travelleth, and thy want as an armed man.
12. A naughty person, a wicked man, walketh with a froward [perverse] mouth.
13. He winketh with his eyes, he speaketh with his feet, he teacheth [points] with his fingers;
—Proverbs 6:6-13
23. In all labour there is profit: but the talk of the lips tendeth only to penury [poverty].
—Proverbs 14:23

THE BLESSING OF REST

31. And He said unto them, Come ye yourselves apart into a desert place, and rest a while: for there were many coming and going, and they had no leisure so much as to eat.
—Mark 6:31

8. Remember the sabbath day, to keep it holy.
9. Six days shalt thou labour, and do all thy work:
10. But the seventh day is the sabbath of the LORD thy God: in it thou shalt not do any work, thou, nor thy son, nor thy daughter, thy manservant, nor thy maidservant, nor thy cattle, nor thy stranger that is within thy gates:
11. For in six days the LORD made heaven and earth, the sea, and all that in them is, and rested the seventh day: wherefore the LORD blessed the sabbath day, and hallowed it.
—Exodus 20:8-11

THE EFFECT OF VIEWING MOVIES, T.V. ETC.

15. Love not the world, neither the things that are in the world. If any man love the world, the love of the Father is not in him.
16. For all that is in the world, the lust of the flesh, and the lust of the eyes, and the pride of life, is not of the Father, but is of the world.
—1 John 2:15, 16

29. And if thy right eye offend thee [cause thee to sin], pluck it out, and cast it from thee: for it is profitable for thee that one of thy members should perish, and not that thy whole body should be cast into hell.
30. And if thy right hand offend thee, cut it off, and cast it from thee: for it is profitable for thee that one of thy members should perish, and not that thy whole body should be cast into hell.
—Matthew 5:29, 30

18. But we all, with open face beholding as in a glass [mirror] the glory of the Lord, are changed into the same image from glory to glory, even as by the Spirit of the Lord.
—2 Corinthians 3:18

8. Finally, brethren, whatsoever things are true, whatsoever things are honest, whatsoever things are just, whatsoever things are pure, whatsoever things are lovely, whatsoever things are of good report; if there be any virtue, and if there be any praise, think on these things.
—Philippians 4:8

WE MUST BE CAREFUL OF OUR MUSIC AND READING

11. And that, knowing the time, that now it is high time to awake out of sleep: for now is our salvation nearer than when we [first] believed.
—Romans 13:11

11. . . . I beseech you as strangers and pilgrims, abstain from fleshly lust, which war against the soul;
—1 Peter 2:11

CAREFUL OF OUR ACTIVITIES

15. Love not the world, neither the things that are in the world. If any man love the world, the love of the Father is not in him.
16. For all that is in the world, the lust of the eyes, and the pride of life, is not of the Father, but is of the world.
17. And the world passeth away, and the lust thereof: but he that doeth the will of God abideth for ever,
—1 John 2:15-17

CAREFUL ABOUT OUR FOOD

29. And God said, Behold, I have given you every herb bearing seed, which is upon the face of all the earth, and every tree, in the which is the fruit of a tree yielding seed; to you it shall be for meat [food].
—Genesis 1:29

2. Of every clean beast thou shalt take to thee by sevens, the male and his female: and of beasts that are not clean by two, the male and female.

3. Of fowls also of the air by sevens, the male and the female; to keep seed alive upon the face of all the earth.
—Genesis 7:2, 3

20. And Noah builded an altar unto the LORD: and took of every clean beast, and of every clean fowl, and offered burnt offerings on the altar.
—Genesis 8:20

2. For thou art an holy people unto the LORD thy God, and the LORD hath chosen thee to be a peculiar [special] people unto Himself, above all the nations that are upon the earth.
—Deuteronomy 14:2

24. But I have said unto you, Ye shall inherit their land, and I will give it unto you to possess it, a land that floweth with milk and honey: I am the LORD your God, which have separated you from other people.
—Leviticus 20:24

4. But flesh with the life thereof, which is the blood thereof, shall ye not eat.
—Genesis 9:4

25. Ye shall therefore put difference between clean beasts and unclean, and between unclean fowls and clean: and ye shall not make your souls abominable by beast, or by fowl, or by any manner of living thing that creepeth on the ground, which I have separated from you as unclean.

26. And ye shall be holy unto me: for I the LORD am holy, and have severed you from other people, that ye should be mine.
—Leviticus 20:25, 26
(Read Also: Leviticus 11 and Deuteronomy 14)

WHAT ABOUT ALCOHOLIC BEVERAGES

29. Who hath woe? who hath sorrow? who hath babbling? who hath wounds without cause? who hath redness of eyes?

30. They that tarry long at the wine; they that go to seek mixed wine.
31. Look not thou upon the wine when it is red, when it giveth his colour in the cup, when it moveth itself aright.
32. At the last it biteth like a serpent, and stingeth like an adder.
33. Thine eyes shall behold strange women, and thine heart shall utter perverse things.
34. Yea, thou shalt be as he that lieth down in the midst of the sea, or as he that lieth upon the top of a mast.
35. They have stricken me, shalt thou say, and I was not sick; they have beaten me, and I felt it not: when shall I awake? I will seek it yet again.
—Proverbs 23:29-35
19. Now the works of the flesh are manifest, which are these; Adultery, fornication, uncleanness, lasciviousness,
20. Idolatry, witchcraft, hatred, variance, emulations, wrath, strife, seditions, heresies,
21. Envyings, murders, *drunkenness*, revellings, and such like: of the which I tell you before, as I have also told you in time past, that they which do such things shall not inherit the kingdom of God.
—Galatians 5:19-21
34. And take heed to yourselves, lest at any time your hearts be overcharged with surfeiting, and drunkenness, and cares of this life, and so that day come upon you unawares.
—Luke 21:34
13. Let us walk honestly, as in the day; not in rioting and drunkenness, not in chambering [licentiousness] and wantonness, not in strife and envying.
—Romans 13:13

HOW SHOULD A CHRISTIAN DRESS

25. Therefore I say unto you, Take no [anxious] thought for your life, what ye shall eat, or what ye shall drink; nor yet

for your body, what ye shall put on. Is not the life more than meat, and the body than raiment?
26. Behold the fowls of the air: for they sow not, neither do they reap, nor gather into barns; yet your heavenly Father feedeth them. Are ye not much better than they:
27. Which of you by taking thought can add one cubit unto his stature?
28. And why take ye thought for raiment? Consider the lilies of the field, how they grow; they toil not, neither do they spin;
29. And yet I say unto you, That even Solomon in all his glory was not arrayed like one of these.
30. Wherefore, if God so clothe the grass of the field, which to day is, and tomorrow is cast into the oven, shall he not much more clothe you, O ye of little faith?
31. Therefore take no thought, saying, What shall we eat? or, What shall we drink? or, Wherewithal shall we be clothed?
32. (For after all these things do the Gentiles seek:) for your heavenly Father knoweth that ye have need of all these things.
33. But seek ye first the kingdom of God, and his righteousness; and all these things shall be added unto you.
—Matthew 6:25-33
16. For all that is in the world, the lust of the flesh, and the lust of the eyes, and the pride of life, is not of the Father, but is of the world.
—1 John 2:16
9. In like manner also, that women adorn themselves in modest apparel, with shamefacedness (modesty of character) and sobriety; not with broided hair, or gold, or pearls, or costly array:
10. But (which becometh women professing godliness) with good works.
—1 Timothy 2:9, 10
1. Likewise, ye wives, be in subjection to your own husbands; that, if any obey not the word, they also may without the word be won by the conversation of the wives;

2. While they behold your chaste conversation coupled with fear.
3. Whose adorning let it not be that outward adorning of plaiting the hair, and of wearing of gold, or of putting on of apparel;
4. But let it be the hidden man of the heart, in that which is not corruptible, even the ornament of a meek and quiet spirit, which is in the sight of God of great price.
—1 Peter 3:1-4

GAUDY COSMETICS ASSOCIATED WITH PAGANISM AND APOSTASY

30. And when Jehu was come to Jezreel, Jezebel heard of it; and she painted her face, and tired [adorned] her head, and looked out at a window.
—2 Kings 9:30
30. And when thou art spoiled, what whilt thou do? Though thou clothest thyself with crimson, though thou deckest thee with ornaments of gold, though thou rentest thy face with painting, in vain shalt thou make thyself fair; thy lovers will despise thee, they will seek thy life.
—Jeremiah 4:30

PRINCIPLES OF CHRISTIAN STANDARDS

8. The wind bloweth where it listeth and thou hearest the sound thereof, but canst not tell whence it cometh, and whither it goeth: so is every one that is born of the Spirit.
—John 3:8
22. But the fruit of the Spirit is love, Joy, Peace, longsuffering, gentleness, goodness, faith,
23. Meekness, temperance: against such there is no law.
—Galatians 5:22, 23

LIVING WITH THE MIND OF CHRIST

5. Let this mind be in you, which was also in Christ Jesus:
—Philippians 2:5

16. For who hath known the mind of the Lord, that He may instruct him? But we have the mind of Christ.
—1 Corinthians 2:16

LIVING TO PRAISE AND GLORIFY GOD

1. O God, Thou art my God; early will I seek thee: my soul thirsteth for thee, my flesh longeth for thee in a dry and thirsty land, where no water is;
2. To see Thy power and Thy glory, so as I have seen thee in the sanctuary.
3. Because thy lovingkindness is better than life, my lips shall praise thee.
4. Thus will I bless thee while I live: I will lift up my hands in thy name.
5. My soul shall be satisfied as with marrow and fatness; and my mouth shall praise thee with joyful lips:
—Psalms 63:1-5
22. And whatsoever we ask, we receive of Him, because we keep His commandments, and do those things that are pleasing in His sight.
—1 John 3:22
15. And that He died for all, that they which live should not henceforth live unto themselves, but unto Him which died for them, and rose again.
—2 Corinthians 5:15
31. Whether therefore ye eat, or drink or whatsoever ye do, do all to the glory of God.
—1 Corinthians 10:31

LIVING TO BE AN EXAMPLE AND TO MINISTER

32. Give none offence, neither to the Jews, nor to the Gentiles, nor to the church of God:
33. Even as I please all men in all things, not seeking mine own profit, but the profit of many, that they may be saved.
—1 Corinthians 10:32, 33

16. And herein do I exercise myself, to have always a conscience void of offence toward God, and toward men.
    —Acts 24:16
6. He that saith he abideth in Him ought himself also so to walk, even as He walked.
    —1 John 2:6
28. Even as the Son of Man came not to be ministered unto, but to minister, and to give His life a ransom for many.
    —Matthew 20:28

CHAPTER 32
MARRIAGE AND THE FAMILY

MALE AND FEMALE IN THE IMAGE OF GOD

26. And God said, Let us make man in Our image, after our likeness: and let them have dominion over the fish of the seas, and over the fowl of the air, and over the cattle, and over the earth, and over every creeping thing that creepeth upon the earth.
27. So God created man in His own image, in the image of God created He Him; male & female created He them.
—Genesis 1:26, 27
31. And God saw every thing that He had made, and, behold, it was very good . . .
—Genesis 1:31
20. . . . for Adam there was not found an help meet for him.
—Genesis 2:20
18. And the Lord God said, It is not good that the man should be alone; I will make him an help meet for him.
—Genesis 2:18
21. And the LORD God caused a deep sleep to fall upon Adam, and he slept; and He took one of his ribs, and closed up the flesh instead thereof;
22. And the rib, which the LORD God had taken from man, made He a woman and brought her unto the man.
23. And Adam said, This is now bone of my bone, and flesh of my flesh: she shall be called a Woman, because she was taken out of man.
—Genesis 2:21-23

MARRIAGE

3. Can two walk together, except they be agreed?
—Amos 3:3

24. Therefore shall a man leave his father and his mother, and shall cleave unto his wife: and they shall be one flesh.
—Genesis 2:24

8. And they twain shall be one flesh: so then they are no more twain, but one flesh.

9. What therefore God hath joined together, let not man put asunder.
—Mark 10:8, 9

21. Submitting yourselves one to another in the fear of God.

22. Wives, submit yourselves unto your own husbands, as unto the Lord.

23. For the husband is the head of the wife, even as Christ is the head of the church: and he is the saviour of the body.

24. Therefore as the church is subject unto Christ, so let the wives be to their own husbands in every thing.

25. Husbands, love your wives, even as Christ also loved the church, and gave Himself for it;

28. So ought men to love their wives as their own bodies. He that loveth his wife loveth himself.

29. For no man ever yet hated his own flesh; but nourisheth and cherisheth it, even as the Lord the church:
—Ephesians 5:21-25, 28, 29

14. Yet ye say, Wherefore? Because the LORD hath been witness between thee and the wife of thy youth, against whom thou hast dealt treacherously: yet is she the companion, and the wife of thy covenant,
—Malachi 2:14

34. My covenant will I not break, nor alter the thing that is gone out of my lips.
—Psalms 89:34

6. Wherefore they are no more twain, but one flesh. What therefore God hath joined together, let not man put asunder.
—Matthew 19:6

18. Let thy fountain be blessed: and rejoice with the wife of thy youth.
19. Let her be as the loving hind and pleasant roe; let her breasts satisfy thee at all times; and be thou ravished always with her love.
—Proverbs 5:18, 19
4. Marriage is honorable among all, and the bed undefiled; but fornicators and adulterers God will judge.
—Hebrews 13:4, NKJV

BIBLICAL LOVE

4. Love suffers long and is kind; love does not envy; love does not parade itself, is not puffed up;
5. does not behave rudely, does not seek its own, is not provoked, thinks no evil;
6. does not rejoice in iniquity, but rejoices in the truth;
7. bears all things, endures all things.
8. Love never fails. . . .
—1 Corinthians 13:4-8, NKJV
10. For we must all appear before the judgment seat of Christ; that every one may receive the things done in his body, according to that he hath done, whether it be good or bad.
—2 Corinthians 5:10

THE FAMILY

28. And God blessed them, and God said unto them, Be fruitful, and multiply, and replenish [fill] the earth, and subdue it: and have dominion over the fish of the sea, and over the fowl of the air, and over every living thing that moveth upon the earth.
—Genesis 1:28

THE FATHER AND MOTHER

18. Wives, submit yourselves unto your own husbands, as it is fit in the Lord.

19. Husbands, love your wives, and be not bitter against them.
20. Children, obey your parents in all things: for this is well pleasing unto the Lord.
21. Father provoke not your children to anger, lest they be discouraged.
—Colossians 3:18-21

1. Likewise, ye wives, be in subjection to you own husbands; that, if any obey not the word, they also may without the word be won by the conversation [behavior] of the wives;
2. While they behold your chaste conversation coupled with fear.
3. Whose adorning let it not be that outward adorning of plaiting the hair, and of wearing of gold, or of putting on of apparel;
4. But let it be the hidden man of the heart, in that which is not corruptible even the ornament of a meek and quiet spirit, which is in the sight of God of great price.
5. For after this manner in the old time the holy women also, who trusted in God, adorned themselves, being in subjection unto their own husbands:
6. Even as Sara obeyed Abraham, calling him lord: whose daughters ye are, as long as ye do well, and are not afraid with any amazement [terror].
7. Likewise, ye husbands, dwell with them according to knowledge, giving honour unto the wife, as unto the weaker vessel, and as being heirs together of the grace of life; that your prayers be not hindered.
8. Finally, be ye all of one mind, having compassion one of another, love as brethren, be pitiful, be courteous;
—1 Peter 3:1-8

20. And Adam called his wife's name Eve; because she was the mother of all living.
—Genesis 3:20

10. Who can find a virtuous woman? for her price is far above rubies.

Marriage and the Family

11. The heart of her husband doth safely trust in her, so that he shall have no need of spoil.
12. She will do him good and not evil all the days of her life.
26. She openeth her mouth with wisdom; and in her tongue is the law of kindness.
27. She looketh well to the ways of her household, and eateth not the bread of idleness.
28. Her children arise up, and call her blessed; her husband also, and he praiseth her.
   —Proverbs 31:10-12, 26-28
   (Read Also: Proverbs 31:29-31)

CHILDREN COMMITTED TO THE LORD

3. Lo, children are an heritage of the LORD: and the fruit of the womb is His reward.
4. As arrows are in the hand of a mighty man; so are children of the youth.
5. Happy is the man that hath his quiver full of them . . .
   —Psalms 127:3-5
7. And thou shalt teach them [God's law] diligently unto thy children, and shalt talk of them when thou sittest in thine house, and when thou walkest by the way, and when thou liest down, and when thou risest up.
   —Deuteronomy 6:7
   (Read Also: Deuteronomy 6:8, 9; 11:18-20)
6. Train up a child in the way he should go: and when he is old, he will not depart from it.
   —Proverbs 2:6

THE EXTENDED FAMILY

18. Now also when I am old an greyheaded, O God, forsake me not; until I have showed thy strength unto this generation, and thy power to every one that is to come.
    —Psalms 71:18
31. The hoary head is a crown of glory, if it be found in the way of righteousness.
    —Proverbs 16:31

4. And even to your old age I am He; and even to hoar hairs will I carry you: I have made, and I will bear; even I will carry, and will deliver you.
—Isaiah 46:4
3. The LORD hath appeared of old unto me saying, yea, I have loved thee with an everlasting love: therefore with lovingkindness have I drawn thee.
—Jeremiah 31:3
27. Pure religion and undefiled before God and the Father is this, To visit the fatherless and widows in their affliction, and to keep himself unspotted from the world.
—James 1:27
22. Ye shall not afflict any widow, or fatherless child.
—Exodus 22:22
17. Thou shalt not pervert the judgment of the stranger, nor of the fatherless; nor take a widows raiment to pledge:
—Deuteronomy 24:17
(Read Also: Deuteronomy 26:12)
10. Remove not the old landmark; and enter not into the fields of the fatherless:
11. For their redeemer is mighty; he shall plead their cause with thee.
—Proverbs 23:10, 11
17. Learn to do well; seek judgment, relieve the oppressed, judge the fatherless, plead for the widow.
—Isaiah 1:17
5. Behold, I will send you Elijah the prophet before the coming of the great and dreadful day of the LORD:
—Malachi 4:5
20. Neither pray I for these alone, but for them also which shall believe on me through their word;
21. That they all may be one; as thou, Father, are in Me, and I in Thee, that they also may be one in Us: that the world may believe that Thou has sent Me.
22. And the glory which Thou gavest Me I have given them; that they may be one, even as we are one:
23. I in them, and Thou in Me, that they may be made perfect

in one; and that the world may know that thou hast sent Me, and hast loved them, as Thou hast loved Me.
—John 17:20-23
6. And He shall turn the heart of the fathers to the children, and the heart of the children to their father, lest I come and smite the earth with a curse.
—Malachi 4:6

CHAPTER 33

WHAT THE BIBLE SAYS ABOUT SINFUL SEXUAL BEHAVIOR

ADULTERY AND FORNICATION

10. And the man that committeth adultery with another man's wife, even he that committeth adultery with his neighbour's wife, the adulterer and the adulteress shall surely be put to death.
11. And the man that lieth with his father's wife hath uncovered his father's nakedness: both of them shall surely be put to death; their blood shall be upon them.
12. And if a man lie with his daughter in law both of them shall surely be put to death: they have wrought confusion; their blood shall be upon them.
14. And if a man take a wife and her mother, it is wickedness: . . .
17. And if a man shall take his sister, his father's daughter, or his mother's daughter, and see her nakedness, and she see his nakedness; it is a wicked thing . . .
    —Leviticus 20:10-12, 14, 17
    (Read Also: Deuteronomy 22:22-30)
28. But I say unto you, That whosoever looketh on a woman to lust after her hath committed adultery with her already in his heart.
    —Matthew 5:28

HOMOSEXUALITY AND LESBIANISM

9. Do you not know that the unrighteous will not inherit the kingdom of God? Do not be deceived. Neither fornicators, nor idolaters, nor adulterers, nor *homosexuals*, nor *sodomites*,
10. nor thieves, nor covetous, nor drunkards, nor revilers, nor extortioners will inherit the kingdom of God.
—1 Corinthians 6:9, 10, NKJV
13. If a man also lie with mankind, as he lieth with a woman, both of them have committed and abomination . . .
—Leviticus 20:13
26. For this cause God gave them up unto *vile* effections: for even their *woman did change the natural use* into that which is *against nature*:
27. And likewise also the *men*, leaving the natural use of the woman, *burned* in their *lust one toward another*; men with men working that which is unseemly, and receiving in themselves that recompense of their error which was meet.
28. And even as they did not like to retain God in their knowledge, God gave them over to a reprobate mind, to do those things which are not convenient [proper];
29. Being filled with all unrighteousness, fornication, wickedness, covetousness, maliciousness; full of envy, murder, debate, deceit, malignity; whisperers,
30. Backbiters, haters of God, despiteful, proud, boasters, inventors of evil things, disobedient to parents.
31. Without understanding, covenant-breakers, without natural affection, implacable, unmerciful:
32. Who knowing the judgment of God, that they which commit such things are worthy of death, not only do the same, but have pleasure in them that do them.
—Romans 1:26-32
5. And they called unto Lot and said unto him, Where are the men [angels] which came in to thee this night? bring them out unto us, that we may *know them* [have sex].

13. For we [Angels] will destroy this place, because the cry of them is waxen great before the face of the LORD; and the LORD hath sent us to destroy it,
   —Genesis 19:5, 13
28. Likewise also as it was in the days of Lot; they did eat, they drank, they bought, they sold, they planted, they builded;
29. But the same day that Lot went out of Sodom it rained fire and brimstone from heaven, and destroyed them all.
30. Even thus shall it be in the day when the Son of Man is revealed.
   —Luke 17:28-30
6. And turning the cities of Sodom and Gomorrha into ashes condemned them with an overthrow, making them an ensample [example] unto those that after should live ungodly;
7. And delivered just Lot, vexed with the filthy conversation [behavior], of the wicked:
8. (For that righteous man dwelling among them, in seeing and hearing, vexed his righteous soul from day to day with their unlawful deeds;)
9. The Lord knoweth how to deliver the godly out of temptation, and to reserve the unjust unto the day of judgment to be punished:
   —2 Peter 2:6-9

BESTIALITY

15. And if a man lie with a beast, he shall be put to death: and ye shall slay the beast.
16. And if a woman approach unto any beast, and lie down thereto, thou shall kill the woman, and the beast: they shall surely be put to death; their blood shall be upon them.
   —Leviticus 20:15, 16

SALVATION IS POSSIBLE FOR EVEN THOSE WHO HAVE COMMITTED THESE SINS

11. And such were some of you: but ye are washed, but ye are sanctified, but ye are justified in the name of the LORD Jesus, and by the Spirit of our God.
    —1 Corinthians 6:11
11. . . . And Jesus said unto her, Neither do I condemn thee: go, and sin no more.
    —John 8:11

CHAPTER 34

THE REMNANT CHURCH

A REMNANT IS A SMALL PORTION LEFT FROM A LARGER WHOLE

NOAH AND HIS FAMILY WERE THE FIRST REMNANT

1. And the LORD said unto Noah, Come thou and all thy house into the ark; for thee have I seen righteous before me in this generation.
23. And every living substance was destroyed which was upon the face of the ground both man, and cattle, and the creeping things, and the fowl of the heaven; and they were destroyed from the earth: and Noah only *remained* alive, but they that were with him in the ark.
—Genesis 7:1, 23

PAUL COMPARES HIS OWN DAY WITH THE TIME OF ELIJAH WHEN ONLY A REMNANT WAS LEFT

2. ... Wot [Know] ye not what the scripture saith of Elias? how he maketh intercession to God against Israel, saying,
3. Lord, they have killed thy prophets, and digged down thine altars; and I am left alone, and they seek my life.
4. But what saith the answer of God unto him? I have reserved to myself seven thousand, men, who have not bowed the knee to the image of Baal.

5. Even so them at this present time also there is a remnant according to the election of grace.
—Romans 11:2-5

ONLY A REMNANT WAS LEFT IN JUDEA DURING THE BABYLONIAN CAPTIVITY.

9. Except the LORD of hosts had left unto us a very small remnant, We should have been as Sodom, and we should have been like unto Gomorrah.
—Isaiah 1:9
7. For thus saith the LORD; Sing with gladness for Jacob, and shout among the chief, of the nations: publish ye, praise ye, and say, O LORD, save the people, the remnant of Israel.
—Jeremiah 31:7
3. And I will gather the remnant of my flock out of all countries whither I have driven them, and will bring them again to their folds; and they shall be fruitful and increase.
—Jeremiah 23:3

A REMNANT RETURNED FROM BABYLON TO JUDEA

8. Yet will I leave a remnant, that ye may have some that shall escape the sword among the nations, when ye shall be scattered through the countries.
—Ezekiel 6:8
3. And they said unto me, The remnant that are left of the captivity there in the province are in great affliction and reproach: the wall of Jerusalem also is broken down, and the gates thereof are burned with fire.
—Nehemiah 1:3

PAUL PREDICTED A FALLING AWAY FROM THE CHURCH AFTER HIS TIME.

3. Let no man deceive you by any means: for that day shall not come except there come a falling away first, and that man of sin be revealed, the son of perdition;
—2 Thessalonians 2:3

THE TRUE CHURCH (A REMNANT) WAS IN HIDING DURING THE DARK AGES.

6. And the woman [the church] fled into the wilderness, where she hath a place prepared of God, that they should feed her there a thousand two hundred and threescore days [years].
—Revelation 12:6

HOW IS THE REMNANT CHURCH IDENTIFIED?

17. And the dragon [Satan] was wroth with the woman [church], and went to make war with the remnant of her seed, which (1) keep the *commandments* of God, and (2) have the *testimony* of Jesus Christ.
—Revelation 12:17

WHAT IS THE TESTIMONY OF JESUS CHRIST?

10. And I fell at his [an angel's] feet to worship him. And he said unto me, See thou do it not: I am thy fellowservant, and of thy brethren that have the *testimony* of Jesus: worship God: for the testimony of Jesus is the *spirit of prophecy*.
—Revelation 19:10

WHAT CHURCH DOES OR HAS BOTH OF THESE?

(1) KEEPS THE COMMANDMENTS OF GOD

12. Here is the patience of the saints: here are they that keep the commandments of God, and the faith of Jesus.
—Revelation 14:12
10. For whosoever shall keep the whole law, and yet offend in one point, he is guilty of all.
11. For He that said, Do not commit adultery, said also, Do not kill. Now if thou commit no adultery, yet if thou kill, thou art become a transgressor of the law.
—James 2:10, 11

THE LAW WAS NOT NAILED TO THE CROSS.

31. Do we then make void the law through faith? God forbid: yea, we establish the law.
—Romans 3:31
17. Think not that I am come to destroy the law, or the prophets: I am not come to destroy, but to fulfil.
18. For verily I say unto you, Till heaven and earth pass, one jot or one tittle shall in no wise pass from the law [including the fourth commandment], till all be fulfilled.
—Matthew 5:17, 18
15. If ye love Me, keep My commandments [including the fourth one].
—John 14:15
14. Blessed are they that do His commandments, that they may have right to the tree of life, and may enter in through the gates into the city.
—Revelation 22:14

(2) AND HAS THE SPIRIT OF PROPHECY.

The "testimony of Jesus" is defined as the "spirit of prophecy," meaning that Jesus is witnessing to the church through the medium of prophecy. The Seventh-day Adventist church has the prophetic writings of E. G. White.

CHAPTER 35

HELL, FIRE, WHEN? WHERE? HOW?

HELL, FIRE, When? Where? How?

7. And when the thousand year [millennium] are expired, Satan shall be loosed out of his prison,
8. And shall go out to deceive the nations which are in the four quarters of the earth, God and Magog, to gather them together to battle: the number of whom is as the sand of the sea.
9. And they went up on the breadth of the earth, and compassed the camp of the saints about, and the beloved city: and fire came down from God out of heaven, and devoured them [burned them up].
10. And the devil that deceived them was cast into the lake of fire and brimstone, where the beast and the false prophets are, and shall be tormented day and night for *ever and ever*.
—Revelation 20:7-10
10. ... and he shall be tormented with fire and brimstone in the presence of the holy angels, and in the presence of the lamb:
11. And the smoke of their torment ascendeth up *for ever and ever*: and they have no rest day nor night, who worship the beast and his image, and whosoever receiveth the mark of his name.
—Revelation 14:10, 11

["for ever and ever"—(Gr. the adjective AIONIOS) literally, "age-lasting", also translated "eternal", or ever-lasting". The death is everlasting not the burning. "Rest"—(Gr. ANAPAUSIS) "cessation", "rest", and "refreshment". The meaning here is that for the duration of the punishment, which continues until death ensues, there will be no relaxation or rest from the punishment.]

22. But Hannah went not up; for she said unto her husband, I will not go up until the child is weaned, and then I will bring him, that he may appear before the LORD, and there abide *for ever*.
28. Therefore also I have lent him to the LORD; *as long as he liveth* he shall be lent to the LORD. and he worshipped the LORD there.
—1 Samuel 1:22, 28
6. Then his master shall bring him [the slave] unto the judges; he shall also bring him to the door, or unto the door post; and his master shall bore his ear through with an awl; and he shall serve him *for ever*.
—Exodus 21:6
(Read Also: Exodus 12:24)
17. Now the LORD had prepared a great fish to swallow up Jonah, and Jonah was in the belly of the fish three days and three nights.
—Jonah 1:17
2. I went down to the bottoms of the mountains; the earth with her bars was about me *for ever*: yet hast thou brought up my life from corruption, O LORD my God.
—Jonah 2:6
Here "for ever" was used for a length of time of three days and three nights.
7. Even as Sodom and Gomorrha, and the cities about them in like manner, giving themselves over to fornication, and going after strange flesh, are set forth for an example, suffering the vengeance of *eternal fire*.(Those cities are not still burning.)
—Jude 7

6. And turning the cities of Sodom and Gomorrha *into ashes* condemned them with an overthrow, making them an ensample [example] unto those that after should live ungodly;
9. The LORD knoweth how to deliver the godly out of temptations, and to reserve the unjust unto the day of judgment to be punished:
—2 Peter 2:6, 9
28. And fear not them which kill the body, but are not able to kill the soul: but rather fear Him which is able to *destroy* both soul and body in hell.
—Matthew 10:28
41. Then shall He say also unto them on the left hand, Depart from me, ye cursed, into *everlasting fire*, prepared for the devil and his angels:
—Matthew 25:41.
(Read Also: Mark 9:43-48)
12. Whose fan is in His hand and He will thoroughly purge His floor, and gather His wheat into the garner; but He will *burn up* the chaff with *unquenchable fire*.(Cannot be extinguished until burned up.)
—Matthew 3:12
27. But if ye will not hearken unto me to hallow the sabbath day, and not to bear a burden, even entering in at the gates of Jerusalem on the sabbath day; then will I kindle a fire in the gates thereof, and it shall devour the palaces of Jerusalem, and it *shall not be quenched*.
—Jeremiah 17:27

It happened twice, 582 B.C. and 70 A.D. but it's not still burning. (Read Also: 2 Chronicles 36:19)

40. As therefore the tares are gathered and *burned in the fire*; so shall it be in the end of this world.
41. The Son of Man shall send forth His angels, and they shall gather out of His kingdom all things that offend, and them which do iniquity.

Hell Fire, When? Where? How?

42. And shall cast them into a *furnace of fire*: there shall be wailing and gnashing of teeth.
—Matthew 13:40-42
(Read Also: Matthew 13:30)

30. And if thy right hand offend thee [cause thee to sin], cut it off, and cast it from thee: for it is profitable for thee that one of thy members should perish, and not that thy whole body should be cast into hell.
—Matthew 5:30

14. Behold, they shall *be as stubble*; the fire shall burn them; they shall not deliver themselves from the power of the flame: there shall not be a *coal to warm at, nor fire to sit before it.*
—Isaiah 47:14

1. For, behold, the day cometh, that shall *burn as an oven*; and all the proud, yea, and all that do wickedly, *shall be stubble*: and the day that cometh shall *burn them up*, saith the LORD of hosts, that it shall leave them *neither root nor branch.*

3. And ye shall tread down the wicked; for they shall be *ashes* under the soles of your feet in the day that I shall do this, saith the LORD of hosts.
—Malachi 4:1, 3

20. The soul that sinneth, *it shall die . . .*
—Ezekiel 18:20
(Read Also: 2 Thessalonians 1:7-9)

18. Thou hast defiled thy sanctuaries by the multitude of thine iniquities by the iniquity of thy traffic; therefore will I bring forth a *fire* from the midst of thee, it shall *devour thee*, and I will bring thee to *ashes* upon the earth in the sight of all them that behold thee.

19. All they that know thee among the people shall be astonished at thee: thou shalt be a terror, and *never shalt thou be any more.*
—Ezekiel 28:18, 19
(Read Also: Psalms 145:20 and Hebrews 2:14)

11. Say unto them, as I live saith the LORD God, I have no pleasure in the *death* of the wicked; but that the wicked turn from his way and live: turn ye, turn ye from your evil ways; for why will ye die, O house of Israel?
—Ezekiel 33:11
(Read Also: Isaiah 28:21)

9. For evildoers shall be cut off: but those that wait upon the LORD, they shall inherit the earth.
10. For yet a little while, and *the wicked shall not be*: yea, thou shalt diligently consider his place, and it *shall not be*.
20. But the wicked shall *perish*, and the enemies of the LORD shall be as the fat of lambs: they shall *consume*; into smoke shall they *consume away*.
38. But the transgressors shall be *destroyed* together: the end of the wicked shall be cut off.
—Psalms 37:9, 10, 20, 38

9. Thou shalt make them as a fiery oven in the time of thine anger: the LORD shall swallow them up in His wrath, and the fire shall *devour them*.
—Psalms 21:9
(Read Also: Psalms 104:35)

5. The mountains quake at Him, and the hills *melt*, and the earth is *burned* at His presence, yea, the world, and all that dwell therein.
6. Who can stand before His indignation? and who can abide in the fierceness of His anger? His fury is poured out like fire, and the rocks are thrown down by Him.
8. But with an overrunning flood He will make an *utter end* of the place thereof, and darkness shall pursue His enemies.
9. What do ye imagine against the LORD? He will make an *utter end*; affliction shall not rise up the second time.
—Nahum 1:5, 6, 8, 9

8. But the fearful, and unbelieving, and the abominable, and murderers, and whoremongers, and sorcerers, and idolaters, and all liars, shall have their part in the lake which

burneth with fire and brimstone: which is the *second death*.
—Revelation 21:8
(Read Also: Revelation 21:4)

6. Whereby the world that then was [time of Noah], being overflowed with water, *perished*: [people not still drowning]
7. But the heavens and the earth, which are now, by the same word are kept in store, reserved unto *fire* against the day of judgment and perdition of ungodly men,
9. The Lord is not slack concerning His promise, as some men count slackness; but is lonsuffering to us-ward [to us], not willing that any should perish, but that all should come to repentance.
10. But the day of the LORD will come as a thief in the night; in the which the heavens shall pass away with a great noise, and the *elements shall melt with fervent heat*, the earth also and the works that are therein shall *be burned up*.
11. Seeing then that all these things shall be *dissolved*, what manner of persons ought ye to be in all holy conversation [behavior], and godliness.
12. Whose fan is in His hand and He will thoroughly purge His floor, and gather His wheat into the garner; but He will *burn up* the chaff with *unquenchable fire*. [Can't extinguish until consumed].
13. Nevertheless we, according to His promise, look for new heavens and a new earth, wherein dwelleth righteousness.
—2 Peter 3:6, 7, 9-13
(Read Also: Romans 6:23)
22. For as the new heavens and the new earth, which I will make, shall remain before me, saith the Lord, so shall your seed and your name remain.
23. And it shall come to pass, that from one new moon to another, and from one Sabbath to another, shall all flesh come to worship before me, saith the Lord.

24. And they shall go forth [the translated and resurrected righteous], and look upon [during the millennium] the carcases [corpses] of the men that have transgressed against me: for their worm [maggot] shall not die [till its work is complete], neither shall their fire be quenched [until its work is done]; and they shall be an abhorring into all flesh [until the earth is cleansed].
   —Isaiah 66:22-24
17. For, behold, I create new heavens and a new earth: and the former shall not be remembered, not come into mind.
   —Isaiah 65:17

CHAPTER 36
WHERE ARE THE DEAD?

WHERE ARE THE DEAD?

7. And the LORD God formed man of the dust of the ground, and breathed into his nostrils, the breath of life; and man became a living soul.
—Genesis 2:7

DUST + BREATH OF LIFE = LIVING SOUL

19. In the sweat of thy face shalt thou eat bread, till thou return unto the ground; for out of it wast thou taken: for dust thou art, and unto dust shalt thou return.
—Genesis 3:19
20. All go unto one place; all are of the dust, and all turn to dust again.
—Ecclesiastes 3:20
13. If I wait, the grave is mine house: I have made my bed in the darkness.
—Job 17:13

DUST (minus) BREATH OF LIFE = DEAD SOUL

28. And fear not them which kill the body, but are not able to kill the *soul*: but rather fear him which is able to destroy both *soul* and body in hell.
—Matthew 10:28

18. He keepeth back his *soul* from the pit and his life from perishing by the sword.
22. Yea, his *soul* draweth near unto the grave, and his life to the destroyers.
28. He will deliver his *soul* from going into the pit [grave], and his life shall see the light.
30. To bring back his *soul* from the pit, to be enlightened with the light of the living.
—Job 33:18, 22, 28, 30
(Read Also: Psalms 89:48)
20. The *soul* that sinneth, it shall die. The son shall not bear the iniquity of the father, neither shall the father bear the iniquity of the son: the righteousness of the righteous shall be upon him, and the wickedness of the wicked shall be upon him.
—Ezekiel 18:20

WHERE DOES THE SPIRIT GO AT TIME OF DEATH?

7. Then shall the dust return to the earth as it was: and the *spirit* (Heb. *rauch*) shall return unto God who gave it.
—Ecclesiastes 12:7

[note: (Hebrew word *rauch*) translated Spirit, breath, wind. Of all the times used, rauch never denotes and intelligent entity capable of living apart from the physical body.]

26. For as the body without the *spirit [breath]* is dead, so faith without works is dead also.
—James 2:26
3. All the while my breath is in me, and the spirit of God is in my nostrils;
—Job 27:3

DO THE DEAD KNOW WHAT THE LIVING ARE DOING?

4. His *breath* goeth forth, he returneth to his earth; in that very day his thoughts perish.
—Psalms 146:4

5. For the living know that they shall die: but the dead know not anything, neither have they any more a reward; for the memory of them is forgotten.
6. Also their love, and their hatred, and their envy, is now perished; neither have they any more a portion for ever in anything that is done under the sun.
—Ecclesiastes 9:5, 6
21. His sons come to honour, and he knowth it not; and they are brought low, but he perceiveth it not of them.
—Job 14:21
18. For the grave cannot praise thee, death cannot celebrate thee: they that go down into the pit cannot hope for thy truth.
—Isaiah 38:18
(Read Also: Psalms 115:17)

WILL THE DEAD LIVE AGAIN?

12. So man lieth down, and riseth not: till the heavens be no more, they shall not awake, nor be raised out of their sleep.
14. If a man die, shall he live again? All the days of my appointed time will I wait till my change come.
—Job 14:12, 14
15. But God will redeem my SOUL from the power of the *grave*: for he shall receive me.
—Psalms 49:15
13. But I would not have you to be ignorant, brethren, concerning them which are *asleep*, that ye sorrow not, even as others which have no hope.
14. For if we believe that Jesus died and rose again, even so them also which *sleep* in Jesus will God bring with him.
15. For this we say unto you by the word of the Lord, that we which are alive and remain unto the coming of the Lord shall not prevent [precede] them which are asleep.
16. For the Lord Himself shall descend from heaven with a shout with the voice of the Archangel, and with the trump of God: and the dead in Christ shall rise first:

17. Then we which are alive and remain shall be caught up together with them in the clouds, to meet the Lord in the air: and so shall we ever be with the Lord.
—1 Thessalonians 4:13-17

THERE WILL BE A RESURRECTION

23. Jesus saith unto her, Thy brother shall rise again.
24. Martha saith unto Him, I know that he shall rise again in the resurrection at the last day.
25. Jesus said unto her, I am the resurrection, and the life: he that believeth in Me, though he were dead, yet shall he live:
26. And whosoever liveth and believeth in Me shall never die. Believest thou this?
—John 11:23-26

3. When Christ, who is our life, shall appear, then shall ye also appear with him in glory.
—Colossians 3:4

28. Marvel not at this: for the hour is coming, in the which all that are in the graves shall hear His voice,
29. And shall come forth; they that have done good, unto the resurrection of life; and they that have done evil, unto the resurrection of damnation.
—John 5:28, 29

36. Neither can they die anymore: for they are equal unto the angels: and are the children of God, being the children of resurrection.
—Luke 20:36

7. To open the blind eyes, to bring out the prisoners from the prison, and them that sit in darkness out of the prison house.
—Isaiah 42:7

15. As for me, I will behold thy face in righteousness; I shall be satisfied, when I wake, with thy likeness.
—Psalms 17:15

4. And God shall wipe away all tears from their eyes; and there shall be no more death, neither sorrow, nor crying, neither shall there be any more pain: for the former things are passed away.
—Revelation 21:4

ONLY GOD HAS INHERENT IMMORTALITY

15. Which in his times he shall show, who is the blessed and only Potentate, the King of Kings, and Lord of lords;
16. Who only hath *immortality*, dwelling in the light which no man can approach into; whom no man hath seen, nor can see: to whom be honour and power everlasting.
—1 Timothy 6:15, 16
17. Shall *mortal* man be more just than God? shall a man be more pure than his maker?
—Job 4:17

GOD GIVES IMMORTALITY TO THE RIGHTEOUS SAVED AT THE SECOND COMING OF CHRIST

51. Behold, I show you a mystery: We shall not all *sleep*, but we shall all be changed,
52. In a moment, in the twinkling of an eye, at the last trump: for the trumpet shall sound, and the dead shall be raised incorruptible, and we shall be changed.
53. For this corruptible must put on incorruption, and this *mortal* must put on *immortality*.
54. So when this corruptible shall have put on incorruption, and this *mortal* shall have put on *immortality*, then shall be brought to pass the saying that is written, Death is swallowed up in victory.
55. O death, where is thy sting? O grave, where is thy victory?
—1 Corinthians 15:51-55
54. Whoso eateth my flesh, and drinketh my blood, hath eternal life; and I will raise him up at the last day.
—John 6:54

GOD CONSIDERS DEATH A SLEEP

11. These things said He: and after that He saith . . . , our friend Lazarus sleepeth; but I go, that I may awake him out of sleep.
13. Howbeit Jesus spake of his death . . .
—John 11:11, 13
(Read Also: 1 Corinthians 15:5, 6)

WHO ARE THE DEAD BROUGHT UP BY MEDIUMS?

9. And the great dragon was cast out, that old serpent, called the Devil, and Satan, which deceiveth the whole world: he was cast out into the earth, and his angels were cast out with him.
—Revelation 12:9
19. And when they shall say unto you, Seek unto them that have familiar spirits [mediums], and unto wizards that peep, and that mutter: should not a people seek unto their God? for the living to the dead?
20. To the law and to the testimony: if they speak not according to this word, it is because there is no light in them.
—Isaiah 8:19, 20

WHAT DOES GOD THINK OF SPIRIT MEDIUMS?

27. A man also or woman that hath a familiar spirit, or that is a wizard, shall surely be put to death . . .
—Leviticus 20:27
18. Thou shalt not suffer a witch to live.
—Exodus 22:18
3. Your eyes have seen what the LORD did because of Baalpeor: for all the men that followed Baalpeor, the LORD thy God hath destroyed them from amoung you.
—Deuteronomy 4:3
28. They [the Israelites] joined themselves also unto Baalpeor, and ate the sacrifices of the dead.

29. Thus they provoked Him [God] to anger with their inventions: and the plague brake in upon them.
—Psalms 106:28, 29
9. And those that died in the plague were twenty and four thousand.
—Numbers 25:9
(Read full account in Numbers 25)

KING SAUL FALLS INTO THE DEVIL'S TRAP

3. Now Samuel was dead, and all Israel had lamented him, and buried him in Ramah, even in his own city, And Saul had put away those that had familiar spirits, and the wizards, out of the land.
6. And when Saul inquired of the LORD, the LORD answered him not, neither by dreams, nor by Urim, nor by prophets.
11. Then said the woman [witch of Endor], Whom shall I bring up unto thee? And he said, Bring me up Samuel.
13. And the king said unto her, Be not afraid: for what sawest thou? And the woman said unto Saul, I saw gods ascending out of the earth
14. And he said unto her, What form is he of? And she said, an old man cometh up; and he is covered with a mantle. And Saul [only] perceived that it was Samuel, and he stooped with his face to the ground, and bowed himself.
—1 Samuel 28:6, 11-14
(Read Also: 1 Samuel 28:3-25)

WHO IS TELLING THE TRUTH, GOD OR SATAN?

4. And the serpent [Satan] said unto the woman [Eve], ye shall not surely die:
—Genesis 3:4
5. And all the days that Adam lived were nine hundred and thirty years: and he died.
—Genesis 5:5

2. In hope of eternal life, which GOD, that *cannot lie*, promised before the world began.
   —Titus 1:2
44. ... there is no truth in him [the *devil*]. When he speaketh a lie, he speaketh of his own: for *he is a lier*, and the father of it.
    —John 8:44
11. Now all these things happened unto them for ensamples [examples], and they are written for our admonitions, upon whom the ends of the world are come.
    —1 Corinthians 10:11

CHAPTER 37
THE SECOND COMING

THE SECOND COMING OF CHRIST. MATTHEW 24.

3. . . . the disciples came unto Him [Christ] privately, saying, Tell us when shall these things be? and what shall be the sign of thy coming, and the end of the world?
4. And Jesus answered and said unto them, Take heed that no man deceive you.
5. For many shall come in my name, saying, I am Christ; and shall deceive many.
6. And ye shall hear of wars and rumors of wars; see that ye be not troubled; for all these things must come to pass, but the end is not yet.
7. For nation shall rise against nation, and kingdom against kingdom: and there shall be famines, and pestilences, and earthquakes, in divers places.
8. All these things are the beginning of sorrows.
9. Then shall they deliver you up to be afflicted, and shall kill you: and ye shall be hated of all nations for my names' sake.
10. And then shall many be offended, and shall betray one another, and shall hate one another.
11. And many false prophets shall rise, and shall deceive many.
12. And because iniquity shall abound, the love of many shall wax cold.

13. But he that shall endure unto the end, the same shall be saved.
14. And this gospel of the kingdom shall be preached in all the world for a witness unto all nations; and then shall the end come.
   —Matthew 24:3-14
21. For then shall be great tribulation, such as was not since the beginning of the world to this time, no, nor ever shall be.
22. And except those days should be shortened, there should no flesh be saved: but for the elect's sake those days shall be shortened.
23. Then if any man shall say unto you, Lo, here is Christ, or there; believe it not.
24. For there shall arise false Christs and false prophets, and shall show great signs and wonders; insomuch that, if it were possible, they shall deceive the very elect.
26. Wherefore if they shall say unto you, Behold, he is in the desert; go not forth: behold, he is in the secret chambers; believe it not.
27. For as the lightning cometh out of the east, and shineth even unto the west; so shall also the coming of the Son of Man be.
29. Immediately after the tribulation of those days shall the sun be darkened, and the moon shall not give her light, and the stars shall fall from heaven, and the powers of the heaven shall be shaken:
30. And then shall appear the sign of the Son of Man in heaven: and then shall all the tribes of the earth mourn, and they shall see the Son of Man coming in the clouds of heaven with power and great glory.
31. And He shall send His angles with great sound of a trumpet, and they shall gather together His elect from the four winds, from one end of the heaven to the other.
33. So likewise ye, when ye shall see all these things, know that it is near, even at the doors.
   —Matthew 24:21-24, 26, 27, 29-31, 33

The Second Coming

35. Heaven and earth shall pass way, but my words shall not pass away.
36. But of the day and hour knoweth no man, no, not the angels of heaven, but my Father only.
37. But as the days of Noe were, so shall also the coming of the Son of Man be.
38. For as in the days that were before the flood they were eating and drinking, marrying and giving in marriage, until the day that Noe entered into the ark,
39. And knew not until the flood came, and took them all away; so shall also the coming of the Son of Man be.
40. Then shall two be in the field; the one shall be taken, and other left.
41. Two women shall be grinding at the mill; the one shall be taken and the other left.
42. Watch therefore: for ye know not what hour your Lord doth come.
44. Therefore be ye also ready: for in such an hour as ye think not the Son of Man cometh.
—Matthew 24:35-42, 44
(Read Also: Mark 13; Luke 21)

CHRIST RETURNS TO HEAVEN AFTER HIS RESURRECTION

50. And He led them out as far as to Bethany, and He lifted up His hands, and blessed them.
51. And it came to pass, while He blessed them, He was parted from them and carried up into heaven.
—Luke 24:50, 51
9. And when He had spoken these things, while they beheld, He was taken up; and a cloud received Him out of their sight.
10. And while they looked stedfastly toward heaven as He went up, behold, two men stood by them in white apparel;
11. Which also said, Ye men of Galilee, why stand ye gazing up into heaven? this same Jesus, which is taken up from

you into heaven, shall so come in like manner as ye have seen Him go into heaven.
—Acts 1:9-11

CHRIST WANTS US WITH HIM IN HEAVEN

24. Father, I will that they also, whom thou hast given me, be with me where I am; that they may behold my glory, which thou hast given me: for thou lovest me before the foundation of the world.
—John 17:24
2. In my Father's house are many mansions: if it were not so, I would have told you, I go to prepare a place for you.
3. And if I go and prepare a place for you, I will come again, and receive you unto myself; that where I am, there ye may be also.
—John 14:2, 3

WE HAVE A FUTURE HOME IN HEAVEN

20. For our conversations [citizenship] is in heaven; from whence also we look for the Saviour, the Lord Jesus Christ:
21. Who shall change our vile [lowly] body, that it may be fashioned like unto His glorious body, according to the working whereby He is able even to subdue all things unto Himself.
—Philippians 3:20, 21
13. Looking for that blessed hope, and the glorious appearing of the great God and our Savior Jesus Christ;
—Titus 2:13
12. And, behold, I come quickly; and my reward is with me, to give every man according as his works shall be.
—Revelation 22:12
28. So Christ was once offered to bear the sins of many; and unto them that look for Him shall He appear the second time without sin unto salvation.
—Hebrews 9:28

CHRIST WILL COME IN A CLOUD OF ANGELS

31. When the Son of Man shall come in His glory, and all the holy angels with Him, then shall He sit upon the throne of His glory:
32. And before Him shall be gathered all nations . . .
—Matthew 25:31, 32

64. Jesus saith unto Him, Thou hast said: nevertheless I say unto you, Hereafter shall ye see the Son of Man sitting on the right hand of power, and coming in the clouds of heaven.
—Matthew 26:64

16. For the Lord himself shall descend from heaven with a shout, with the voice of the Archangel, and with the trump of God: and the dead in Christ shall rise first:
17. Then we which are alive and remain shall be caught up together with them in the clouds, to meet the Lord in the air: and so shall we ever be with the Lord.
—1 Thessalonians 4:16, 17

14. And I looked, and behold a white cloud, and upon the cloud one sat, like unto the Son of Man, having on His head a golden crown, and in His hand a sharp sickle.
—Revelation 14:14

27. For the Son of Man shall come in the glory of His Father with His angels; and then He shall reward every man according to His works.
—Matthew 16:27

22. But ye are come unto mount Sion, and unto the city of the living God, the heavenly Jerusalem, and to an innumerable company of angels,
—Hebrews 12:22

11. And I beheld, and I heard the voice of many angels round about the throne and the beasts [living creatures] and the elders: and the number of them was ten thousand times ten thousand, and thousands of thousands;
—Revelation 5:11

14. And Enoch also, the seventh from Adam prophesied of these, saying, Behold, the Lord cometh with ten thousand of His saints.
15. To execute judgment upon all,
   —Jude 14,15

CHRIST WILL NOT COME IN SECRET

7. Behold, He cometh with clouds; and every eye shall see Him, and they also which pierced Him: and all kindreds of the earth shall wail because of Him,
   —Revelation 1:7
3. Our God shall come, and shall not keep silence: a fire shall devour before Him, and it shall be very tempestuous round about Him.
4. He shall call to the heavens from above, and to the earth, that He may judge His people.
5. Gather my saints together unto me; those that have made a covenant with me by sacrifice.
   —Psalms 50:3-5
8. And then shall that wicked be revealed, whom the Lord shall consume with the spirit of His mouth, and shall destroy with the brightness of His coming:
   —2 Thessalonians 2:8
7. . . . the Lord Jesus shall be revealed from heaven with His mighty angels,
8. In flaming fire taking vengeance on them that know not God, and that obey not the gospel of our Lord Jesus Chirst:
   —2 Thessalonians 1:7, 8
   (Read Also: 2 Timothy 3:1-5)

THE RIGHTEOUS LIVING WILL BE CAUGHT UP WITH THE RIGHTEOUS DEAD

(Read Also: 1 Corinthians 15:51-54)

51. Behold, I show you a mystery: We shall not all sleep, but we shall all be changed,

52. In a moment, in the twinkling of any eye, at the last trump: for the trumpet shall sound, and the dead shall be raised incorruptible, and we shall be changed.
—1 Corinthians 15:51-52
2. For yourselves know perfectly that the day of the Lord so cometh as a thief in the night.
3. For when they shall say, Peace and safety; then sudden destruction cometh upon them, as travail upon a woman with child; and they shall not escape.
—1 Thessalonians 5:2, 3
(Read Also: 1 Thessalonians 5:1-6)
9. And it shall be said in that day, Lo, this is our God; we have waited for Him, and He will save us: this is the LORD; we have waited for Him, we will be glad and rejoice in His salvation.
—Isaiah 25:9

CHAPTER 38

THE NEARNESS OF HIS COMING

THE NEARNESS OF THE RETURN OF JESUS CHRIST

3. And as He set upon the mount of Olives, the disciples came unto Him privately, saying, Tell us, *when* shall these things be? And *what shall be the sign* of thy coming and of the *end of the world*?
—Matthew 24:3

36. But of that day and hour knoweth no man, no, not the angels of heaven, but my Father only.
—Matthew 24:36
(Read Also: Matthew 24)

THESE SIGNS TELL US HIS COMING IS NEAR.

32. Now learn a parable of the fig tree; When his branch is yet tender, and putteth forth leaves, ye know that summer is nigh:
33. So likewise ye, when ye shall see all these things know that it is near, even at the doors.
—Matthew 24:32, 33

PEOPLE WILL LOSE INTEREST IN CHURCH GOING

25. Not forsaking the assembling of ourselves together, as the manner of some is; but exhorting one another: and so much the more, as ye see *the day approaching*.
—Hebrews 10:25

3. For the time will come when they *will not endure sound doctrine*; but after their own lusts shall they heap to themselves teachers, having itching ears;
4. And they shall turn away their ears from the truth, and shall be *turned unto fables.*
—2 Timothy 4:3, 4
1. Now the Spirit speaketh expressly, that in the latter times some shall depart from the faith, giving heed to seducing spirits, and doctrines of devils;
—1 Timothy 4:1
20. To the law and to the testimony: if they speak not according to the word, it is because there is no light in them.
—Isaiah 8:20
4. But ye, brethren, are not in darkness, that *that day* should overtake you as a thief.
—1 Thessalonians 5:4

THERE WILL BE FALSE CHRISTS AND FALSE PROPHETS

24. For there shall arise *false christs*, and *false prophets*, and shall show *great signs and wonders*; insomuch that, if it were possible, they shall deceive the very elect.
—Matthew 24:24
14. For they are the *spirits of devils, working miracles*, which go forth unto the kings of the earth and of the whole world, to gather them to the battle of that great day of God Almighty.
—Revelation 16:14

THE RICH WILL PILE UP GREAT FORTUNES

3. Your gold and silver is cankered; and the rust of them shall be a witness against you, and shall eat your flesh as it were fire. *Ye have heaped treasure* together for the *last days.*
—James 5:3

THERE WILL BE MANY POOR ON THE EARTH

4. Behold, the hire of the labourers who have reaped down your fields, which is of you kept back by fraud, crieth: and the cries of them which have reaped are entered into the ears of the Lord of sabaoth.
8. Be ye also patient; stablish you hearts: for the *coming* of the Lord *draweth nigh*.
—James 5:4, 8

KNOWLEDGE WILL BE INCREASED AND TRAVEL WILL BE SPEEDED UP

4. But thou, O Daniel, shut up the words, and seal the book, even to the time of the end: many shall *run to and fro*, and *knowledge* shall be *increased*.
—Daniel 12:4

3. ... the Chariots shall be with flaming torches in the *day of His preparation*, and the fir trees shall be terribly shaken.
4. The chariots shall rage in the streets, they shall justle one against another in the broad ways: they shall seem like torches, they shall run like the lightnings.
—Nahum 2:3, 4

FEARFUL CALAMITIES ON THE INCREASE

11. And great *earthquakes* shall be in divers places, and *famines*, and *pestilences*: and fearful sights and great signs shall there be from heaven.
—Luke 21:11

A CRAZE FOR PLEASURE/DECLINE IN TRUE RELIGION

1. This know also, that in the last days *perilous time* shall come.
2. For men shall be lovers of their own selves covetous, boasters, proud, blasphemers, disobedient to parents, unthankful, unholy,
3. Without natural affection, Trucebreakers, false accusers,

incontinent [without self-control], fierce, despisers of those that are good,
4. Traitors, heady [reckless], highminded [proud, arrogant], *lovers of pleasure more than lovers of God;*
5. Having a form of godliness, but denying the power thereof: from such turn away.
—2 Timothy 3:1-5

CRIME AND WICKEDNESS ON INCREASE

12. And because iniquity shall abound, the love of many shall wax cold.
—Matthew 24:12
37. But as the days of Noe [Noah] were, so shall also the coming of the Son of Man be.
38. For as in the days that were before the flood they were *eating* and *drinking, marrying* and giving in marriage, until the day that Noe [Noah] entered into the ark,
—Matthew 24:37, 38
5. And God saw that the wickedness of man was great in the earth, and that every *imagination* of the thoughts of his heart was only *evil continually.*
—Genesis 6:5
11. The earth also was corrupt before God, and the earth was filled with violence.
—Genesis 6:11

SOCIETY WILL ACT AS IN THE DAYS OF LOT

49. Behold, this was the iniquity of thy sister Sodom, pride, fulness of bread, and abundance of idleness was in her and in her daughters, neither did she strengthen the hand of the poor and needy.
50. And they were haughty, and *committed abomination* before me: therefore I took them away as I saw good.
—Ezekiel 16:49, 50
28. Likewise also as it was in the days of Lot; they did *eat,*

they *drank*, they bought, they sold, they planted, they builded;
29. But the same day that Lot went out of Sodom it rained fire and brimstone from heaven, and destroyed them all.
30. Even thus shall it be in the day when the Son of Man is revealed.
—Luke 17:28-30

MISSIONARIES SPREADING GOSPEL WORLD WIDE

1. Blow ye the trumpet in Zion, and sound an alarm in my holy mountain: let all the inhabitants of the land tremble: for *the day of the LORD* cometh, for it is *nigh at hand*.
—Joel 2:1
14. And this gospel of the kingdom shall be preached in all the world for a *witness unto all nations*; and then shall the end come.
—Matthew 24:14
(Read Also: Revelation 14:6-14)

PEOPLE WILL SCOFF AT THE IDEA

3. Knowing this first, that there shall come in the last days *scoffers*, walking after their own lusts,
4. And saying, Where is the promise of His coming? for since the fathers fell asleep, all things continue as they were from the beginning of the creation.
5. For this *they willingly are ignorant* of, that by the word of God the heavens were of old, and the earth standing out of the water and in the water:
—2 Peter 3:3-5

THE NATIONS WILL TALK PEACE

2. And it shall come to pass in the last days, that the mountain of the LORD's house shall be established in the top of the mountains, and shall be exalted above the hills; and all nations shall flow unto it.

3. And many people shall go and say, come ye, and let us go up to the mountain of the LORD, to the house of the God of Jacob; and He will teach us of His ways, and we will walk in His paths: for out of Zion shall go forth the law, and the word of the LORD from Jerusalem.
4. And He shall judge amoung the nations, and shall rebuke many people: and they shall beat their swords into plowshares, and their spears into pruning hooks, nation shall not lift up sword against nation, neither shall they learn war any more.
—Isaiah 2:2-4
3. For when they shall say, peace and safety; then sudden destruction cometh upon them, as travail upon a woman with child; and they shall not escape.
—1 Thessalonians 5:3

BUT THEY WILL PREPARE FOR WAR

9. Proclaim ye this amoung the Gentiles; Prepare war, wake up the mighty men, let all the men of war draw near; let them come up:
10. Beat your plowshares into swords, and your pruning hooks into spears: let the weak say, I am strong.
14. Multitudes, multitudes in the valley of decision: for THE DAY of the LORD IS NEAR in the valley of decision.
—Joel 3:9, 10, 14

WHEN THESE THINGS ARE HAPPENING CHRIST'S COMING IS NEAR

11. And great earthquakes shall be in divers places, and famines, and pestilences; and fearful sights and great signs shall there be from heaven.
—Luke 21:11
25. And there shall be *signs* in the *sun*, and in the *moon*, and in the *stars*; and upon the earth distress of nations, with perplexity; the sea and the waves roaring;

26. Men's hearts failing then for fear, and for looking after those things which are coming on the earth: for the powers of heaven shall be shaken,
27. And then shall they see the Son of Man coming in a cloud with power and great glory.
28. And when these things begin to come to pass, *look up*, and lift up your heads; for *your redemption draweth nigh*.
—Luke 21:25-28
29. Immediately after the (1) tribulation of those days shall the (2) sun be darkened, and the (3) moon shall not give her light, and the (4) stars shall fall from heaven, and the powers of the heavens shall be shaken:
30. And then shall appear the sign of the Son of Man in heavens: and then shall all the tribes of the earth mourn, and they shall see the (5) Son of Man coming in the clouds of heaven with power and great glory.
—Matthew 24:29, 30 *(see below)
29. So ye in like manner, when ye shall see these things come to pass, know that it is nigh, even at the doors.
—Mark 13:29
34. And take heed to yourselves, lest at any time your hearts be overcharged with surfeiting, and drunkenness, and cares of this life, and so that day come upon you unawares.
—Luke 21:34
28. For He will finish the work, and cut it short in righteousness: because a short work will the Lord make upon the earth.
—Romans 9:28
34. Verily I say unto you, This generation shall not pass, till all these things be fulfilled.
—Matthew 24:34
44. Therefore be ye also ready: for in such an hour as ye think not the Son of Man cometh.
—Matthew 24:44

*(1) The great tribulation ended with the beginning of the reformation in the 16th century.

(2) This was fulfilled by a day of supernatural darkness on May 19, 1780. It was not an eclipse.

(3) The moon became red as blood on the night of May 19, 1780.

(4) The great star shower (meteors) took place on the night of November 13, 1833.

(5) Christ's second coming is the next event. Are you ready?

CHAPTER 39
THE TIME OF THE END

THE TIME OF THE END AND THE MILLENNIUM

1. And I saw another mighty angel come down from heaven, clothed with a cloud: and a rainbow was upon his head, and his face was as it were the sun, and his feet as pillars of fire:
2. And he had in his hand a *little book open*: and he set his right foot upon the *sea* [represents heavily populated areas], and his left foot on the *earth* [represents sparsely populated areas],
5. And the angel which I saw stand upon the sea and upon the earth lifted up his hand to heaven,
6. And sware by Him that liveth for ever and ever, who created heaven, and the things that therein are, and the earth, and the things that therein are, and the sea, and the things which are therein, that there should be time *no longer*: [The end of prophetic time].
—Revelation 10:1, 2, 5, 6

WHEN IS THE END OF PROPHETIC TIME?

14. And when he said unto me, Unto two thousand and three hundred days; then shall the sanctuary be cleaned. [In prophecy a day represents a year.]
—Daniel 8:14

6. And when thou hast accomplished them, lie again on the right side, and thou shalt bear the iniquity of the house of Judah forty days: *I have appointed thee each day for a year*.
—Ezekiel 4:6
34. After the number of days in which ye searched the land, even forty days, *each day for a year*, shall ye bear your iniquities, even forty years, and ye shall know my breach of promise. [The 2300 days/years started at the command of Artaxerxes, king of Persia (reigns 464-425), to restore and rebuild Jerusalem, in 457 B.C.]
—Numbers 14:34
7. And there went up some of the children of Israel, and of the priests, and the Levites, . . . in the seventh year of Artaxerxes the king.
8. And He [Ezra] came to Jerusalem in the fifth month, which was in the seventh year of the king. [The 2300 years from 457 B.C. takes you to the year 1844 A.D., remember, there is no zero year.]
—Ezra 7:7, 8

HOW DO WE KNOW THAT PROPHETIC TIME BEGINS WITH THE YEAR 457 B.C.?

24. Seventy weeks are determined upon thy people and upon the holy city, to finish the transgression, and to make and end of sins, and to make reconciliation [Christ's death] for iniquity, and to bring in everlasting righteousness, and to seal up the vision and prophecy, and to anoint the most Holy.
[seventy weeks = 70 X 7 = 490 days/years.]
25. Know therefore and understand, that from the going forth of the commandment to restore and build Jerusalem unto the Messiah the Prince [Christ] shall be seven weeks [49 years], and three score and two weeks [434 years]: the street shall be built again, and the wall, even in troublous times.
[Above equals 69 weeks X 7 = 483 years.]

26. And after three score and two weeks shall Messiah be cut off [crucified], but not for himself: and the people of the prince (Satan) that shall come shall destroy the city the sanctuary; and the end thereof shalt be with a flood [Roman Army], and unto the end of the war desolations [to lay waste] are determined.
[The above adds to 62 weeks or 434 years.]
27. And he shall confirm the covenant with many for one week: and in the midst of the week he shall cause the sacrifice and the oblation [religious offerings] to cease, and He shall make it desolate [lay it waste], even until the consummation [make complete], and that determined shall be poured upon the desolate.
—Daniel 9:25-27

1. 457 B.C. to 408 B.C. = 7 weeks or 49 years, Jerusalem and temple rebuilt.
2. 408 B.C. to 27 A.D. = 3 score and two weeks or 434 years, ends at Christ's Baptism and anointing with the Holy Spirit.
(See: verses 25, 26 above)
3. 27 A.D. to 31 A.D. = $3\frac{1}{2}$ years or one half week, the time of Jesus' ministry, ending at the crucifixion.
4. 31 A.D. to 34 A.D. = $3\frac{1}{2}$ years or one half week, the time message given primarily to the Jews.
(See: verse 27 above)

This ended the 70 weeks determined upon thy people [the Jews] or 490 years. After this the gospel went also to the Gentiles This proves the prophetic time of Daniel started at 457 B.C.

IN THE DAYS OF THE TIME OF THE END THE BOOKS OF DANIEL AND REVELATION WOULD BEGIN TO BE UNDERSTOOD BY GOD'S PEOPLE

7. But in the days of the voice of the seventh angel, when he shall begin to sound, the *mystery* of God should be *finished* [understood], as he hath declared to his servants the prophets.

8. And the voice which I heard from heaven spake unto me again, and said, Go and take the *little book* which is *open* [to be understood] in the hand of the angel which standeth upon the sea and upon the earth.
9. And I went unto the angel, and said unto him, Give me the *little book*. And he said unto me, Take it, and eat it up; and it shall make thy *belly bitter*, but it shall be in thy mouth *sweet as honey*.
10. And I took the *little book* out of the angel's hand, and ate it up; and it was in my mouth *sweet as honey* [The message sounded sweet and desirable]: and as soon as I had eaten it, my *belly was bitter* [The message was misunderstood and caused bitter disappointment].
—Revelation 10:7-10
4. But thou, O Daniel, shut up the words and *seal up the book*, even to the time of the end: many shall run *to and fro* (1), and *knowledge* shall be *increased* (2).
—Daniel 12:4
[1. Missionaries spreading the gospel.]
[2. Understanding of God's word.]
6. And I saw another *angel* [heavenly messenger] fly in the midst of heaven, having the *everlasting gospel* to preach unto them that dwell on the earth, and to every nation, and kindred, and tongue, and people,
7. Saying with a loud voice, Fear God, and give glory to him; for the hour of His judgment is come [Investigative Judgment]: and worship Him that made heaven, and earth and the sea, and the fountains of water.
8. And there followed another angel, saying, Babylon [false religion] is fallen, is fallen, that great city, because she made all nations drink of the wine of the wrath of her fornication [illicit religion].
9. And the third angel followed them, saying with a loud voice, If *any man* worship the beast and his image, and received his mark in his forehead (1.), or in his hand (2.),
[1. Propagate the false theology.]
[2. Accept for economic convenience.]

10. The same [*any man*] shall drink of the wine of the wrath of God, which is poured out without mixture into the cup of His indignation; and he shall be tormented with fire and brimstone in the presence of the holy angels, and in the presence of the Lamb [Christ]:
—Revelation 14:6-10

36. But of that day and hour *knoweth no man*, no, not the angels of heaven, but *my father only*.
—Matthew 24:36

[Christ did not know the time while a man on earth. He may know now, that He sits next to His Father in Heaven.]

32. Now learn a parable of the fig tree; When his branch is yet tender, and putteth forth leaves, ye know that summer is nigh:
33. So likewise ye, when ye shall see all these things, know that it is near, even at the doors. [Those who understand Bible prophecy can foresee Christ's soon return, just as the signs of approaching Summer.]
—Matthew 24:32, 33

1. But of the times and the seasons, brethren, ye have no need that I write unto you.
2. For yourselves know perfectly that the day of the Lord so cometh as a thief in the night.
3. For when they shall say, Peace and safety; then sudden destruction cometh upon them, as travail (labor pains) upon a woman with child; and they shall not escape.
4. But ye, brethren, are not in darkness, that that day should overtake you as a thief.
5. Ye are all the children of light, and the children of the day: we are not of the night, nor of darkness.
6. Therefore let us not sleep, as do others; but let us watch and be sober.
—1 Thessalonians 5:1-6

CHRIST CAME RIGHT ON TIME AT HIS FIRST ADVENT

4. But when the fulness of the time was come, God sent forth His Son, made of a woman, made under the law,
—Galatians 4:4

JESUS' CRUCIFIXION HAPPENED ON THE VERY HOUR FOR WHICH IT WAS PROPHESIED

4. Jesus saith unto her, Woman, What have I to do with thee? mine hour is not yet come.
—John 2:4

30. When Jesus therefore had received the vinegar, he said, It [His Father's business] is finished: and he bowed his head, and gave up the ghost.
—John 19:30
(Read Also: John 4:34; Luke 2:49)

MOST OF THE WORLD WILL NOT EXPECT HIS SECOND COMING

3. Knowing this first, that there shall come in the last days scoffers, walking after their own lusts,
4. And saying, Where is the promise of his coming? for since the fathers fell asleep, all things continue as they were from the beginning of the creation.
5. For this they willingly are ignorant of, that by the word of God the heavens were of old, and the earth standing out of the water and in the water:

[Much of the world refuses to believe in a six day creation.]

6. Whereby the world that then was, being overflowed with water, perished: [Much of the world's people refuse to accept the story of the flood as true.]
7. But the heavens and the earth, which are now, by the same word are kept in store, reserved unto fire against the day of judgment and perdition of ungodly men. [The

great coal and oil reserves are in store to help burn up and cleanse the world by fire.]
8. But, beloved, be not ignorant of this one thing, that one day is with the Lord as a thousand years, and a thousand years as one day.
—2 Peter 3:3-8

[Some believe this means that the first 6,000 years of the earth's history represents the six days of creation. The 7th day of creation, the Sabbath, is represented by the 1,000 year period or millennium that begins at Christ 2nd coming, when the earth will rest.]

FOLLOWING IS A DESCRIPTION OF SOCIETY ON EARTH JUST BEFORE CHRIST RETURNS

37. But as the days of Noe [Noah] were, so shall also the coming of the Son of Man be.
38. For as in the days that were before the flood they were eating and drinking, marrying and giving in marriage, until the day that Noe [Noah] entered into the ark,
39. And knew not until the flood came, and took them all away; so shall also the coming of the Son of Man be.
—Matthew 24:37-39
9. The Lord is not slack concerning his promise, as some men count slackness; but is longsuffering to us ward (toward us), not willing that any should perish, but that all should come to repentance.
—2 Peter 3:9

[Just when many think the Lord is not coming He will come as a *thief* in the night and surprise most of the world.]

EVENTS DURING THE MILLENNIUM

2. And he laid hold on the dragon, that old serpent, which is the Devil, and Satan, and bound him a thousand years,
3. And cast him into the bottomless pit, and shut him up,

and set a seal upon him, that he should deceive the nations no more, till the thousand years should be fulfilled: and after that he must be loosed a little season.
—Revelation 20:2, 3

[Satan is bound to this earth by circumstances because there is no one left to tempt. The wicked are dead and the righteous are in heaven during the millennium.]

4. But in the seventh year shall be a sabbath of rest unto the land, a sabbath for the LORD: thou shalt neither sow thy field, nor prune thy vineyard.
—Leviticus 25:4
34. Then shall the land enjoy her sabbaths, as long as it lieth desolate, and ye be in your enemies' land; even then shall the land rest, and enjoy her sabbaths.
—Leviticus 26:34

[Predictions of Babylonian captivity]

21. To fulfil the word of the LORD by the mouth of Jeremiah, until the land had enjoyed her sabbaths: for as long as she lay desolate she kept sabbath, to fulfil threescore and ten years.
—2 Chronicles 36:21
11. And this whole land shall be a desolation, and an astonishment; and these nations shall serve the king of Babylon seventy years,
—Jeremiah 25:11

[The children of Israel were supposed to allow the earth to rest every seventh year, but they didn't do it. So the earth was allowed to rest 70 years while they were in Babylonian captivity. The earth will rest again during the millennium because mankind has not allowed it to rest as God intended.]

A DESCRIPTION OF THE EARTH DURING THE MILLENIUM FOLLOWS

23. I beheld the earth, and, lo, it was without form, and void; and the heavens, and they had no light.
24. I beheld the mountains, and, lo, they trembled, and all hills moved lightly.
25. I beheld, and, lo, there was no man, and all the birds of the heavens were fled.
26. I beheld, and, lo, the fruitful place was a wilderness, and all the cities thereof were broken down at the presence of the LORD, and by his fierce anger.
—Jeremiah 4:23-26

[The time of the end began in 1844 and all prophetic time is now past.]

CHAPTER 40
THE MILLENNIUM

(The word "millennium" not found in English Bible. It comes from two Latin words, mille, which means 1000; and annus, year.)

TWO RESURRECTIONS SEPERATED BY 1,000 YEARS

28. Marvel not at this: for the hour is coming, in the which all that are in the graves shall hear his voice,
29. And shall come forth; they that have done good, unto the resurrection of life; and they that have done evil, unto the resurrection of damnation.
—John 5:28, 29

5. But the rest of the dead lived not again until the thousand years were finished. This is the first resurrection.
—Revelation 20:5

THE RIGHTEOUS DEAD ARE RAISED IN THE FIRST RESURRECTION AND WITH THE RIGHTEOUS LIVING GO TO LIVE WITH CHRIST FOR 1,000 YEARS.

2. In my Father's house are many mansions: if it were no so, I would have told you. I go to prepare a place for you.
3. And if I go and prepare a place for you, I will come again, and receive you unto myself; that where I am, there ye may be also.

—John 14:2, 3

18. And there were voices, and thunders, and lightnings; and there was a great earthquake, such as was not since men were upon the earth, so mighty an earthquake, and so great.
20. And every island fled away, and the mountains were not found.
21. And there fell upon men a great hail out of heaven, every stone about the weigh of a talent [75 pounds]: and men blasphemed God because of the plague of the hail; for the plague thereof was exceeding great.
—Revelation 16:18, 20, 21

16. For the Lord himself shall descend from heaven with a shout, with the voice of the archangel, and with the trump of God: and the dead in Christ shall rise first:
17. Then we which are alive and remain shall be caught up together with them in the clouds, to meet the Lord in the air: and so shall we ever be with the Lord.
—1 Thessalonians 4:16, 17

51. Behold, I show you a mystery: We shall not all sleep, but we shall all be changed,
52. In a moment, in the twinkling of an eye, at the last trump: for the trumpet shall sound, and the dead shall be raised incorruptible, and we shall be changed.
—1 Corinthians 15:51, 52

21. Who shall change our vile [lowly] body, that it may be fashioned like unto His glorious body, according to the working whereby, He is able even to subdue all things unto Himself.
—Philippians 3:21

8. And then shall that wicked be revealed, whom the Lord shall consume with the spirit of His mouth, and shall destroy with the brightness of His coming:
—2 Thessalonians 2:8

6. Blessed and holy is he that hath part in the first resurrection: on such the second death hath no power, but they shall be priests of God and of Christ, and shall reign with him a thousand years.

—Revelation 20:6

THE RIGHTEOUS SAVED WILL JUDGE THE WICKED WHO ARE STILL DEAD UPON THE EARTH

2. Do ye not know that the saints shall judge the world? and if the world shall be judged by you, are ye unworthy to judge the smallest matters?
3. Know ye not that we shall judge angels? how much more things that pertain to this life?
—1 Corinthians 6:2, 3
4. And I saw thrones, and they sat upon them, and judgment was given unto them: and I saw the souls of them that were beheaded for the witness of Jesus and for the word of God, and which had not worshipped the beast, neither his image, neither, had received his mark upon their foreheads, or in their hands; and they lived and reigned with Christ a thousand years.
—Revelation 20:4
11. And I saw a great white throne, and Him that sat on it, from whose face the earth and the heavens fled away; and there was found no place for them.
12. And I saw the dead, small and great, stand before God: and the books were opened: and another book was opened, which is the book of life: and the dead were judged out of those things which were written in the books, according to their works.
—Revelation 20:11, 12
1. And after these things I heard a great voice of much people in heaven, saying, alleluia; Salvation, and glory, and honour, and power, unto the Lord our God:
2. For true and righteous are His judgments: for He hath judged the great whore, which did corrupt the earth with her fornication, and hath avenged blood of his servants at her hand.
—Revelation 19:1, 2

15. And whosoever was not found written in the *book of life* was cast into the lake of fire.
    —Revelation 20:15

THE WICKED DEAD WILL REMAIN DEAD ANOTHER 1,000 YEARS. THE WICKED WHO ARE ALIVE WILL BE STRUCK DEAD BY CHRIST'S SECOND COMING.

33. And the slain of the LORD shall be at that day from one end of the earth even unto the other end of the earth: they shall not be lamented, neither gathered, nor buried; they shall be dung upon the ground.
    —Jeremiah 25:33
1. Behold, the LORD maketh the earth empty, and maketh it waste, and turneth it upside down, and scattereth abroad the inhabitants thereof.
    —Isaiah 24:1
23. I beheld the earth, and, lo, it was without form, and void; and the heavens, and they had no light.
24. I beheld the mountains, and, lo, they trembled, and all the hills moved lightly.
25. I beheld, and, lo, there was no man, and all the birds of the heavens were fled.
26. I beheld, and, lo, the fruitful place was a wilderness and all the cities thereof were broken down at the presence of the LORD, and by His fierce anger.
27. For thus hath the LORD said, the whole land shall be desolate; yet will I not make a full end.
    —Jeremiah 4:23-27

SATAN WILL BE LEFT ON THE EARTH WITH NO ONE TO TEMPT FOR 1,000 YEARS.

1. And I saw an angel come down from heaven, having the key of the bottomless pit and a great chain in his hand.
2. And he laid hold on the dragon, that old serpent, which is the Devil, and Satan, and bound him a thousand years,
3. And cast him into the bottomless pit, and shut him up,

and set a seal upon him, that he should deceive the nations no more, till the thousand years should be fulfilled: after that he must be loosed a little season.
—Revelation 20:1-3

THERE IS NO SECOND CHANCE FOR THE WICKED

11. He that is unjust, let him be unjust still: and he that is righteous, let him be righteous still: and he that is holy, let him be holy still.
12. And, behold, I come quickly; and my reward is with me, to give every man according as his work shall be.
—Revelation 22:11, 12

NEW JERUSALEM DESCENDS AFTER 1,000 YEARS.

2. And I John saw the holy city, New Jerusalem, coming down from God out of heaven, prepared as a bride adorned for her husband.
—Revelation 21:2
4. And His feet shall stand in that day upon the mount of Olives, which is before Jerusalem on the east, and the mount of Olives shall cleave in the midst thereof toward the east and toward the west, and there shall be a very great valley; and half of the mountain shall remove toward the north, and half of it towards the south.
5. And ye shall flee to the valley of the mountains; for the valley of the mountains shall reach unto Azel: yea, ye shall flee, like as ye fled from before the earthquake in the days of Uzziah king of Judah: and the LORD my God shall come, and all the saints with thee.
—Zechariah 14:4, 5

THE RESURRECTED WICKED AGREE, GOD IS JUST.

10. That at the name of Jesus every knee should bow, of things in heaven, and things in earth, and things under the earth;

11. And that every tongue should confess that Jesus Christ is the Lord, to the glory of God the Father.
—Philippians 2:10, 11

SATAN'S ARMY OF RESURRECTED WICKED, WILL ATTEMPT TO CAPTURE THE NEW JERUSALEM.

7. And when the thousand years are expired, Satan shall be loosed out of his prison,
8. And shall go out to deceive the nations which are in the four quarters of the earth, Gog and Magog, to gather them together to battle: the number of whom is as the sand of the sea.
9. And they went up on the breadth of the earth, and compassed the camp of the saints about, and the beloved city: and fire came down from God out of heaven, and devoured them.
—Revelation 20:7-9
10. But the day of the Lord will come as a thief in the night; in the which the heavens shall pass away with a great noise, and the elements shall melt with fervent heat, the earth also and the works that are therein shall be burned up.
—2 Peter 3:10
1. For, behold, the day cometh, that shall burn as an oven; and all the proud, yea, and all that do wickedly, shall be stubble: and the day that cometh shall burn them up, saith the LORD of hosts, that it shall leave them neither root nor branch.
2. But unto you that fear my name shall the Sun of righteousness arise with healing in his wings; and ye shall go forth, and grow up as calves of the stall.
3. And ye shall tread down the wicked; for they shall be ashes under the soles of your feet in the day that I shall do this, saith the LORD of hosts.

—Malachi 4:1-3
15. And whosoever was not found written in the book of life was cast into the lake of fire.
—Revelation 20:15

A NEW EARTH IS CREATED AFTER THE FIRE

13. Nevertheless we, according to His promise, look for new heavens and a new earth, wherein dwelleth righteousness.
—2 Peter 3:13

1. And I saw a new heaven and a new earth: for the first heaven and the first earth were passed away; and there was no more sea.
—Revelation 21:1

3. And I heard a great voice out of heaven saying, Behold, the tabernacle of God is with men, and He will dwell with them, and they shall be His people, and God Himself shall be with them, and be their God.
—Revelation 21:3

5. Blessed are the meek: for they shall inherit the earth.
—Matthew 5:5

17. For, behold, I create new heavens and a new earth: and the former shall not be remembered, nor come into mind.
—Isaiah 65:17

9. What do ye imagine against the Lord? He will make an utter end: affliction shall not rise up the second time.
—Nahum 1:9

CHAPTER 41
GOD'S LAW

THE LAW OF GOD

13. And He [*God*] declared unto you His covenant, which He commanded you to perform, even *ten commandments*; and He wrote them upon two tables of stone.
—Deuteronomy 4:13

I

3. Thou shalt have no other gods before me.

II

4. Thou shalt not make unto thee any graven image, or any likeness or anything that is in heaven above, or that is in the earth beneath, or that is in the water under the earth:
5. Thou shalt not bow down thyself to them, nor serve them: for I the LORD thy God am a jealous God, visiting the iniquity of the fathers upon the children unto the third and fourth generation of them that hate me;
6. and showing mercy unto thousands of them that love me, and keep my *commandments*.

III

7. Thou shalt not take the name of the LORD thy God in vain, for the LORD will not hold him guiltless that taketh His name in vain.

IV

8. Remember the Sabbath Day, to keep in Holy.
9. Six days shalt thou labour, and do all thy work:
10. But the seventh day is the Sabbath of the LORD thy God: in it thou shalt not do any work, thou, nor thy son, nor thy daughter, thy manservant, nor thy maidservant, nor thy cattle, nor thy stranger that is within thy gate:
11. For in six days the LORD made heaven and earth, the sea, and all that in them is, and rested the seventh day: wherefore the LORD blessed the Sabbath Day, and Hallowed it.

V

12. Honour thy father and thy mother: that thy days may be long upon the land which the Lord thy God giveth thee.

VI

13. Thou shalt not kill.

VII

14. Thou shalt not commit adultery.

VIII

15. Thou shalt not steal.

IX

16. Thou shalt not bear false witness against thy neighbour.

X

17. Thou shalt not covet thy neighbour's house, thou shalt not covet thy neighbour's wife, nor his manservant, nor his maidservant, nor his ox, nor his ass, nor any thing that is thy neighbour's.
—Exodus 20:3-17

2. Ye shall not add unto the word which I command you, neither shall ye diminish ought from it, that ye may keep the *commandments* of the LORD your God which I command you.
—Deuteronomy 4:2

13. ... Fear God, and keep His *commandments*: for this is the whole duty of man.
    —Ecclesiastes 12:13
7. The LAW of the LORD is perfect, converting the soul: the testimony of the LORD is sure, making wise the simple.
8. The *statutes* of the LORD are right, rejoicing the heart: the *commandment* of the LORD is pure, enlightening the eyes.
    —Psalms 19:7, 8
11. Moreover by them is Thy servant warned: and in keeping of them there is great reward.
    —Psalms 19:11
17. ... but if thou wilt enter into life, keep the *commandments*.
    —Matthew 19:17
12. Wherefore the law is holy, and the *commandment* holy, and just, and good.
    —Romans 7:12
18. And knowest His will, and approvest the things that are more excellent, being instructed out of the LAW:
    —Romans 2:18
21. Not every one that saith unto Me, Lord, Lord, shall enter into the kingdom of heaven; but he that doeth *the will of my father* which is in heaven.
    —Matthew 7:21
3. But He answered and said unto them, Why do ye also transgress the *commandment* of God by your tradition?
    —Matthew 15:3
9. But in vain they do worship Me, teaching for doctrines the *commandments* of men.
    —Matthew 15:9
    (Read Also: Matthew 15:3-9)
4. Whosoever committeth sin transgresseth also the LAW: for sin is the transgression of the LAW.
    —1 John 3:4

God's Law

7. What shall we say then? Is the LAW sin? God forbid. Nay, I had not known sin, but by the LAW: for I had not known lust, except the LAW had said, Thou shalt not covet.
   —Romans 7:7
10. For whosoever shall keep the whole LAW, and yet offend in one point, he is guilty of all.
11. For He that said, Do not commit adultery, said, also, Do not kill. Now if thou commit no adultery, and yet if thou kill, thou art become a transgressor of the LAW.
    —James 2:10, 11
9. If we confess our sins, He is faithful and just to forgive us our sins, and to cleanse us from all unrighteousness.
   —1 John 1:9
13. ... Fear God, and keep His *commandments*: for this is the whole duty of man.
14. For God shall bring every work into judgment, with every secret thing, whether it be good, or whether it be evil.
    —Ecclesiastes 12:13, 14
12. So speak ye, and so do, as they that shall be judged by the LAW of liberty.
    —James 2:12
165. Great peace have they which love Thy LAW: and nothing shall offend them.
     —Psalms 119:165
18. O that thou hadst harkened to My *commandments*! then had thy peace been as a river, and thy righteousness as the waves of the sea.
    —Isaiah 48:18
10. The fear of the Lord is the beginning of wisdom: a good understanding have all they that do His *commandments*.
    —Psalm 111:10
1. Blessed is the man that walketh not in the counsel of the ungodly, nor standeth in the way of sinners, nor sitteth in the seat of the scornful.
2. But his delight is in the LAW of the Lord; and in His LAW doth he meditate day and night.
   —Psalms 1:1, 2

7. Because the carnal mind is enmity against God: for it is not subject to the LAW of God, neither indeed can be.
—Romans 8:7

3. For this is the love of God, that we keep His *commandments*: and His *commandments* are not grievous.
—1 John 5:3

10. Love worketh no ill to his neighbor: therefore love is the fulfilling of the law.
—Romans 13:10

37. Thou shalt love the Lord thy God with all thy heart, and with all thy soul, and with all thy mind.
38. This is the first and great *commandment*.
39. And the second is like unto it, Thou shalt love thy neighbor as thyself.
40. On these two *commandments* hang all the LAW and the prophets.
—Matthew 22:37-40

4. He that saith, I know Him, and keepeth not His *commandments*, is a liar, and the truth is not in him.
—1 John 2:4

19. If ye be willing and obedient, ye shall eat the good of the land.
—Isaiah 1:19

1. Blessed are the undefiled in the way, who walk in the LAW of the Lord.
—Psalms 119:1

THE PERPETUITY OF THE LAW

12. There is one *lawgiver*, who is able to save and to destroy.
—James 4:12

6. For I am the Lord, I change not.
—Malachi 3:6

7. The works of His hands are verity and judgment; all His *commandments* are sure.
1. They stand fast forever and ever, and are done in truth and uprightness.
—Psalms 111:7, 8

God's Law

17. Think not that I am come to destroy the LAW, or the prophets: I am not come to destroy, but to fulfil.
18. For verily I say unto you, Till heaven and earth pass, one jot or one tittle shall in no wise pass from the law, till all be *fulfilled*.
19. Whosoever therefore shall break one of these least commandments, and shall teach men so, he shall be called the least in the kingdom of heaven: but whosoever shall do and teach them, the same shall be called great in the kingdom of heaven.
—Matthew 5:17-19

[Some teach the word "fulfilled" means the ten commandments were abolished at the cross. Only the Jewish ceremonial laws were done away with after the Lamb of God, died on the cross. A Sacrificial lamb was no longer needed. Let us examine other texts with the word fulfill.]

2. Bear ye one another's burdens, and so *fulfil [obey]* the LAW of Christ.
—Galatians 6:2
8. If ye *fulfil [obey]* the royal law according to the scripture, Thou shalt love thy neighbour as thyself, ye do well:
—James 2:8

SOME SYNONYMS, Webster: to make full, make whole, carry out, accomplish, consummate, execute, measure up, finish, answer, satisfy.

10. If ye keep *My commandments*, ye shall abide in My love; even as I have kept *My Father's commandments*, and abide in His love.
—John 15:10
6. He that saith he abideth in Him ought himself also so to walk, even as He walked.
—1 John 2:6
4. Whosoever committeth sin transgresseth also the LAW: for sin is the transgression of the LAW.
—1 John 3:4

23. For all have sinned, and come short of the glory of God.
—Romans 3:23

9. What then? are we better than they? No, in no wise: for we have before proved both Jews and Gentiles, that they are all under sin;
—Romans 3:9

19. Now we know that what things soever the LAW saith, it saith to them who are under the LAW: that every mouth may be stopped, and all the world may become guilty before God.
—Romans 3:19

31. Do we then make void the LAW through faith? God forbid: yea, we establish the LAW.
—Romans 3:31

13. For not the hearers of the LAW are just before God, but the doers of the LAW shall be justified.
—Romans 2:13

25. But he that looketh into the perfect LAW, the LAW of liberty and so continueth, being not a hearer that forgetteth, but a doer that worketh, this man shall be blessed in his doing.
—James 1:25, R.V.

2. By this we know that we love the children of God, when we love God, and keep *His commandments*.

3. For this is the love of God, that we keep *His commandments*.
—1 John 5:2, 3

12. Here is the patience of the saints: here are they that keep the *commandments* of God, and the faith of Jesus.
—Revelation 14:12

CHAPTER 42
THE SABBATH

THE BIBLE SABBATH

1. Thus the heavens and the earth were finished, and all the host of them.
2. And on the seventh day God ended His work which He had made; and He rested on the seventh day from all His work which He had made.
3. And God blessed the seventh day, and sanctified it: because that in it He had rested from all His work which God created and made.
—Genesis 2:1-3

THE SABBATH IMPORTANCE RE-CONFIRMED

15. And when the children of Israel saw it, they said one to another, It is manna: for they wist not what it was and Moses said unto them, This is the bread which the LORD hath given you to eat.
16. This is the thing which the LORD hath commanded, gather of it every man according to his eating, an omer for every man, according to the number of your persons; take ye every man for them which are in his tents.
26. Six days ye shall gather it; but on the seventh day, which is the sabbath, in it *there shall be none*.
—Exodus 16:15, 16, 26

GOD GIVES THE TEN COMMANDMENTS

10. And the LORD delivered unto me [Moses] two tables of stone written with the *finger of God*; and on them was written according to all the words, which the LORD spake with you in the mount out of the midst of the fire in the day of the assembly.
11. And it came to pass at the end of forty days and forty nights, that the LORD gave me the two tables of stone, even the tables of the covenant.
—Deuteronomy 9:10, 11
1. And God spake all these words, saying,
2. I am the LORD thy God, which have brought thee out of the land of Egypt, out of the house of bondage.
3. (I) Thou shalt have no other gods before me.
4. (II) Thou shalt not make unto thee any graven image, or any likeness of anything that is in heaven above, or that is in the earth beneath, or that is in the water under the earth:
5. Thou shalt not bow down thyself to them, nor serve them: for I the LORD thy God am a jealous God, visiting the iniquity of the father upon the children unto the third and fourth generation of them that hate me;
6. And showing mercy unto thousands of them that love me, and keep my commandments.
7. (III) Thou shalt not take the name of the LORD thy God in vain; for the LORD will not hold him guiltless that taketh His name in vain.
8. (IV) *Remember the sabbath day, to keep it holy.*
9. Six days shalt thou labour, and do all thy work:
10. But the seventh day is the sabbath of the LORD thy God; in it thou shalt not do any work, thou, nor thy son, nor thy daughter, thy manservant, nor thy maidservant nor thy cattle, nor thy stranger that is within thy gates:
11. For in six days the LORD made heaven and earth, the sea, and all that in them is, and rested the seventh day: wherefore the *LORD blessed the sabbath day, and hallowed it.* (Read Also: 1 Chronicles 17:27)

12. (V) Honour thy father and thy mother: that thy days may be long upon the land which the Lord thy God giveth thee.
13. (VI) Thou shalt not kill.
14. (VII) Thou shalt not commit adultery.
15. (VIII) Thou shalt not steal.
16. (IX) Thou shalt not bear false witness against thy neighbour.
17. (X) Thou shalt not covet thy neighbour's house, thou shalt not covet thy neighbour's wife, nor his manservant, nor his maidservant, nor his ox, nor his ass, nor anything that is thy neighbour's.
—Exodus 20:1-17

2. Ye shall not add unto the word which I command you, neither shall ye diminish ought from it, that ye may keep the commandments of the LORD your God which I command you.
—Deuteronomy 4:2

THE SABBATH A SIGN BETWEEN GOD AND MAN

12. and the LORD spake unto Moses, saying,
13. Speak thou also unto the children of Israel, saying, Verily my sabbaths ye shall keep: for it is a *sign* between me and you throughout your generations; that ye may know that I am the LORD that doth sanctify you.
15. Six days may work be done; but in the seventh is the sabbath of rest, holy to the LORD; . . .
17. It is a *sign* between Me and the children of Israel for ever: for in six days the LORD made heaven and earth, and on the seventh day He rested, and was refreshed.
—Exodus 31:12, 13, 15, 17

WHAT THE PROPHETS SAID ABOUT THE SABBATH

13. If thou turn away thy foot from the sabbath, from doing thy pleasure on my holy day; and call the sabbath a delight, the holy of the LORD, honourable; and shalt hon-

our Him, not doing thine own ways, nor finding thine own pleasure, nor speaking thine own words:
14. Then shalt thou delight thyself in the LORD; and I will cause thee to ride upon the high places of the earth, and the heritage of Jacob thy father: for the mouth of the LORD hath spoken it.
—Isaiah 58:13, 14
2. Blessed is the man that doeth this, and the Son of Man that layeth hold on it; that keepeth the sabbath form polluting it, and keepeth his hand from doing any evil.
6. Also the sons of the stranger, that join themselves to the LORD, to serve Him, and to love the name of the LORD, to be His servants, everyone that keepeth the sabbath from polluting it, and taketh hold of my covenant;
7. Even them will I bring to my holy mountain, and make them joyful in my house of prayer . . .
—Isaiah 56:2, 6, 7

THE SABBATH TO BE OBSERVED IN THE NEW EARTH

22. For as the new heavens and the new earth, which I will make, shall remain before me, saith the LORD, so shall your seed and your name remain.
23. and it shall come to pass, that from one new moon to another, and from one sabbath to another, shall all flesh come to worship before me, saith the LORD.
—Isaiah 66:22, 23
12. Moreover also I gave them my sabbaths to be a *sign* between me and them, that they might know that I am the LORD that sanctify them.
—Ezekiel 20:12
20. And hallow my sabbaths; and they shall be a SIGN between me and you, that ye may know that I am the LORD you God.
—Ezekiel 20:20

CHRISTIANS TODAY ARE ISRAELITES

11. And I say unto you, That many shall come from the east and west, and shall sit down with Abraham, and Isaac, and Jacob, in the kingdom of heaven.
—Matthew 8:11
14. That the blessing of Abraham might come on the Gentiles through Jesus Christ; that we might receive the promise of the Spirit through faith.
29. And if ye be Christ's then are ye Abraham's seed, and heirs according to the promise.
—Galatians 3:14, 29
(Read Also: Romans 9:6)

CHRIST OBSERVED THE SABBATH

16. And he came to Nazareth, where He had been brought up: and as His custom was, He went into the synagogue on the sabbath day, and stood up for to read.
31. And came down to Capernaum, a city of Galilee, and taught them on the sabbath days.
—Luke 4:16, 31
(Read Also: Matthew 24:20)
10. And He was teaching in one of the synagogues on the sabbath.
—Luke 13:10

CHRIST IS LORD OF THE SABBATH

8. For the Son of Man is Lord even of the sabbath day.
—Matthew 12:8
(Read Also: Revelation 1:10)
27. And He said unto them, The sabbath was made for man, and not man for the sabbath:
28. Therefore the Son of Man is Lord also of the sabbath.
—Mark 2:27, 28

CHRIST CREATED THE SABBATH

3. All things were made by Him [Christ]; and without Him was not anything made that was made.
—John 1:3
(Read Also: Ephesians 3:9)

CHRIST IS LORD OF THE COMMANDMENTS

15. If ye love me, keep my commandments.
—John 14:15

THE COMMANDMENTS ARE NOT CHANGEABLE

17. And it is easier for heaven and earth to pass, than one title of the law to fail.
—Luke 16:17
(Read Also: Matthew 5:18; Romans 6:23)

4. Whosoever committeth sin transgresseth also the law for sin is the transgression of the law.
—1 John 3:4

10. For whosoever shall keep the whole law, and yet offend in one point, he is guilty of all.
—James 2:10
(Read Also: James 4:17)

16. This is the covenant that I will make with them after those days, saith the Lord, I will put my laws into their hearts, and in their minds will I write them;
—Hebrews 10:16

CHRIST RESTED ON THE SABBATH IN THE TOMB

42. And now when the even was come, because it was the preparation, that is, the day before the sabbath,
—Mark 15:42
(Read Also: Luke 23:56)

1. And when the sabbath was past, Mary Magdalene, and Mary the mother of James, and Salome, had bought sweet spices, that they might come and anoint Him.

2. And very early in the morning the first day of the week, they came unto the sepulchre at the rising of the sun.
—Mark 16:1, 2

THE APOSTLE PAUL OBSERVED THE SABBATH

2. And Paul, as his manner was, went in unto them, and three sabbath days reasoned with them out of the scriptures,
—Acts 17:2

4. And he reasoned in the synagogue every sabbath, and persuaded the Jews and the Greeks.
—Acts 18:4

4. For He spake in a certain place of the seventh day on this wise, and God did rest the seventh day from all his works.
—Hebrews 4:4

14. But when they departed form Perga, they came to Antioch in Pisidia, and went into the synagogue on the sabbath day, and sat down.

42. And when the Jews were gone out of the synagogue, the Gentiles besought that these words might be preached to them the next sabbath.

44. And the next sabbath day came almost the whole city together to hear the word of God.
—Acts 13:14, 42, 44

13. and on the sabbath we went out of the city by a river side, where prayer was wont to be made; and we sat down, and spake unto the women which resorted thither.
—Acts 16:13

THE SABBATH KEPT IN NEW JERUSALEM

12. Here is the patients of the saints: here are they that keep the commandments of God, and the faith of Jesus.
—Revelation 14:12

14. Blessed are they that do His commandments, that they may have right to the tree of life, and may enter in through the gates into the city.
—Revelation 22:14

8. Jesus Christ the same yesterday, and today, and forever.
   —Hebrews 13:8
   (Read Also: 2 Timothy 2:15)

CHAPTER 43
THE CHANGE OF THE SABBATH

THE CHANGE OF THE SABBATH

8. Remember the sabbath day, to keep it holy,
9. Six days shalt thou labour, and do all thy work:
10. But the seventh day is the sabbath of the LORD thy God; in it thou shalt not do any work, thou, nor thy son, nor thy daughter, thy manservant, nor thy maidservant, nor thy cattle, nor thy stranger that is within thy gates:
11. For in six days the LORD made heaven and earth, the sea, and all that in them is, and rested the seventh day: wherefore the LORD blessed the sabbath day, and hallowed it.
 —Exodus 20:8-11

[The only weekly Sabbath or weekly holy day ever mentioned in the Bible is the seventh day, which Christ our Creator, blessed and set apart for man at the beginning of the world's history.]
(Read Also: Genesis 2:3)

34. My covenant will I not break, nor altar the things that is gone out of my lips.
 —Psalms 89:43

SABBATH WAS STILL OBSERVED AFTER CHRIST WAS ON EARTH

14. But when they departed from Perga, they came to Antioch in Pisidia, and went into the synagogue on the sabbath day, and sat down.
42. And when the Jews were gone out of the synagogue, the Gentiles besought that these words might be preached to them the next Sabbath.
—Acts 13:14, 42

[This was 13 years after the resurrection.]

4. And he reasoned in the synagogue every sabbath, and persuaded the Jews and the Greeks.
—Acts 18:4

[This was 23 years after the resurrection.]
(Read Also: Acts 13:27; 15:21; 17:1-3)
[If the first day had taken the place of the seventh as God's holy day at the resurrection of Christ, the book of Acts would not have called the seventh day the Sabbath day for 23 years after the resurrection. This proves that the apostles regarded the seventh day as the Sabbath of the Lord. Since the transfer of the day of worship from the seventh to the first was not made in New Testament times, it must have been made by uninspired men later. Hence the change rests only on human authority.]
[The first law every made setting Sunday apart as a day of rest was made by Emperor Constantine on March 7, 321 A.D. The first rule directing that Christians should rest on the first day of the week in place of seventh was in the Council of Laodicea in 364 A.D.]

25. And he shall speak great words against the most High, and shall wear out the saints of the most High, and think to change times and laws: and they shall be given into his hand until a time and times and the dividing of time.
—Daniel 7:25

The Change of the Sabbath

[God foretold that a power would attempt to change the times and law of God. The only place in God's law that mentions time is the fourth commandment, where God directs man to count time, devoting the first six days of the week to labor, and to rest the seventh, or last, day of the week. Under the rule of the Catholic church this arrangement was reversed, so that men would rest on the first day of the week and work the last six. Note: that the substitution was to last for a time, times, and dividing of time, "or 1260 prophetic days, or literal years."
$360 + 720 + 180 = 1260$ or 42 months x 30 days $= 1260$..
You may also read about the 1260 years in Revelation 12:6, 14: 13:4. Using the Jewish calendar, which has 360 days in a year all three add up to the same amount of time—1260 years.]

A DAY IN PROPHECY = A CALENDAR YEAR.

6. . . . and thou shalt bear the iniquity of the house of Judah forty days: I have appointed thee each day for a year.
—Ezekiel 4:6

34. . . . each day for a year, shall ye bear your iniquities, even forty years, and ye shall know my breach of promise.
—Numbers 14:34

[The 1260 year period began in 538 A.D., when the Roman Emperor Justinian made the papal power supreme in Christendom. The period ended in 1798 when Napoleon's general, Alexander Berthier, took the pope captive. It is a fact that light on this wrong substitution of the first day for the seventh day of the week did not come to the whole world until after 1798 A.D.]

SABBATH TRUTH TO BE MADE KNOWN AT END TIME.

4. But thou, O Daniel, shut up the words, and seal the book,

even to the time of the end: many shall run to and fro, and knowledge shall be increased.
—Daniel 12:4

SUNDAY KEEPING IN PAST TIMES NOT CONDEMNED

41. Jesus said unto them, If ye were blind, ye should have no sin: but now ye say, We see; therefore your sin remaineth. John 9:41.
17. Therefore to him that knoweth to do good, and doeth it not, to him it is sin.
—James 4:17
4. Whosoever committeth sin transgresseth also the law: for sin is the transgression of the law.
—1 John 3:4

DO WE OBEY GOD OR MAN?

16. ye not, that to whom ye yield yourselves servants to obey, his servants ye are to whom ye obey; whether of sin unto death or of obedience unto righteousness?
—Romans 6:16
29. Then Peter and the other apostles answered and said, We ought to obey God rather than men.
—Acts 5:29
9. And being made perfect, He became the author of eternal salvation unto all them that obey Him;
—Hebrews 5:9

[We must obey Christ if we hope to be saved, this includes keeping holy the seventh day, which Christ as Creator sanctified for us.]

FIRST DAY OF THE WEEK IN THE NEW TESTAMENT

[Only eight N.T. texts mention the first day of the week. None prove a change in the day of worship.]

The Change of the Sabbath

Text # 1:
9. Now when Jesus was risen early the first day of the week, He appeared first to Mary Magdalene, out of whom He had cast seven devils.
—Mark 16:9

Text # 2:
1. And when the sabbath was past, Mary Magdalene, and Mary the mother of James and Salome, had bought sweet spices, that they might come and anoint Him.
2. And very early in the morning the first day of the week, they came unto the sepulchre at the rising of the sun.
—Mark 16:1, 2

Text #3:
1. In the end of the sabbath, as it began to dawn toward the first day of the week, came Mary Magdalene and the other Mary to see the sepulchres.
—Matthew 28:1

Text # 4:
54. And that day was the preparation, and the sabbath drew on.
55. And the women also, which came with Him from Galilee, followed after, and beheld the sepulchre, and how His body was laid.
56. And they returned and prepared spices and ointments; and rested the sabbath day according to the commandment.
—Luke 23:54-56
1. Now upon the first day of the week, very early in the morning, they came unto the sepulchre, bringing the spices which they had prepared, and certain others with them.
—Luke 24:1

[The women came to the tomb on the first day of the week, Sunday, to embalm the body of Jesus.]

Text # 5:
1. The first day of the week cometh Mary Magdalene early, when it was yet dark, unto the sepulchre, and seeth the stone taken away from the sepulchre.
—John 20:1

Text # 6:
19. Then the same day at evening, being the first day of the week, when the doors where shut where the disciples were assembled for fear of the Jews, came Jesus and stood in the midst and saith unto them Peace be unto you.
—John 20:19
(Read Also: Mark 16:9-14)

[Jesus appeared to His disciples to convince them that He was risen from the dead. The disciples did not meet on the Sunday night of the day that Jesus arose, to honor His resurrections on that day, because they did not believe that He was risen, and Christ had to come and convince them that He was alive. The Bible does not say one word about the first day of the week becoming a holy day in honor of our Lord's resurrection. This proves that the first day of the week was never appointed as a holy day by the Lord Jesus Christ.]

26. And after eight days again His disciples were within, and Thomas with them: then came Jesus, the doors being shut, and stood in the midst, and said, Peace be unto you.
27. Then saith He to Thomas, Reach hither thy finger, and behold my hands; and reach hither thy hand, and thrust it into my side: and be not faithless, but believing.
28. And Thomas answered and said unto Him my Lord and my God.
—John 20:26-28

[The second meeting with the disciples was to convince Thomas of His resurrection.]

Text # 7:
1. Now concerning the collection for the saints, as I have given order to the churches of Galatia, even so do ye.

The Change of the Sabbath

2. Upon the first day of the week let every one of you lay by him in store, as God hath prospered him, that there be no gathering when I come.
—1 Corinthians 16:1, 2

[This was not an order for a public collection at church, but a private laying by at home on the first of each week of something for the poor saints at Jerusalem, which Paul was to carry up to Jerusalem when he came to Corinth.]

Text # 8:

7. And upon the first day of the week, when the disciples came together to break bread, Paul preached unto them, ready to depart on the morrow; and continued his speech until the midnight.
—Acts 20:7

[This was a farewell meeting that Paul held with the Christians at Troas. There are eight different places, from thirteen to twenty-three years after Christ's resurrection in the book of Acts that plainly refers to the seventh day as the Sabbath day. (Acts 13:14, 27, 42, 44; 15:21; 16:13; 17:1-3; 18:4.) The book of Acts would not have done this these eight times, if the first day of the week had taken the place of the seventh. Baptism and the Lord's supper did come in as new ordinances under the new covenant, and they are fully explained and commanded in the N.T. If Sunday had come in as a new day to be kept, it would also have been fully explained.]

26. For as often as ye eat this bread, and drink this cup, ye do show the Lord's death till He come.
—1 Corinthians 11:26

[No one needs to keep Friday to honor our Lord's crucifixion on that day, because the Lord's supper is the divinely appointed way of commemorating the Savior's death.]

12. Buried with Him in baptism, wherein also ye are risen with Him through the faith of the operation of God, who hath raised Him from the dead.
—Colossians 2:12

[No one needs to keep Sunday to honor Christ's resurrection on that day, because baptism is God's memorial of the resurrection.]

13. But He answered and said, Every plant, which my heavenly Father hath not planted shall be rooted up.
 —Matthew 15:13

[God never planted Sunday, the first day, as a holy day, and it is certain to be rooted up forever at Christ's second coming.]

CHAPTER 44
THE TRUTH ABOUT THE SABBATH

THE TRUTH ABOUT THE SABBATH

32. And ye shall know the *truth*, and the *truth* shall make you free.
   —John 8:32
6. Jesus saith unto him, I AM the way, the *truth*, and the life: no man cometh unto the Father, but by Me.
   —John 14:6
17. Sanctify them through Thy *truth*: Thy word is *truth*.
   —John 17:17

THE BIBLE = ABSOLUTE TRUTH

142. Thy righteousness is an everlasting righteousness, and Thy law is the *truth*.
   —Psalms 119:142

THERE ARE THREE SPECIAL WORDS IN THE BIBLE: HALLOWED 23 TIMES, SANCTIFIED 40 TIMES, BLESSED 307 TIMES.

EXAMPLES:

9. After this manner therefore pray ye: Our Father which art in heaven, *hallowed* be Thy name.
   —Matthew 6:9

19. And for their sakes I *sanctify* Myself, that they also might be *sanctified* through the *truth*.
—John 17:19
21. If a man therefore purge himself from these, he shall be a vessel unto honour, *sanctified*, and meet for the master's use, and prepared unto every good work.
—2 Timothy 2:21
27. Now therefore let it please thee to *bless* the house of thy servant, that it may be before thee for ever: for thou *blessest*, O LORD, and it shall be *blessed* for ever.
—1 Chronicles 17:27
6. *Blessed* and holy is he that hath part in the first resurrection: on such the second death has no power, but they shall be priests of God and of Christ, and shall reign with him a thousand years.
—Revelation 20:6

THE ONLY PLACE WHERE ALL THREE WORDS ARE FOUND IS WHERE GOD SPEAKS OF THE SABBATH

3. And God *blessed* the seventh day, and *sanctified* it: because that in it He had rested from all His work which God created and made.
—Genesis 2:3
8. Remember the Sabbath day, to keep it *holy*.
9. Six days shalt thou labour, and do all thy work:
10. But the seventh day is the sabbath of the LORD thy God: in it thou shalt not do any work, thou, nor thy son, nor thy daughter, thy manservant, nor thy maidservant, nor thy cattle, nor thy stranger that is within thy gates:
11. For in six days the LORD made heaven and earth, the sea, and all that in them is, and rested the seventh day: wherefore the *LORD blessed the sabbath day, and hallowed it.*
—Exodus 20:8-11

[Synonyms: Sanctify = To Hallow and Hallowed = Blessed; From: Webster's Third New International Dictionary]

ANCIENT ISRAEL ALSO HAD TROUBLE HALLOWING THE SABBATH

21. Thus saith the LORD; Take heed to yourselves, and bear no burden on the sabbath day, nor bring it in by the gates of Jerusalem;
22. Neither carry forth a burden out of your houses on the sabbath day, neither do ye any work, but *hallow* ye the sabbath day, as I commanded your fathers.
23. But they obeyed not, neither inclined their ear, but made their neck stiff, that they might not hear, nor receive instruction.
24. And it shall come to pass, if ye diligently hearken unto me, saith the LORD, to bring in no burden through the gates of this city on the sabbath day, but hallow the sabbath day, to do no work therein;
25. Then shall there enter into the gates of this city kings and princes sitting upon the throne of David, riding in chariots and on horses they, and their princes, the men of Judah, and the inhabitants of Jerusalem: and this city shall remain for ever.
—Jeremiah 17:21-25 [Would not go into Babylon captivity.]

2. *Blessed* is the man that doeth this, and the Son of Man that layeth hold on it; that keepeth the sabbath from polluting it, and keepeth his hand from doing any evil.
—Isaiah 56:2

CHRIST IS LORD OF THE SABBATH

28. Therefore the Son of Man is Lord also of the sabbath.
—Mark 2:28

CHRIST IS THE WORD WHO CREATED WORLDS

1. In the beginning was the Word, and the Word was with God, and the Word was God.
2. The same was in the beginning with God.

3. All things were made by Him; and without Him was not any thing made that was made.
14. And the Word was made flesh, and dwelt among us, (and we beheld His glory, the glory as of the only begotten of the Father,) full of grace and truth.
—John 1:1-3, 14
1. God, who at sundry times and in divers manners spake in time past unto the fathers by the prophets,
2. Hath in these last days spoken unto us by His Son, whom He hath appointed heir of all things, by whom also he made the worlds;
—Hebrews 1:1, 2

CHRIST CREATED THE SABBATH, A GIFT FOR HUMANITY, TO LAST FOR ETERNITY

15. Who is the image of the invisible God, the firstborn of every creature:
16. For by Him were all things created, that are in heaven, and that are in earth, visible and invisible, whether they be thrones, or dominions, or principalities, or powers: all things were created by him, and for him:
—Colossians 1:15, 16
1. Thus the heavens and the earth were finished, and all the host of them.
2. And on the seventh day God ended his work which he had made; and he rested on the seventh day from all his work which he had made.
3. And God *blessed* the seventh day, and sanctified it: because that in it he had rested from all his work which *God created and made*.
—Genesis 2:1-3 [Christ the Word is God the Creator.]
27. And He said unto them, The sabbath was made for man, and not man for the sabbath:
—Mark 2:27
17. It is a sign between Me and the children of Israel for ever: for in six days the LORD made heaven and earth, and on the seventh day he rested, and was refreshed.

The Truth About the Sabbath

—Exodus 31:17

2. Six days shall work be done, but on the seventh day there shall be to you an Holy day, a sabbath of rest to the LORD: whosoever doeth work therein shall be put to death.
—Exodus 35:2

4. For He spake in a certain place of the seventh day on this wise, And God did rest the seventh day from all His works.
—Hebrews 4:4

9. There remaineth therefore a rest to the people of God.
—Hebrews 4:9

10. For he that is entered into his rest, he also hath ceased from his own works, as God did from His.
—Hebrews 4:10

15. For thus saith the Lord GOD, the HOLY One of Israel; In returning and rest shall ye be saved; in quietness and in confidence shall be your strength: and ye would not.
—Isaiah 30:15

42. And when the Jews were gone out of the synagogue, the Gentiles besought that these words might be preached to them the next sabbath.

43. Now when the congregation was broken up, many of the Jews and religious proselytes followed Paul and Barnabas: who speaking to them, persuaded them to continue in the grace of God.

44. And the next sabbath day came almost the whole city together to hear the word of God.
—Acts 13:42-44 [Years after Christ left earth Paul and Barnabas still keep the Sabbath.]

22. For as the new heavens and the new earth, which I will make, shall remain before me, saith the LORD, so shall your seed and your name remain.

23. And it shall come to pass, that from one new moon to another, and from one Sabbath to another, shall all flesh come to worship before me, saith the LORD.
—Isaiah 66:22, 23

25. Not forsaking the assembling of ourselves together, as the manner of some is; but exhorting one another: and so much the more, as ye see the day approaching.
—Hebrews 10:25

GOD PROMISES A GREAT BLESSING ON THOSE WHO HONOR HIS SABBATH.

13. If thou turn away thy foot from the sabbath, from doing thy pleasure on My holy day; and call the sabbath a delight, the holy of the LORD, honourable; and shalt honour Him, not doing thine own words:
14. Then shalt thou delight thyself in the LORD; and I will cause thee to ride upon the high places of the earth, and feed thee with the heritage of Jacob thy father: for the mouth of the LORD hath spoken it.
—Isaiah 58:13, 14

HOW DO WE KNOW FOR SURE WHICH DAY IS THE SEVENTH DAY?

54. And that day [Good Friday] was the preparation, and the sabbath drew on.
55. And the women also, which came with him from Galilee, followed after, and beheld the sepulchre, and how his body was laid.
56. And they returned, and prepared spices and ointments; and rested the sabbath day according to the commandment.
—Luke 23:54-56
1. Now upon the first day of the week, very early in the [Easter] morning, they came unto the sepulchre, bringing the spices which they had prepared, and certain others with them.
2. And they found the stone rolled away from the sepulchre.
—Luke 24:1, 2

[Jews scattered all over the world still keep the same day as Sabbath.]

CHAPTER 45
THE EVERLASTING COVENANT

THE EVERLASTING COVENANT

11. And I saw heaven opened, and behold a white horse; and He [Christ] that sat upon him was called Faithful and True, and in righteousness he doth judge and make war.
—Revelation 19:11

16. And He hath on His vesture and on His *thigh* a name written, *KING OF KING, AND LORD OF LORDS*.
—Revelation 19:16

[In ancient times placing ones hand under another's *thigh* when taking an oath was like raising your right hand and swearing to tell the truth or shaking hands to seal a verbal agreement. That is why Christ had His *name, title and authority*, written on His *thigh*.]

29. And the time drew nigh that Israel must die: and he called his son Joseph, and said unto him, If now I have found grace in thy sight, put, I pray thee, thy hand under my *thigh*, and deal kindly and truly with me; bury me not, I pray thee, in Egypt:
—Genesis 47:29

CHRIST WISHES TO HAVE A COVENANT IN THE HEARTS AND MINDS OF HIS PEOPLE

16. This is the *covenant* that I will make with them after those days, saith the Lord, *I will put My laws into their hearts, and in their minds* will I write them;
—Hebrews 10:16
17. And their sins and iniquities will I remember no more.
—Hebrews 10:17

COVENANT = AGREEMENT = WILL = TESTAMENT

5. Now therefore, if ye will obey My voice indeed, and keep *My covenant*, then ye shall be a peculiar (special) treasure unto Me above all people: for all the earth is mine:
—Exodus 19:5

[Commandment keepers are special to God.]

10. For this is the *covenant* that I will make with the house of Israel after those days, saith the Lord; I will put *My laws* into their mind, and write them in their hearts: and I will be to them a God, and they shall be to me a people:
—Hebrews 8:10
23. But this thing *commanded* I them, saying, Obey My voice, and I will be your God, and ye shall be My people: and walk ye in all the ways that I have *commanded* you, that it may be well unto you.
—Jeremiah 7:23
7. And I will give them an heart to know Me, that I Am the LORD: and they shall be My people, and I will be their God: for they shall return unto Me with their *whole heart*.
—Jeremiah 24:7
5. And said, I beseech thee, O LORD God of heaven, the great and terrible God, that keepeth *covenant* and mercy for them that love Him and observe His *commandments*:
—Nehemiah 1:5

The Everlasting Covenant

THE RAINBOW IS AN EVERLASTING COVENANT

16. And the BOW shall be in the cloud; and I will look upon it, that I may remember the *everlasting covenant* between God and every living creature of all flesh that is upon the earth.
—Genesis 9:16

GOD HAS ANOTHER EVERLASTING COVENANT

7. And I will establish *My covenant* between Me and thee and thy seed after thee in their generations for an *everlasting covenant*, to be a God unto thee, and to thy seed after thee.
—Genesis 17:7

MANKIND'S PART TOWARD THE COVENANT IS TO OBEY HIS COMMANDMENTS

9. Know therefore that the LORD thy God, He is God, the faithful God, which keepeth *covenant* and mercy with them that love Him and keep His *commandments* to a thousand generations [or forever];
—Deuteronomy 7:9
15. Be ye mindful always of His *covenant*; the word which He *commanded* to a thousand generations;
16. Even of the covenant which He made with Abraham, and of His oath unto Isaac;
17. And hath confirmed the same to Jacob for a LAW, and to Israel for an *everlasting covenant*,
—1 Chronicles 16:15-17

COVENANT FOR ALL PEOPLE NOT JUST ISRAEL

14. Neither with you only do I make this covenant and this oath; [Also included the Egyptians that came out with the Israelites.]

15. But with him that standeth here with us this day before the LORD our God, and also with him that is not here with us this day [future generations]:
—Deuteronomy 29:14, 15

6. And he said, It is a light thing that thou shouldest be my servant to raise up the tribes of Jacob, and to restore the preserved of *Israel*: I will also give thee for a light to the *Gentiles*, that thou mayest be my salvation unto the end of the earth.

8. Thus saith the LORD, . . . I will preserve thee, and give thee for a *covenant* of the people, to establish the earth, to cause to inherit the desolate heritages;
—Isaiah 49:6, 8

3. And the *Gentiles* shall come to thy light, and kings to the brightness of thy rising.
—Isaiah 60:3

14. That the blessing of Abraham might come on the *gentiles through Jesus Christ*; that we might receive the promise of the Spirit through faith.
—Galatians 3:14

33. And they departed from the mount of the LORD three days' journey: and the *ark* of the *covenant* of the LORD went before them in the three days' journey, to search out a resting place for them.
—Numbers 10:33 [The ark contained the covenant of ten commandments on stone.]

MOSES MADE A COPY OF THE ORIGINAL ARK OF THE TESTAMENT AS LATER SEEN BY JOHN IN VISION

19. And the temple of God was opened in heaven, and there was *seen* [by John] in His [Christ's] temple *the ark* of His *testament* [*covenant*]:
—Revelation 11:19

CHRIST MADE A NEW COVENANT AT THE LAST SUPPER THEN RATIFIED IT WITH HIS DEATH

25. After the same manner also He took the cup, when He had supped, saying, This cup is the *new testament [new covenant]* in My blood: this do ye, as oft as ye drink it, in remembrance of me.
—1 Corinthians 11:25

GENTILE CHRISTIANS ARE ABRAHAM'S SEED BY ADOPTION THROUGH CHRIST

29. And if ye be Christ's then are ye Abraham's seed, and heirs according to the promise.
—Galatians 3:29
11. Wherefore remember, that ye being in time past Gentiles in the flesh, who are called Uncircumcision by that which is called the Circumcision in the flesh made by hands;
12. That at the time ye were without Christ, being aliens from the commonwealth of Israel, and strangers from the *covenants* of promise, having no hope, and without God in the world:
—Ephesians 2:11, 12

WHY DO WE NEED A NEW COVENANT?

7. And he took the book of the *covenant*, and read in the audience of the people: and they said, All that the LORD hath said will we do, and be obedient.
—Exodus 24:7

WAS THE OLD COVENANT OBEDIENCE BY WORKS?

7. For if that first *covenant* had been faultless, then should no place have been sought for the second.
8. For finding fault with them, he saith, Behold, the days come, saith the LORD, when I will make a new *covenant* with the house of Israel and with the house of Judah:

[There was nothing wrong with the first covenant but the people tried to keep it in their own strength and failed.]

9. Not according to the *covenant* that I made with their fathers in the day when I took them by the hand to lead them out of the land of Egypt; because they continued not in my *covenant*, and I regarded them not, saith the Lord.
—Hebrews 8:7-9

CHRIST IS TESTATOR OF THE NEW COVENANT

6. But now hath he obtained a more excellent ministry, by how much also he is the mediator of a better *covenant*, which was established upon better promises.
—Hebrews 8:6

15. And for this cause he is the mediator of the *new testament*, that by means of death, for the redemption of the transgressions that were under the *first testament*, they which are called might receive the promise of eternal inheritance.

16. For where a *testament* is, there must also of necessity be the *death* of the *testator [one leaving a will]*.
—Hebrews 9:15, 16

[Before the proceeds of a will are distributed the *testator* must die.]

17. For a *testament [will]* is of force after men are dead: otherwise it is of no strength at all while the testator liveth.
—Hebrews 9:17

18. Whereupon neither the first *testament [covenant]* was dedicated without blood.
—Hebrews 9:18

[A will or agreement can be easily changed while both parties are still alive. They just need to write in the change, and have both parties initial it before witnesses.] [After a person dies a will cannot be changed. When Christ died the covenant was sealed forever.]

CHRIST LIVED A PERFECT LIFE FOR US

16. Let us therefore come boldly unto the throne of grace, that we may obtain mercy, and find grace to help in time of need.
—Hebrews 4:16
15. For we have not an high priest which cannot be touched with the feeling of our infirmities; but was in all points tempted like as we are, yet without sin.
—Hebrews 4:15
20. Not the God of peace, that brought again from the dead our Lord Jesus, that great shepherd of the sheep.
21. Make you perfect in every good work to do his will, working in you that which is well pleasing in his sight, through Jesus Christ; to whom be glory for ever and ever.
—Hebrews 13:20, 21

THROUGH THE BLOOD OF THE EVERLASTING COVENANT

9. Not according to the *covenant* that I made with their fathers in the day when I took them by the hand to lead them out of the land of Egypt; because they continued not in my *covenant*, and I regarded them not, saith the Lord.
10. For this is the *covenant* that I will make with the house of Israel after those days, saith the Lord; I will put my laws into *their mind*, and write them in *their hearts*: and I will be to them a God, and they shall be to me a people:
—Hebrews 8:9, 10
16. Wherefore the children of Israel shall keep the *Sabbath*, to observe the *Sabbath* throughout their generations, for a *perpetual covenant*.
—Exodus 31:16
12. Moreover also I gave them My *Sabbath*, to be a *SIGN* [just like the rainbow] between Me and them, that they might know that *I Am* the LORD that sanctify them.

20. And hallow My *Sabbaths*; and they shall be a sign between Me an you, that ye may know that *I Am* the LORD your God.
—Ezekiel 20:12, 20
13. Speak thou also unto the children of Israel, saying, Verily *My Sabbaths* ye shall keep: for it is a *sign* between Me and you *throughout your generations*; that ye may know that I Am the LORD that doth sanctify you.
17. It is a *sign* between Me and the children of Israel *for ever*: for in six days the LORD made heaven and earth, and on the seventh day He rested, and was refreshed.
—Exodus 31:13, 17

[The covenant of the rainbow and the covenant of the Sabbath are both a sign. They must be: universal, tangible, well defined, incorruptible, and personal. Both the Sabbath and rainbow have all these elements.]

6. Also the sons of the *stranger that join themselves* to the LORD, to serve him, and to love the name of the LORD, to *be his servants, every one that keepeth the Sabbath* from polluting it, and *taketh hold of My covenant*;
7. *Even them [the Gentiles]* will I bring to My holy mountain, and make them joyful in my house of prayer: their burnt offerings and their *sacrifices shall be accepted* upon mine altar; for *Mine house* shall be called an house of prayer for *all people*.
—Isaiah 56:6, 7
48. And when the gentiles heard this, they *were glad*, and glorified the word of the Lord:
—Acts 13:48

CHRISTIANS CONTINUED TO KEEP THE SABBATH AFTER CHRIST DIED

44. And the next *sabbath* day came almost the whole city together to hear the word of God.
—Acts 13:44

12. And from thence to Philippi . . . and we were in that city abiding certain days.
13. And on the Sabbath we went out of the city by a river side, where prayer was wont to be made; and we sat down, and spake unto the women which resorted thither.
—Acts 16:12, 13
2. And Paul, as his manner was, went in unto them, and *three Sabbath days* reasoned with them out of the scriptures,
17. Therefore *dispute* he in the synagogue *with the Jews*, and *with the devout persons*, and in the market daily with them that meet with him.
—Acts 17:2, 17
4. And he reasoned in the synagogue every *Sabbath*, and *persuaded the Jews and the Greeks*.
—Acts 18:4
22. For as the new heavens and the new earth, which I will make, shall remain before me, saith the LORD, so shall your seed and your name remain.
—Isaiah 66:22

[If Christ had wanted to change the day of His Sabbath (as testator) He would have done it before He died.]

THE SABBATH WILL BE KEPT IN THE NEW EARTH

23. And it shall come to pass that from one new moon to another, and from *one Sabbath to another* shall all flesh come to *worship before Me*, saith the LORD.
—Isaiah 66:23
13. If thou turn away thy foot from the *Sabbath*, from doing thy pleasure on My holy day; and call the Sabbath a delight, the holy of the LORD, honourable; and shalt honour him, not doing thine own ways, nor finding thine own pleasure, nor speaking thine own words:
14. Then shalt thou delight thyself in the LORD; and *I will cause thee to ride upon the high places of the earth*, and

feed thee with the heritage of Jacob thy fathers: for the mouth of the LORD hath spoken it.
—Isaiah 58:13, 14

9. There remaineth therefore a rest to the people of God.
10. For he that is entered into His rest, he also hath ceased from his own works, as God did from His.
—Hebrews 4:9, 10

CHAPTER 46
SUPPORT OF GOD'S WORK

BIBLE PLAN FOR THE SUPPORT OF GOD'S WORK

18. But thou shalt *remember* the LORD thy God: for it is He that giveth thee power to get wealth . . .
—Deuteronomy 8:18
32. And concerning the tithe of the herd, or of the flock even of whatsoever passeth under the rod, the *tenth* shall be holy unto the LORD.
—Leviticus 27:32
22. Thou shalt truly tithe all the increase of thy seed, that the field bringeth forth year by year.
—Deuteronomy 14:22
20. And blessed be the most high God, which hath delivered thine enemies into thy hand. And he [Abraham] gave him [Melchizedek King of Salem] tithes of all.
—Genesis 14:20
2. To whom [Melchesedec] also Abraham gave a tenth part of all; first being by interpretation King of righteousness, and after that also King of Salem, which is, King of peace;
—Hebrews 7:2

EVERYTHING IN THE WORLD BELONGS TO GOD

1. The earth is the LORD's and the fulness thereof; the world, and they that dwell therein.
—Psalms 24:1

8. The silver is mine, and the gold is mine, saith the LORD of hosts.
   —Haggai 2:8
10. For every beast of the forest is mine, and the cattle upon a thousand hills.
11. I know all the fowls of the mountains: and the wild beasts of the field are mine.
12. If I were hungry I would not tell thee: for the world is mine, and the fulness thereof.
    —Psalms 50:10-12

WE EACH BELONG TO GOD

19. What? Know ye not that your body is the temple of the Holy Ghost which is in you, which ye have of God, and ye are not your own?
20. For ye are bought with a price: therefore glorify God in your body, and in your spirit, which are God's.
    —1 Corinthians 6:19, 20

THE MINISTERS OF THE GOSPEL ARE TO BE SUPPORTED BY THE TITHE.

20. And the LORD spake unto Aaron, Thou shalt have no inheritance in their land, neither shalt thou have any part among them: I am the part and thine inheritance among the children of Israel.
21. And, behold, I have given the children of Levi all the tenth of Israel for an inheritance, for their service which they serve, even the service of the tabernacle of the congregation.
    —Numbers 18:20, 21
13. Do ye not know that they which minister about holy things live of the things of the temple? And they which wait at the alter are partakers with the alter?
14. Even so hath the Lord ordained that they which preach the gospel should live of the gospel.
    —1 Corinthians 9:13, 14

14. And this gospel of the kingdom shall be preached in all the world for a witness unto all nations; and then shall the end come.
—Matthew 24:14
8. And here men [preachers of gospel] that die receive tithes; but there [in Heaven] He [Christ] receiveth them, of whom it is witnessed that He liveth.
—Hebrews 7:8

CHRIST ENDORSED TITHING

23. Woe unto you, scribes and Pharisees, hypocrites? for ye pay tithe of mint and anise and cummin, and have omitted the weightier matters of the law, judgment, mercy, and faith: these ought ye to have done, and not to leave the other undone.
—Matthew 23:23

WE ARE TO GIVE OFFERINGS IN ADDITION TO THE TITHE AS WE ARE ABLE.

17. Every man shall give as he is able, according to the blessing of the LORD thy God which he hath given thee.
—Deuteronomy 16:17
9. Honour the LORD with thy substance, and with the firstfruits of all thine increase.
10. So shall thy barns be filled with plenty, and thy presses shall burst out with new wine.
—Proverbs 3:9, 10
6. . . . He which soweth sparingly shall reap also sparingly; and he which soweth bountifully shall reap also bountifully.
7. Every man according as he purposeth in his heart, so let him give; not grudgingly, or of necessity: for God loveth a cheerful giver.
8. And God is able to make all grace abound toward you; that ye, always having all sufficiency in all things, may abound to every good work:
—2 Corinthians 9:6-8

WHEN THE LORD SPEAKS TO OUR HEARTS WE SHOULD GIVE WILLINGLY.

21. Then everyone came whose heart was stirred, and everyone whose spirit was willing, and they brought the LORD's offering for the work of the tabernacle of meeting, for all its service, and for the holy garments.
—Exodus 35:21

THERE ARE MORE THAN ENOUGH FUNDS TO SPREAD THE GOSPEL IF EVERYONE GAVE GENEROUSLY.

6. So Moses gave a commandment, and they caused it to be proclaimed throughout the camp, saying. "let neither man nor woman do any more work for the offering of the sanctuary." and the people were restrained from bringing,
7. for the stuff they had was sufficient for all the work to be done indeed too much.
—Exodus 36:6, 7

MANY MEN ROB GOD

8. Will a man rob God? Yet ye have robbed Me. But ye say, Wherein have we robbed thee? In tithes and offerings.
—Malachi 3:8
9. Ye are cursed with a curse: for ye have robbed me, even this whole nation.
—Malachi 3:9

GOD BLESSES TITHE GIVERS AND HE WILL PROVIDE FOR OUR NEEDS

10. Bring ye all the tithes into the storehouse, that there may be meat [food] in mine house, and prove me now herewith, saith the LORD of hosts, if I will not open you the windows of heaven, and pour you out a blessing, that there shall not be room enough to receive it.

11. And I will rebuke the devourer for your sakes, and he shall not destroy the fruits of your ground; neither shall your vine cast her fruit before the time in the field, saith the LORD of hosts.
—Malachi 3:10, 11
24. No man can serve two masters: for either he will hate the one, and lover the other; or else he will hold to the one, and despise the other. Ye cannot serve God and mammon.
25. Therefore I say unto you, Take no thought [anxious thought] for your life, what ye shall eat, or what ye shall drink; nor yet for your body, what ye shall put on. Is not the life more than meat [food], and the body then raiment?
26. Behold the fowls of the air: for they sow not, neither do they reap, nor gather into barns; yet your heavenly Father feedeth them. Are ye not much better than they?
—Matthew 6:24-26
25. I have been young, and now am old; yet have I not seen the righteous forsaken, nor His seed begging bread.
—Psalms 37:25

IF WE DO OUR PART GOD WILL KEEP HIS PROMISE

20. And Jacob vowed a vow, saying, If God will be with me, and will keep me in this way that I go, and will give me bread to eat, and raiment to put on,
21. So that I come again to my father's house in peace; then shall the LORD be my God:
22. And this stone, which I have set for a pillar shall be God's house: and of all that thou shalt give me I will surely give the tenth unto thee.
—Genesis 28:20-22
10. He that is faithful in that which is least is faithful also in much: and he that is unjust in the least is unjust also in much.

11. If therefore ye have not been faithful in the unrighteous mammon, who will commit to your trust the true riches [of heaven]?
12. And if ye have not been faithful in that which is another man's, who shall give you that which is your own?
—Luke 16:10-12

IT IS HARD FOR A RICH MAN TO ENTER HEAVEN

17. And when He was gone forth into the way, there came one running, and kneeled to Him, and asked Him, Good Master, what shall I do that I may inherit eternal life?
18. And Jesus said unto him, Why callest thou Me good? There is none good but one, that is, God.
19. Thou knowest the commandments, Do not commit adultery, Do not kill, Do not steal, Do not bear false witness, Defraud not, Honour thy father and mother.
20. And he answered and said unto Him, Master, all these have I observed from my youth.
21. Then Jesus beholding him loved him, and said unto him, One thing thou lackest: go thy way, sell whatsoever thou hast, and give to the poor, and thou shalt have treasure in heaven: and come, take up the cross, and follow me.
22. And he was sad at that saying, and went away grieved: for he had great possessions.
23. And Jesus looked round about, and saith unto His disciples, How hardly shall they that have riches enter into the kingdom of God.
—Mark 10:17-23

9. For what is a man profited, if he shall gain the whole world, and lose his own soul? or what shall a man give in exchange for his soul?
—Matthew 16:26

1. Go to now, ye rich men, weep and howl for your miseries that shall come upon you.
2. Your riches are corrupted, and your garments are moth eaten.

3. Your gold and silver is cankered; and the rust of them shall be a witness against you, and shall eat your flesh as it were fire.
—James 5:1-3

OUR GIVING IS MEANS TESTED

41. And Jesus sat over against the treasury, and beheld how the people cast money into the treasury: and many that were rich cast in much.
42. And there came a certain poor widow, and she threw in two mites, which make a farthing.
43. And he called unto him his disciples, and saith unto them, Verily I say unto you, That this poor widow hath cast more in, than all they which have cast into the treasury:
44. For all they did cast in of their abundance; but she of her want did cast in all that she had, even all her living.
—Mark 12:41-44

CHAPTER 47
FOOD GOOD TO EAT

WHAT BIBLE SAYS ABOUT FOOD GOOD TO EAT

29. And God said, Behold, I have given you every herb bearing seed, which is upon the face of all the earth, and every tree, in the which is the fruit of a tree yielding seed; to you it shall be for meat [food or nourishment].
—Genesis 1:29

GOD LATER ALLOWED MEN TO EAT OF CERTAIN FLESH FOODS

2. . . . These are the beast which ye shall eat among all the beasts that are on the earth.
3. Whatsoever parteth the hoof, and is clovenfooted, and cheweth the cud, among the beast, that shall ye eat.
—Leviticus 11:2, 3

SEA CREATURES ALLOWED FOR FOOD

9. These shall ye eat of all that are in the waters: whatsoever hath fins and scales in the waters, in the seas, and in the rivers, them shall ye eat.
10. And all that have not fins and scales in the seas, and in the rivers, of all that move in the waters, and of any living thing which is in the waters, they shall be an abomination unto you:
11. They shall be even an abomination unto you; ye shall not

eat of their flesh, but ye shall have their carcases in abomination.
12. Whatsoever hath no fins nor scales in the waters, that shall be an abomination unto you.
—Leviticus 11:9-12

FOWLS GOOD FOR FOOD

13. 'And these you shall regard as an abomination among the birds; they shall not be eaten, they are an abomination: the eagle, the vulture, the buzzard,
14. 'the kite, and the falcon after its kind;
15. 'every raven after its kind;
16. 'the ostrich, the short-eared owl, the seagull, and the hawk after its kind;
17. 'the little owl, the fisher owl, and the screech owl.
18. 'the white owl, the jackdaw, and the carrion vulture;
19. 'the stork, the heron after its kind . . .
—Leviticus 11:13-19

THE STORY OF CORNELIUS USED AS ARGUMENT FOR EATING ANYTHING AND EVERYTHING

Entire story: Acts 10:1-48; 11:1-18

LET US EXAMINE THE KEY VERSES

10. And he [Peter] became very hungry, and would have eaten: but while they made ready, he fell into a trance,
11. And saw heaven open, and a certain vessel descending unto him, as it had been a great sheet knit at the four corners, and let down to the earth:
12. Wherein were all manner of fourfooted beasts of the earth, and wild beasts, and creeping things, and fowls of the air.
13. And there came a voice to him, Rise, Peter; kill, and eat.
14. But Peter said, Not so, Lord; for I have never eaten any thing that is common or unclean.

15. And the voice spake unto him again the second time, What God hath cleansed, that call not thou common,
16. This was done thrice: and the vessel was received up again into heaven.
17. Now while Peter doubted in himself what this vision which he had seen should mean, behold, the men which were sent from Cornelius had made inquiry for Simon's house, and stood before the gate,
—Acts 10:10-17

LATER ON PETER GIVES TRUE MEANING OF DREAM

28. And he said unto them, Ye know how that it is an unlawful thing for a man that is a Jew to keep company, or come unto one of another nation; but God hath showed me that I should not call any man common or unclean.
29. Therefore came I unto you without gainsaying, as soon as I was sent for:
—Acts 10:28, 29
34. Then Peter opened his mouth, and said, Of a truth I perceive that God is no respecter of persons:
35. But in every nation he that feareth him, and worketh righteousness, is accepted with him.
—Acts 10:34, 35

LATER PETER TOLD THE JEWS WHAT HAPPENED

4. But Peter rehearsed the matter from the beginning, and expounded it by order unto them, saying,
5. I was in the city of Joppa praying: and in a trance I saw a vision, A certain vessel descend, as it had been a great sheet, let down from heaven by four corners; and it came even to me:
6. Upon the which when I had fastened mine eyes, I considered, and saw fourfooted beasts of the earth, and wild beasts, and creeping things, and fowl of the air.

Food Good to Eat

7. And I heard a voice saying unto me, Arise, Peter; slay and eat.
8. But I said, Not so, Lord: for nothing common or unclean hath at any time entered into my mouth.
9. But the voice answered me again from heaven, What God hath cleansed, that call not thou common.
10. And this was done three times: and all were drawn up again into heaven.
18. When they heard these things, they held their peace, and glorified God, saying, Then hath God also to the Gentiles granted repentance unto life.
—Acts 11:4-10, 18

ROMANS 14 USED AS AN EXCUSE TO EAT ANYTHING

2. For one believeth that he may eat all things: another, who is weak, eateth herbs [vegetables].
3. Let not him that eateth despise him that eateth not; and let not him which eateth not judge him that eateth: for God hath received him.
6. . . . He that eateth, eateth, to the Lord, for he giveth God thanks; and he that eateth not, to the Lord he eateth not, and giveth God thanks.
14. I know, and am persuaded by the Lord Jesus, that there is nothing unclean of itself: but him that esteemeth any thing to be unclean, to him it is unclean.
15. But if thy brother be grieved with thy meat, now walkest thou not charitably. Destroy not him with thy meat, for whom Christ died.
17. For the kingdom of God is not meat and drink; but righteousness, and peace, and joy in the Holy Ghost.
20. For meat destroy not the work of God. All things indeed are pure; but it is evil for that man who eateth with offence.

21. It is good neither to eat flesh, nor to drink wine, nor anything whereby thy brother stumbleth, or is offended, or is made weak.
—Romans 14:2, 3, 6, 14, 15, 17, 20, 21

[Paul here is talking about eating meat first offered to idols. Some thought it was wrong and some thought it didn't make any difference. 1 Corinthians 8 is talking about the same thing but makes is clearer.]

4. As concerning therefore the eating of those things that are offered in sacrifice unto idols, we know that an idol is nothing in the world, and that there is none other God but one.
7. Howbeit there is not in every man that knowledge: for some with conscience of the idol unto this hour eat it as a thing offered unto an idol; and their conscience being weak is defiled.
8. But meat commendeth us not to God: for neither, if we eat, are we the better; neither, if we eat not, are we the worse.
9. But take heed lest by any means this liberty of yours become a stumbling block to them that are weak.
10. For if any man see thee which hast knowledge sit at meat in the idol's temple, shall not the conscience of him which is weak be emboldened to eat those things which are offered to idols;
13. Wherefore, if meat make my brother to offend, I will eat no flesh while the world standeth, lest I make my brother to offend.
—1 Corinthians 8:4, 7-10, 13

[Paul is arguing here in 1 Corinthians 8 that Christians should be sensitive to one another's feelings.]

31. Whether therefore ye eat, or drink, or whatsoever ye do, do all to the glory of God.
—1 Corinthians 10:31

Food Good to Eat

ANOTHER TEXT OFTEN CITED THAT UNCLEAN MEAT(S) ARE O.K. FOR FOOD IS IN 1 Timothy 4.

1. Now the Spirit speaketh expressly, that in the latter times some shall depart from the faith, giving heed to seducing spirits, and doctrines of devils;
2. Speaking lies in hypocrisy; having their conscience seared with a hot iron;
3. Forbidding to marry, and commanding to abstain from meats, which God hath created to be received with thanksgiving of them which believe and know the truth.
4. For every creature of God is good, and nothing to be refused, if it be received with thanksgiving:
5. For it is *SANCTIFIED BY THE WORD OF GOD* and prayer.
—1 Timothy 4:1-5

[The word of God in the book Leviticus 11 tells us what flesh food God has sanctified. Some people read only verses 3 and 4 and stop there.]

MARK 7 SOMETIMES USED AS AN EXCUSE TO EAT ANYTHING

Christ said to His disciples:

15. There is nothing from without a man [food], that entering into him can defile him: but the things which come out of him [thoughts and words], those are they that defile the man.
18. . . . Do ye not perceive, that whatsoever thing from without entereth into the man, it cannot defile him;
19. Because it entereth not unto his heart, but into the belly, and goeth out into the draught, purging all meats [foods]?
20. And He said, That which cometh out of the man, that defileth the man.
21. For from within, out of the heart of men, proceed evil thoughts, adulteries, fornications, murders,
—Mark 7:15, 18-21

CHRIST WAS ANSWERING THE PHARISEES QUESTION

5. Then the Pharisees and scribes asked Him, Why walk not thy disciples according to the tradition of the elders, but eat bread with unwashen hands?
—Mark 7:5

MODERN MEDICINE AGREES WITH LEVITCUS

17. It shall be a perpetual statute for your generation throughout all your dwellings, that ye eat neither fat nor blood.
—Leviticus 3:17
14. For it is the life of all flesh; the blood of it is for the life thereof . . .
—Leviticus 17:14
6. For I AM the LORD, I change not . . .
—Malachi 3:6

CHAPTER 48
CHRIST'S MINISTRY IN THE HEAVENLY SANCTUARY

FIRST: THE EARTHLY SANCTUARY REPLICA

8. And let them make me a sanctuary; that *I may dwell among them*.
—Exodus 25:8
1. Then verily the first covenant had also ordinances of divine service, and a *worldly sanctuary*.
—Hebrews 9:1
9. According to all that I show thee, *after the pattern* of the tabernacle, and the patters of all the instruments thereof, even so shall ye make it.
—Exodus 25:9
40. And look that thou make them after the pattern, which was showed thee in the mount.
—Exodus 25:40

SECOND: THE HEAVENLY SANCTUARY OR TEMPLE

1. Now of the things which we have spoken this is the sum: We have such an *high priest*, who is set on the *right hand* of the *throne* of the *majesty* in the *heavens*;
2. A minister of the sanctuary, and of the *true tabernacle*, which the Lord pitched, and not man.
—Hebrews 8:1, 2
23. It was therefore necessary that the patterns of things in the heavens should be purified with these; but the heavenly things themselves with better sacrifices than these.

24. For *Christ is not entered* into the holy places made with hands, which are the figures of the true; but *into heaven itself,* now to appear in the *presence of God* for us:
—Hebrews 9:23, 24

GOD'S THRONE IS IN THE HEAVENLY SANCTUARY

4. The LORD is in His *holy temple,* the LORD's throne is *in heaven*: His eyes behold, His eyelids try, the children of men.
—Psalms 11:4

19. For He hath looked down from the height of His sanctuary; from heaven did the LORD behold the earth;
—Psalms 102:19

2. Hear, all ye people; hearken, O earth, and all that therein is: and let the Lord GOD be witness against you, *the LORD from His holy temple.*

3. For, behold, the LORD cometh forth out of His place, and will come down, and tread upon the high places of the earth.
—Micah 1:2, 3

SEEN BY JOHN THE REVELATOR

15. And after that I looked, and, behold, the temple of the tabernacle of the testimony in heaven was opened:
—Revelation 15:5

19. And the temple of God was opened in heaven, and there was *seen in His temple the ark* of His testament [covenant or agreement]: and there were lightnings, and voices, and thunderings, and an earthquake, and great hail.
—Revelation 11:19

12. And I turned to see the voice that spake with me. And being turned, I saw seven *golden candlesticks [lampstands]*;
—Revelation 1:12
(Read Also: Exodus 25:31-40)

3. And another angel came and stood at the altar, having a *golden censer*; and there was given unto him much in-

cense, that he should offer it with the prayers of all saints upon the *golden altar* which was before the throne.
—Revelation 8:3
(Read Also: Leviticus 10:1, 2; Numbers 16:46; Hebrews 9:4)

13. And the sixth angel sounded, and I heard a voice form the four horns of the *golden altar* which is before God,
—Revelation 9:13
(Read Also: Exodus 40:26; Numbers 4:11; 2 Chronicles 4:19)

17. And the seventh angel poured out his vial into the air; and there came a great voice out of the *temple* of heaven, from the throne, saying, It is done.
—Revelation 16:17

5. And after that I looked, and, behold, the *temple* of the tabernacle of the testimony in heaven was opened:
6. And the seven angels came out of the *temple*, having the seven plagues, clothed in pure and white linen, and having their breasts girded with golden girdles.
7. And one of the four beasts [living creatures] gave unto the seven angels seven golden vials full of the wrath of God, who liveth for ever and ever.
8. And the *temple* was filled with smoke from the glory of God, and from His power; and no man was able to enter into the *temple*, till the seven plagues of the seven angels were fulfilled.
—Revelation 15:5-8
(Read Also: Revelation 4:2, 3)

THE SUBSTITUTIONARY SACRIFICE OF CHRIST

22. And almost all things are by the law purged with blood; and without *shedding of blood* is no remission.
—Hebrews 9:22

6. All we like sheep have gone astray; we have turned every one to his own way; and the LORD hath laid on Him the iniquity of us all.
—Isaiah 53:6

26. For then must He [*Christ*] often have suffered since the foundation of the world: but now once in the end of the world hath He appeared to put away sin by the *sacrifice of Himself.*
27. And as it is appointed unto men once to die, but after this the judgment:
28. So Christ was once offered to bear the sins of many; and unto them that look for Him shall He appeared the second time without sin unto salvation.
—Hebrews 9:26-28
10. By the which will we are sanctified through the *offering of the body of Jesus Christ* once for all.
11. And every priest standeth daily ministering and offering oftentimes the same sacrifices, which can never take away sins:
12. But this man [Jesus], after He had *offered one sacrifice* for sins for ever, sat down on the right hand of God;
13. From henceforth expecting [waiting] till His enemies be made His footstool.
14. For *by one offering He [Christ Himself]* hath perfected for ever them that are sanctified.
—Hebrews 10:10-14
18. Therefore as by the offense of one [Adam] judgment came upon all men to condemnation; even so by the righteousness of one the free gift came upon all men unto justification of life.
—Romans 5:18
(Read Also: John 1:29; 1 Peter 1:18–20)

GOD'S JUDGMENT ON SIN

23. For the wages of sin is death; but the *gift of God is eternal life* through Jesus Christ our Lord.
—Romans 6:23

MINISTRY OF CHRIST IN HEAVEN'S SANCTUARY

5. For there is one God, and *one mediator* between God and men, the man *Christ Jesus;*

Christ's Ministry In the Heavenly Sanctuary

—1 Timothy 2:5

18. For through Him we both have access by one Spirit unto the Father.
—Ephesians 2:18

14. Seeing then that we have a *great High Priest*, that is passed into the heavens, *Jesus the Son of God*, let us hold fast our profession.

15. For we have not an *High Priest* which cannot be touched with the feeling of our infirmities; but [*Christ*] was in all points tempted like as we are, yet without sin.

16. Let us therefore come boldly unto the throne of grace, that we may obtain mercy, and find grace to help in time of need.
—Hebrews 4:14-16

25. Wherefore He is able also to save them to the uttermost that come unto God by Him, seeing He [*Christ*] ever liveth to make intercession for them.
—Hebrews 7:25

24. For Christ is not entered into the holy places made with hands, which are the figures of the true; but into heaven itself, now to appear in the presence of God for us:
—Hebrews 9:24

19. Having therefore, brethren, boldness to enter into the holiest by the blood of Jesus,

20. By a new and living way, which He hath consecrated for us, through the *veil*, that is to say, His *flesh*; (veil = flesh of Christ)

21. And having an high priest over the house of God;

22. Let us draw near with a true heart in full assurance of faith, having our hearts sprinkled from an evil conscience, and our bodies washed with pure water.
—Hebrews 10:19-22

THE WORK OF EARTHLY PRIESTS

17. And the priest shall dip his finger in some of the blood, and sprinkle it seven times before the LORD, even before the veil.
(LORD = Jehovah = Christ = Veil)

18. And he shall put some of the blood upon the horns of the altar which is before the LORD, that is in the tabernacle of the congregation, and shall pour out all the blood at the bottom of the altar of the burnt offering, which is at the door of the tabernacle of the congregation.
—Leviticus 4:17, 18
25. Speak unto Aaron and to his sons, saying, This is the law of the sin offering: In the place where the burnt offering is killed shall the sin offering be killed before the LORD: it is most holy.
26. The priest that offereth it for sin shall eat it: in the holy place shall it be eaten, in the court of the tabernacle of the congregation.
30. And no sin offering, whereof any of the blood is brought into the tabernacle of the congregation to reconcile withal in the holy place, shall be eaten: it shall be burnt in the fire.
—Leviticus 6:25, 26, 30

THE RESULT OF BEING FORGIVEN AND OF HAVING A FORGIVING SPIRIT

32. And be ye kind one to another, tenderhearted, forgiving one another, even as God for Christ's sake hath forgiven you.
—Ephesians 4:32
9. If we confess our sins, He is faithful and just to forgive us our sins, and to cleanse us from all unrighteousness.
—1 John 1:9
21. For He hath made Him to be sin for us, who knew no sin; that we might be made the righteousness of God in Him.
—2 Corinthians 5:21
24. Being justified freely by His grace through the redemption that is in Christ Jesus:
—Romans 3:24
20. Notwithstanding in this rejoice not, that the spirits are

subject unto you; but rather rejoice, because your names are written in heaven.
—Luke 10:20

THE MINISTRY OF THE EARTHLY MOST HOLY PLACE

THE DAY OF ATONEMENT ONCE EACH YEAR

16. And he shall make an atonement for the holy place, because of the uncleanness of the children of Israel, and because of their transgressions in all their sins: and so shall he do for the tabernacle of the congregation, that remaineth among them in the midst of their uncleanness.
17. And there shall be no man in the tabernacle of the congregation when he goeth in to make an atonement in the holy place, until he come out, and have made an atonement for himself, and for his household, and for all the congregation of Israel.
18. And he shall go out unto the altar that is before the LORD, and make an atonement [at-one-ment] for it; and shall take of the blood of the bullock, and of the blood of the goat, and put it upon the horns of the altar round about.
19. And he shall sprinkle of the blood upon it with his finger seven times, and cleanse it, and hallow it from the uncleanness of the children of Israel.
—Leviticus 16:16-19

AZEZEL'S REMOVAL REPRESENTED THE COMPLETE AND FINAL REMOVAL OF SIN FROM THE UNIVERSE

8. And Aaron shall cast lots upon the two goats; one lot for the LORD, and the other lot for the scapegoat.
—Leviticus 16:8
20. And when he hath made an end of reconciling the holy place, and the tabernacle of the congregation, and the altar, he shall bring the live goat:
21. And Aaron shall lay both his hands upon the head of the

live goat, and confess over him all the iniquities of the children of Israel, and all their transgressions in all their sins, putting them upon the head of the goat, and shall send him away by the hand of a fit man into the wilderness:
22. And the goat shall bear upon him all their iniquities unto a land not inhabited: and he shall let go the goat in the wilderness.
30. For on the day shall the priest make an atonement for you, to cleanse you, that ye may be clean from all your sins before the LORD.
31. It shall be a sabbath [not seventh day Sabbath] of rest unto you, and ye shall afflict your souls, by a statute for ever.
32. And the priest [High Priest], whom he shall anoint, and whom he shall consecrate to minister in the priest's office in his father's stead, shall make the atonement, and shall put on the linen clothes, even the holy garments:
33. And he shall make an atonement for the holy sanctuary, and he shall make an atonement for the tabernacle of the congregation, and for the altar, and he shall make an atonement for the priests, and for all the people of the congregation.
—Leviticus 16:20-22; 30-33
19. To wit, that God was in Christ, reconciling the world unto himself, not imputing their trespasses unto them; and hath committed unto us the word of reconciliation.
—2 Corinthians 5:19
22. And almost all things are by the law purged with blood; and without shedding of blood is no remission.
—Hebrews 9:22

THERE ARE THREE DIFFERENT PHASES OF THE JUDGMENT IN HEAVEN

PHASE ONE: [The investigative judgment in heaven much like our Grand Jury to look at the body of evidence to separate

the righteous from the wicked. This takes place before the Christ's Second coming.]
PHASE TWO: [The judgment of the wicked, both man-kind and Satan and His Angels. This takes place during the millennium and the righteous saved will take part in this work.]
PHASE THREE: [Executive judgment or the punishment of the Wicked which takes place after the Millennium and when Christ comes to the earth the third time.]

EXACT TIME OF CHRIST'S SECOND COMING IS NOT KNOWN BUT WE MUST ALWAYS REMAIN READY

10. That in the dispensation of the *fulness of times* he might gather together in one all things in Christ, both which are in heaven, and which are on earth; even in him:
    —Ephesians 1:10
13. I saw in the night vision, and, behold, one like the Son of Man came with the clouds of heaven, and came to the Ancient of days, and they brought Him [Christ] near before Him [God the Father].
14. And there was given Him dominion, and glory, and a kingdom, that all people, nations, and languages, should serve Him: His dominion is an everlasting dominion, which shall not pass away, and His kingdom that which shall not be destroyed.
    —Daniel 7:13, 14
25. Wherefore He is able also to save them to the uttermost that come unto God by Him, seeing He ever liveth to make intercession for them.
    —Hebrews 7:25
7. But the heavens and the earth, which are now, by the same word are kept in store, reserved unto fire against the day of judgment and perdition of ungodly men.
8. But, beloved, be not ignorant of this one things, that one day is with the Lord as a thousand years, and a thousand years as one day.
9. The Lord is not slack concerning His promise, as some

men count slackness; but is longsuffering to us-ward, not willing that any should perish, but that all should come to repentance.
10. But the day of the Lord will come as a thief in the night; in the which the heavens shall pass away with a great noise, and the elements shall melt with fervent heat, the earth also and the works that are therein shall be burned up.
11. Seeing then that all these things shall be dissolved, what manner of person ought ye to be in all holy conversation and godliness,
12. Looking for and hasting unto the coming of the day of God, wherein the heavens being on fire shall be dissolved, and the elements shall melt with fervent heat?
13. Nevertheless we, according to His promise, look for new heavens and a new earth, wherein dwelleth righteousness.
—2 Peter 3:7-13

PHASE ONE: THE PRE-ADVENT INVESTIGATIVE JUDGMENT (WE MUST BE WRITTEN IN THE BOOK)

9. I beheld till the thrones were cast down [placed], and the Ancient of days did sit, whose garment was white as snow, and the hair of His head like the pure wool: His throne was like the fiery flame, and His [its] wheels as burning fire.
10. A fiery stream issued and came forth from before Him: thousand thousands ministered unto Him, and ten thousand times ten thousand stood before Him: the judgment was set, and the *books* were opened.
—Daniel 7:9, 10
20. Notwithstanding in this rejoice not, that the spirits are subject unto you; but rather rejoice, because your *names* are *written* in heaven.
—Luke 10:20
3. And I entreat thee also, true yokefellow, help those women which laboured with me in the gospel, with Clement also,

and with other my fellowlabourers, whose *names* are in the *book* of life.
—Philippians 4:3

1. And at that time shall Michael [Christ] stand up, the great prince which standeth for the children of thy people: and there shall be a time of trouble, such as never was since there was a nation even to that same time: and at that time thy people shall be delivered, *every one* that shall be found written in the *book*.
—Daniel 12:1

27. And there shall in no wise enter into it any thing that defileth, neither whatsoever worketh abomination, or maketh a lie: but *they which are written* in the *Lamb's book of life*.
—Revelation 21:27

5. He that overcometh, the same shall be clothed in white raiment; and I will not blot out his name out of the *book of life*, but I will confess his name before My Father, and before His angels.
—Revelation 3:5

SEPARATING THE RIGHTEOUS FROM THE WICKED

31. When the Son of Man [Christ] shall come in His glory, and all the holy angels with Him, then shall He sit upon the throne of His glory:
32. And before Him shall be gathered all nations: and He shall separate them one from another, as a shepherd divideth his sheep from the goats:
33. And He shall set the sheep on His right hand, but the goats on the left.
34. Then shall the King say unto them on His right hand, Come, ye blessed of My Father, inherit the kingdom prepared for you from the foundation of the world:
35. For I was an hungered, and ye gave Me meat: I was thirsty, and ye gave Me drink: I was a stranger, and ye took Me in:
36. Naked, and ye clothed Me: I was sick, and ye visited Me: I was in prison, and ye came unto Me.

37. Then shall the righteous answer Him, saying, Lord, when saw we Thee and hungered, and fed Thee? or thirsty, and gave Thee drink?
38. When saw we Thee a stranger, and took Thee in? or naked, and clothed Thee?
39. Or when saw we Thee sick, or in prison, and came unto Thee?
40. And the King shall answer and say unto them, Verily I say unto you, Inasmuch as ye have done it unto one of the least of these My brethren, ye have done it unto Me.
41. Then shall He say also unto them on the left hand, Depart from Me, ye cursed, into everlasting fire, prepared for the devil and his angels:
42. For I was and hungered and ye gave Me no meat: I was thirsty, and ye gave Me no drink:
43. I was a stranger, and ye took Me not in: naked, and ye clothed Me not: sick, and in prison, and ye visited Me not.
44. Then shall they also answer Him, saying, Lord, when saw we Thee and hungered, or athirst, or a stranger, or naked, or sick, or in prison, and did not minister unto Thee?
45. Then shall He answer them, saying, Verily I say unto you, Inasmuch as ye did it not to one of the least of these, ye did it not to Me.
46. And these shall go away into everlasting punishment: but the righteous into life eternal.
—Matthew 25:31-46
12. And, behold, I come quickly; and My reward is with Me, to give every man according as his work shall be.
—Revelation 22:12
10. And I heard a loud voice saying in heaven, Now is come salvation, and strength, and the kingdom of our God and the power of His Christ: for the accuser of our brethren is cast down, which accused them before our God day and night.
—Revelation 12:10

PHASE TWO: THE JUDGMENT OF THE WICKED BY THE RIGHTEOUS DURING THE 1000 YEARS

4. And I saw *thrones*, and they *[saints] sat upon them*, and judgment was given unto them: and I saw the souls of them that were beheaded for the witness of Jesus, and for the word of God, and which had not worshipped the beast, neither his image, neither had received his mark upon their foreheads, or in their hands; and they lived and reigned with Christ a thousand years.
—Revelation 20:4

1. Dare any of you, having a matter against another, go to law before the unjust, and not before the saints?
2. Do ye not know that the saints shall judge the world and if the world shall be judged by you, are ye unworthy to judge the smallest matters?
3. Know ye not that we shall judge angels? how much more things that pertain to this life?
—1 Corinthians 6:1-3

35. But they which shall be accounted worthy to obtain that world, and the resurrection from the dead, neither marry, nor are given in marriage:
36. Neither can they die any more: for they are equal unto angels; and are the children of God, being the children of the resurrection.
—Luke 20:35, 36

PHASE THREE: PUNISHMENT OF WICKED AFTER THE 1000 YEARS (THE MILLENNIUM)

11. And I saw a great white throne, and Him that sat on it, from whose face the earth and the heaven fled away; and there was found no place for them.
12. And I saw the dead, small and great, and another book was opened, which is the book of life: and the dead were judged out of those things which were written in the books, according to their works.
13. And the sea gave up the dead which were in it; and death

and hell delivered up the dead which were in them: and they were judged every man according to their works.
14. And death and hell were cast into the lake of fire. This is the second death.
15. And whosoever was not found written in the book of life was cast into the lake of fire.
—Revelation 20:11-15
27. That He [Christ] might present it to Himself a glorious church, not having spot, or wrinkle, or any such thing; but that it should be holy and without blemish.
—Ephesians 5:27

THE CLEANSING OF THE HEAVENLY SANCTUARY

22. And almost all things are by the law purged with blood; and without shedding of blood is no remission.
23. It was therefore necessary that the patterns of things in the heavens should be purified with these; but the heavenly things themselves with better sacrifices than these.
—Hebrews 9:22, 23
1. Now of the things which we have spoken this is the sum: We have such an high priest, who is set on the right hand of the throne of the Majesty in the heavens;
2. A minister of the sanctuary, and of the true tabernacle, which the Lord pitched, and not man.
12. For I will be merciful to their unrighteousness, and their sins and their iniquities will I remember no more.
—Hebrews 8:1, 2, 12

THE TIME OF RESTORATION, AND CLEANSING, OF THE HEAVENLY SANCTUARY AND JUDGMENT.

17. So he came near where I stood: and when he came, I was afraid, and fell upon my face: but he said unto me, Understand, O Son of Man: for at the time of the end shall be the vision.
—Daniel 8:17
25. Wherefore He is able also to save them to the uttermost

Christ's Ministry In the Heavenly Sanctuary

that come unto God by Him, seeing He ever liveth to make intercession for them.
—Hebrews 7:25

14. And he said unto me, Unto two thousand and three hundred days; then shall the sanctuary be cleansed.
—Daniel 8:14

2300 DAYS IN PROPHECY = 2300 ACTUAL YEARS
ONE DAY = ONE YEAR IN PROPHECY

34. After the number of the days in which ye searched the land, even FORTY DAYS, each day for a year, shall ye bear your iniquities, even FORTY YEARS, and ye shall know my breach of promise.
—Numbers 14:34

3. And when thou hast accomplished them, lie again on thy right side, and thou shalt bear the iniquity of the house of Judah forty days: I HAVE APPOINTED THEE EACH DAY FOR A YEAR.
—Ezekiel 4:6

THE ANGEL GABRIEL EXPLAINS THE VISION

16. And I heard a man's voice between the banks of Ulai, which called, and said, Gabriel, make this man to understand the vision.
—Daniel 8:16

27. And I Daniel fainted, and was sick certain days; afterward I rose up, and did the king's business; and I was astonished at the vision, but none understood it.
—Daniel 8:27

23. At the beginning of thy supplication the commandment came forth, and I am come to show thee; for thou art greatly beloved: therefore understand the matter, and consider the vision.
—Daniel 9:23

THE 70 WEEK PROPHECY

24. Seventy weeks are determined upon thy people [the Jews] and upon thy holy city [Jerusalem], to finish the transgression, and to make and end of sins, and to make reconciliation for iniquity [Christ's death], and to bring in everlasting righteousness, and to seal up the vision and prophecy, and to anoint the most Holy.
25. Know therefore and understand, that from the going forth of the commandment to restore and to build Jerusalem [took place in 457 BC, a historical fact] unto the Messiah the Prince [Jesus Christ] shall be seven weeks, and threescore and two weeks [69 prophetic weeks]: the street shall be built again, and the wall, even in troublous times.
—Daniel 9:24, 25

69 PROPHETIC WEEKS = 69 x 7 = 483 ACTUAL YEARS

27. And he shall confirm the covenant with many for one week: and in the midst of the week he shall cause the sacrifice and the oblation to cease, and for the overspreading of abomination he shall make it desolate, even until the consummation, and that determined shall be poured upon the desolate.
—Daniel 9:27
(2300—490 = 1810 years left)
(34 + 1810 = 1844 the year beginning the "cleansing of the Sanctuary" in heaven.)

THE VINDICATION OF GOD'S PEOPLE

22. Until the Ancient of days came, and judgment was given to the saints of the most High; and the time came that the saints possessed the kingdom,
—Daniel 7:22
32. Whosoever therefore shall confess Me before men, him will I confess also before My Father which is in heaven.
—Matthew 10:32

8. Also I say unto you, Whosoever shall confess Me before men, him shall the Son of Man also confess before the angels of God:
9. But he that denieth Me before men shall be denied before the angels of God.
—Luke 12:8, 9
5. He that overcometh, the same shall be clothed in white raiment; and I will not blot out his name out of the book of life, but I will confess his name before My Father, and before His angels.
—Revelation 3:5

JUDGMENT AND SALVATION

34. Who is he that condemneth? It is Christ that died, yea rather, that is risen again, who is even *at the right hand of God*, who also maketh intercession for us.
—Romans 8:34
1. My little children, these things write I unto you, that ye sin not. And if any man sin, we have an *advocate* with the Father, Jesus Christ the righteous:
—1 John 2:1

CHURCH ALSO HAS FALSE BELIEVERS

28. He said unto them, An enemy hath done this. The servants said unto him, Wilt thou then that we go and gather them up?
29. But he said, Nay; lest while ye gather up the tares, ye root up also the wheat with them.
30. *LET BOTH GROW TOGETHER UNTIL THE HARVEST*: and in the time of harvest I will say to the reapers, Gather ye together first the tares, and bind them in bundles to burn them: but gather the wheat into my barn.
—Matthew 13:28-30
33. And the LORD said unto Moses, *whosoever hath sinned against Me, him will I blot out of My book*.
—Exodus 32:33

21. Not every one that saith unto Me, Lord, Lord, shall enter into the kingdom of heaven; but *He that doeth the will of My Father* which is in heaven.
22. Many will say to Me in that day, Lord, Lord, have we not prophesied in thy name? and in thy name have cast out devils? and in thy name done many wonderful works?
23. And then will I profess unto them, I never knew you: depart from Me, ye that work iniquity.
—Matthew 7:21-23

IT IS TIME TO BE READY

7. Saying with a loud voice, Fear God, and give glory to him; for *the hour of His judgment is come:* and worship him that made heaven, and earth, and the sea, and the fountains of waters.
—Revelation 14:7
27. Also on the tenth day of this seventh month there shall be a *day of atonement*: it shall be an holy convocation unto you; and *ye shall afflict your souls*, and offer an offering made by fire unto the LORD.
—Leviticus 23:27
33. Take ye heed, *WATCH AND PRAY*: for *YE KNOW NOT WHEN THE TIME IS.*
—Mark 13:33
14. Seeing then that we have a great high priest, that is passed into the heavens, Jesus the Son of God, let *us hold fast our profession.*
15. For we have not an high priest which cannot be touched with the feeling of our infirmities; but was in all points tempted like as we are, yet without sin.
16. Let us therefore *come boldly* unto the throne of grace, that we may *obtain mercy*, and find grace to help in time of need.
—Hebrews 4:14-16

CHAPTER 49
HEAVEN

HEAVEN

2. I knew a man in Christ above fourteen years ago, (whether in the body, I cannot tell [do not know]; or whether out of the body, I cannot tell: God knoweth;) such an one caught up to the *third heaven*.
—2 Corinthians 12:2

[Since there is a third heaven there must be a first and second heaven too.]

FIRST HEAVEN, ATMOSPHERE WHERE BIRDS FLY

17. And I saw an angel standing in the sun; and he cried with a loud voice, saying to all the fowls that fly in the midst of *heaven*, come and gather yourselves together unto the supper of the Great God;
—Revelation 19:17

THE SECOND HEAVEN IS THE STELLER HEAVEN WERE THE SUN, MOON AND STARS MOVE IN THEIR ORBITS

1. The *heavens* declare the glory of God; and the firmament showeth His handiwork.
2. Day unto day uttereth speech and night unto night showeth knowledge.

3. There is no speech nor language, where their voice is not heard.
4. Their line is gone out through all the earth, and their words to the end of the world. In them hath He set a tabernacle for the sun,
—Psalms 19:1-4

THE THIRD HEAVEN IS PARADISE WHERE THE THRONE OF GOD IS, WHERE JESUS IS NOW

4. Now that he was caught up into paradise, and heard unspeakable words, which it is not lawful for a man to utter.
—2 Corinthians 12:4

JESUS IS PREPARING A PLACE FOR HIS PEOPLE

3. And if I go and prepare a place for you, I will come again, and receive you unto myself; that where I am, there ye may be also.
—John 14:3
10. For he [Abraham] looked for a city which hath foundations, whose builder and maker is God.
16. But now they desire a better country, that is, and *heavenly*: wherefore God is not ashamed to be called their God: for He hath prepared for them a city.
—Hebrews 11:10, 16

THE NEW JERUSALEM IS 375 MILES ON EACH OF FOUR SIDES. IT IS 140,625 MILES SQUARE. LARGER THAN OH, IL, IN, AND NJ ALL TOGETHER.

10. ... He ... showed me that great city, the holy Jerusalem, descending out of heaven from God,
11. Having the glory of God: and her light was like unto a stone most precious, even like a jasper stone [diamond], clear as crystal;
12. And had a wall great and high, and had twelve gates, and at the gates twelve angels, and names written thereon,

which are the names of the twelves tribes of the children of Israel:
13. On the east three gates; on the north three gates; on the south three gates; and on the west three gates.
14. And the wall of the city had twelve foundations, and in them the names of the twelve apostles of the Lamb.
15. And he that talked with me had a golden read to measure the city, and the gates thereof, and the wall thereof.
16. And the city lieth foursquare, and the length is as large as the breadth: and he measured the city with the read, twelve thousand furlongs. The length and the breadth and the height of it are equal.
17. And he measured the wall thereof, and hundred and forty and four cubits, according to the measure of a men, that is, of the angel.
18. And the building of the wall of it was of jasper: and the city was pure gold, like unto clear glass.
19. And the foundations of the wall of the city were garnished with all manner of precious stones. . . .
21. And the twelve gates were twelve pearls; every several gate was of one pearl: and the street of the city was pure gold, as it were transparent glass.
22. And I saw no temple therein: for the Lord God Almighty and the Lamb are the temple of it.
23. And the city had not need of the sun, neither of the moon, to shine in it: for the glory of God did lighten it, and the Lamb is the light thereof.
24. And the nations of them which are saved shall walk in the light of it . . .
25. And the gates of it shall not be shut at all by day: for there shall be no night there.
27. And there shall no wise enter into it any thing that defileth, neither whatsoever worketh abomination, or maketh a lie: but they which are written in the Lamb's book of life.
—Revelation 21:10-27

1. And he showed me a pure river of water of life, clear as crystal, proceeding out of the throne of God and of the Lamb.
2. In the midst of the street of it, and on either side of the river, was there a tree of life, which bare twelve manner of fruits, and yielded her fruit every month: and the leaves of the tree were for the healing of the nations.
3. And there shall be no more curse: but the throne of God and of the Lamb shall be in it: and His servants shall serve Him:
4. And they shall see His face; and His name shall be in their foreheads.
5. And there shall be no night there; and they need no candle [lamp], neither light of the sun; for the Lord God giveth them light: and they shall reign for ever and ever.
—Revelation 22:1-5

A CITY OF PERFECT HEALTH

4. And God shall wipe away all tears from their eyes; and there shall be no more death, neither sorrow, nor crying, neither shall there be any more pain: for the former things are passed away.
—Revelation 21:4

WE MUST OBEY ALL GOD'S COMMANDMENTS TO GET THERE

14. Blessed are they that do His commandments, that they may have right to the tree of life, and may enter in through the gates into the city.
—Revelation 22:14

WE WILL HAVE GLORIOUS SPIRITUAL BODIES, SAME AS JESUS

20. For our conversation [citizenship] is in heaven; from whence also we look for the Saviour, the Lord Jesus Christ:

21. Who shall change our vile [lowly] body, that it may be fashioned like unto His glorious body, according to the working whereby He is able even to subdue all things unto Himself.
—Philippians 3:20, 21
2. Beloved, now are we the sons of God, and it doth not yet appear what we shall be: but we know that, when he shall appear, we shall be like Him; for we shall see Him as He is.
—1 John 3:2
44. It is sown a natural body; it is raised a spiritual body. There is a natural body, and there is a spiritual body.
—1 Corinthians 15:44

JESUS' FOLLOWERS RECOGNIZED JESUS IN HIS RESURRECTED BODY, SO WILL WE KNOW ONE ANOTHER IN HEAVEN.

16. Jesus saith unto her, Mary. She turned herself, and saith unto Him, Rabboni; which is to say, Master.
—John 20:16
(Read Also: John 20:11-15)
27. Then saith He to Thomas, Reach hither thy finger, and behold my hands; and reach hither thy hand, and thrust it into my side: and be not faithless, but believing.
28. And Thomas answered and said unto Him, My Lord and My God.
—John 20:27, 28

[Just as the disciples on the Mount of Transfiguration recognized Moses and Elijah, Men whom they had never seen before, so our glorious spiritual bodies will have the power of recognition to know millions of people in heaven that we have never seen before.]

3. And, behold, there appeared unto them Moses and Elias talking with Him.
4. Then answered Peter, and said unto Jesus, Lord, it is good

for us to be here: if thou wilt, let us make here three tabernacles: one for thee, and one for Moses, and one for Elias.
—Matthew 17:3, 4

[We will know each other fully then, as God knows us now.]

12. For now we see through a glass [mirror], darkly; but then face to face: now I know in part; but then shall I know even as also I am known.
—1 Corinthians 13:12

AFTER THE MILLENIUM GOD WILL MAKE A NEW FIRST HEAVEN WITH A NEW PURE ATMOSPHERE

10. But the day of the Lord will come as a thief in the night; in the which the heavens shall pass away with a great noise, and the elements shall melt with fervent heat, the earth also and the works that are therein shall be burned up.
13. Nevertheless we, according to His promise, look for new heavens and a new earth, wherein dwelleth righteousness.
—2 Peter 3:10, 13

THE NEW JERUSALEM WILL BECOME THE CAPITAL OF THE NEW EARTH

1. And I saw a new heaven and a new earth: for the first heaven and the first earth were passed away; and there was nor more sea.
2. And I John saw the holy city, new Jerusalem, coming down from God out of heaven, prepared as a bride adorned for her husband.
3. And I heard a great voice out of heaven saying, Behold, the tabernacle of God is with men, and He will dwell with them, and they shall be his people, and God Himself, shall be with them, and be their God.
—Revelation 21:1-3

A DESCRIPTION OF THE NEW EARTH

6. The wolf also shall dwell with the lamb, and the leopard shall lie down with the kid; and the calf and the young lion and the fatling together; and a little child shall lead them.
7. And the cow and the bear shall feed; their young ones shall lie down together: and the lion shall eat straw like the ox.
8. And the sucking child shall play on the hole of the asp, and the weaned child shall put his hand on the cockatrice' den.
9. They shall not hurt nor destroy in all my holy mountain: for the earth shall be full of the knowledge of the LORD, as the water covers the sea.
—Isaiah 11:6-9
23. And it shall come to pass, that from one new moon to another, and from one sabbath to another, shall all flesh come to worship before me, saith the LORD.
—Isaiah 66:23

REFERENCES

The books that were most helpful in bringing together the Bible Texts for the Various topics and sub-topics were these.

Helps to Bible Study, by J. L. Shuler; TEACH Services, Inc., Brushton, NY 1995.

Bible Readings for the Home, Contributions by a Large Number of Bible Students; Review and Herald Publishing Association, Takoma Park, Washington, D.C. 1945.

The Story of Patriarchs and Prophets, by Ellen G. White; Review and Herald Publishing Association, Washington, D.C. 1958.

Seventh-day Adventists Believe . . . A Biblical Exposition of 27 Fundamental Doctrines, Ministerial Association General Conference of Seventh-day Adventist; Review and Herald Publishing Association, Hagerstown, Maryland 21740, 1988.

Seventh-day Adventist BIBLE COMMENTARY: Review and Herald Publishing Association, Washington, D.C.

The Franklin Hand Held Computerized Holy Bible, King James Version, was especially useful to find texts, when only a phrase or a few words were remembered.

Scriptures used are from the King James Version of the Bible unless otherwise noted.

Personal pronouns for Persons of the God-Head are capitalized as is often done in more modern translations.

Words in italics within the texts are placed there for emphasis by the compiler.

We invite you to view the complete
selection of titles we publish at:

www.TEACHServices.com

or write or email us your praises,
reactions, or thoughts about this
or any other book we publish at:

TEACH Services, Inc.
P.O. Box 954
Ringgold, GA 30736

info@TEACHServices.com

Finally, if you are interested in seeing
your own book in print, please contact us at

publishing@teachservices.com.

We would be happy to review your manuscript for free.

www.ingramcontent.com/pod-product-compliance
Lightning Source LLC
Chambersburg PA
CBHW070620230426
43670CB00010B/1592